The Ambuja Story

Praise for *The Ambuja Story*

Once I asked Narotamji, what is the hallmark of a great leader? He said, 'The job of a leader is to get ordinary people to do extraordinary things.' This book is a practical lesson and a brilliant case study of his leadership philosophy… It is a must-read for any entrepreneur and leader.

Puneet Dalmia, managing director, Dalmia Bharat Group

I have followed Mr Sekhsaria's journey from my early days and have known him as one of the most dynamic leaders of our time. He is a visionary who turned Gujarat Ambuja into a world-class conglomerate and brand. This book says it all. Thank you for sharing this remarkable story—one that must be told to motivate and inspire aspirants to reach the stars.

Hemendra Kothari, chairman, DSP Investment Managers Private Limited

This book is not just a story of how Mr Narotam Sekhsaria and his colleagues built a much-admired cement company. It is a splendid story of how the pursuit of excellence, a commitment to virtue and the generation of wealth can be wonderfully interwoven.

Bimal Patel, architect, president, CEPT University, Ahmedabad

This is an extraordinary account of a formidable entrepreneurial journey, a successful transformation of 20th-century traders into 21st-century industrialists and, by extension, a story of India's modern capitalism. Shri Sekhsaria opens up like never before for the reading pleasure of aspiring entrepreneurs, fellow deal-makers and anyone looking for leadership inspiration.

Haigreve Khaitan, senior partner, Khaitan & Co.

This is one of the most honest and best books that I have read in business history through the journey of an iconic entrepreneur. Nothing is hidden. Everything is shared, the good and the bad. It is a must-read book because it is informative and brilliantly drafted. Kudos to the author.

Dr Omkar Goswami, chairman, CERG Advisory Private Limited

A riveting story of the journey from cotton trading to building one of India's most efficient cement plants. Two things stood out for me: the early focus on ethics, environment and communities when ESG and CSR were not the buzz words they are today. And the second, the can-do attitude. Nothing can keep a good man down, not even cancer! A fascinating read indeed.

Shikha Sharma, former MD and CEO, Axis Bank

Narotambhai's autobiography is a powerful lesson in humility, simplicity, transparency and human potential. He hands out credit so abundantly that his awesome leadership and charisma that all have experienced are invisible but potently present. This is a mesmerising tale of an outstanding Indian enterprise, a 'globally acknowledged jewel' today.

Shailesh Haribhakti, chartered accountant

The world knows Narotambhai as a super-successful entrepreneur. But I have known him as a human being with sterling values—compassion, courage, generosity, humility, perfectionism and patriotism. This book encapsulates his philosophy, personality and extraordinary achievements during his Ambuja years and after. It is an inspiring guide to those who want to learn the art of business and those keen to learn the higher art of loving and living life even in the face of the most daunting adversities.

Sudheendra Kulkarni, columnist and editor

I have known Narotamji for at least 40 years, as we shared the same office premises. I have always looked up to him. His business and investment acumen, philanthropy and the way he holds friends and family are so impressive. After reading this most inspiring book, I would recommend all entrepreneurs and youngsters pick up a copy.

Anil Agarwal, chairman, Vedanta Resources

A remarkable story of an exceptional individual—gifted with a surfeit of wisdom, intellect, grace, and a large heart—building an iconic company founded on principles of ethics, integrity, transparency, empowerment and trust, and fairness. A company resolutely producing the best quality cement at the lowest cost with minimal environmental impact and maximum community welfare—all in an industry where such virtuous confluence was unthinkable. A tale beyond inspirational!

Rajendra Chitale, managing partner, M. P. Chitale & Co.

From trading in cotton to manufacturing cement in a community-friendly and environmentally sustainable manner in the then backward region of Gujarat, Mr Narotam Sekhsaria was a trailblazer. Even among the enterprising Marwari community, he stands tall. The history of Ambuja Cements is a remarkable story of a human being.

R.V. Pandit, publisher and film producer

The story of Mr Narotam Sekhsaria, from a cotton trader to an industrialist, makes for a fascinating read. It provides a peep into the life of a young Marwari boy growing up in South Mumbai with a commitment to family, passion for business and appreciation of the good life. Ambuja transformed the cement business with innovation in manufacturing, logistics, distribution, sales, branding, acquisitions, and finance. I admire most how he created a distinctive culture at Ambuja—the spirit of 'I Can'. I have seen it at play.

Sudhir Soni, partner, S. R. Batliboi & Co. LLP

Narotam is an exceptional raconteur and storyteller. This book is a recollection of the minutest fragments of his successful journey to create a cement business and successfully manage the multiple labyrinths of an enterprise. The thoughtful and skilfully narrated vignettes, including his personal journey, will encourage other entrepreneurs to extend beyond their conventional paths. Truly inspiring!

Ranjit Shahani, former VC and MD, Novartis

This book captures the indomitable spirit of Mr Sekhsaria. It is a great read about the glorious journey of Ambuja Cement and how he went on to build one of India's foremost and trusted cement brands, peppered with rare insights and personal anecdotes. It's an engaging memoir with an interesting narrative that reintroduces a few business fundamentals and priceless learnings which growth-focused modern corporates must internalise.

Nimesh Kampani, non-executive chairman, JM Financial Limited

Mr Narotam Sekhsaria's autobiography makes a fascinating read and is inspirational. I have worked as his advisor for over 20 years and have seen him at close quarters. This book captures the essence of what he stands for, the struggles and the exceptional resilience. It is a must on the bookshelf of every entrepreneur.

Cyril Shroff, managing partner, Cyril Amarchand Mangaldas

The Ambuja Story is a treatise on the courage, conviction, confidence, commitment, conversion of opportunities, networking, talent and industry of many missionary zeal-fired ordinary individuals who help build an icon of the cement industry. People with the ambition to scale the heights of glory in business will be amply rewarded by reading this book.

G.N. Bajpai, ex-chairman, SEBI and LIC

Narotamji has always had a clear sense of purpose, a bold vision, and strong family values. He disrupted the cement industry in the late '80s and created an iconic consumer brand which no one in the industry thought was possible. This autobiography is a wonderful read and has many wonderful life lessons. I encourage all young entrepreneurs to read it and embody the spirit of 'I Can'.

Jay Mehta, executive vice chairman, Saurashtra Cement, The Mehta Group

An observant and astute entrepreneur, Narotam Sekhsaria's autobiography reveals a narrative of business struggles and triumphs etched with honour. Some ideas arrived by luck but more often were the careful plans to build sturdy organisations and teams. A fascinating must-read.

Gita Piramal, writer and business historian

This book is a treasure for today's generation to learn from. N.S.'s penchant for driving commerce with passion, building and preserving a cohesive team, believing in Karma which sees his journey through so many ups and downs, are some of the values that stand out in the book. Thank you for this gift!

Sanjay Nayar, chairman, KKR India

I first met Mr Narotam Sekhsaria over 25 years ago when establishing Warburg Pincus' presence in India. One of the most compelling elements of the India story to me—then and now—are the stories of immensely talented entrepreneurs who defy the odds and whose success changes the landscape. *The Ambuja Story* tells one of those great stories—by the person who made it all happen. The story is as compelling now as it was then.

Charles Kaye, CEO, Warburg Pincus LLC

Mr Narotam Sekhsaria's journey in the cement industry is truly fascinating. It is a remarkable story of a start-up cement company that became the most profitable and respected company in India. Ambuja Cement is a jewel in the Holcim Group of companies. We are proud of Ambuja Cement and our association with Mr Narotam Sekhsaria.

Jan Jenisch, CEO, Holcim Group

Seldom does one come across a book so compelling regarding a personal journey that resulted in the creation of a company that emerged from its first days as innovative and profitable, and challenged conventional wisdom in every aspect, big and small. I would not hesitate to recommend this book to all who wish to delve deeper into how this was achieved, particularly young entrepreneurs. It should be required reading in all management schools.

Nasser Munjee, chairman, DCB Bank

Narotam Sekhsaria and I go back many years. He always wanted his facilities to be beautiful, safe, and user-friendly for his workers. Buzz words like reuse, recycle, and sustainable were part of his language even then. With him I never felt I was meeting an industrialist, but a creative, inspiring and caring humanitarian. This book captures everything in vivid detail.

Hafeez Contractor, architect

I joined the Ambuja Board in September 1985 when Ambuja was about to start production. I witnessed how Narotam Sekhsaria and his colleagues, despite no knowledge of cement or experience in running an industry, turned a small unit into one of the most successful cement manufacturers in the country. Reading this book brought back those great memories.

M.L. Bhakta, senior partner, Kanga & Co.

India is replete with examples of how ordinary men created extraordinary companies. Fate and destiny pick persons who are bright, energetic, visionary and risk-taking. In the case of Narotambhai the extra dimensions were warmth, humility, empathy and compassion, as is evident in this book that captures his journey.

Vinayak Chatterjee, chairman of CII's National Council on Infrastructure

The Ambuja Story

How a Group of Ordinary Men Created an Extraordinary Company

NAROTAM SEKHSARIA

HARPER BUSINESS

An Imprint of HarperCollins *Publishers*

First published hardback in India by Harper Business 2022
An imprint of HarperCollins *Publishers*
4th Floor, Tower A, Building No. 10, Phase II, DLF Cyber City,
Gurugram, Haryana – 122002
www.harpercollins.co.in

This edition published by Harper Business 2024

2 4 6 8 10 9 7 5 3 1

P-ISBN: 978-93-6213-580-3
E-ISBN: 978-93-5489-199-1

Typeset in 11.5/15.4 Adobe Garamond
Manipal Technologies Limited, Manipal

Printed and bound at
Manipal Technologies Limited

This book is produced from independently certified FSC® paper
to ensure responsible forest management.

For
my wife Nalini,
son Pulkit, and daughter Padmini
whose unconditional love energised me every day

Contents

Prologue

On a sweltering day in the summer of June 1982, Suresh Neotia and I flew to Lucknow to explore the possibility of setting up a cement plant in Uttar Pradesh. Suresh, who had arrived from Calcutta, was a relative and a mentor to me. We had come to Lucknow to meet Mr Narayan Dutt Tiwari, the Union Industry Minister, to submit the initial proposal for the plant, and to gauge the response. Mr Tiwari had been the Chief Minister of Uttar Pradesh till a few years ago and retained considerable clout in the state capital.

We were waiting in the lobby of the iconic Clarks Hotel on our way to the meeting when I saw a distinguished, tall, and fair gentleman walk in with a retinue of people. I recognized him immediately. It was Mr N.N. Pai, the chairman and managing director of Industrial Development Bank of India (IDBI), the country's premier bank for development finance in those days. I had known him well for a few years. He saw me and stopped. 'Narotam, what are you doing here in Lucknow?' he asked. I told him about our mission. He looked slightly amused and indulgently told me, 'You are wasting your time. If you are serious about investing, you should consider Gujarat.'I was taken aback by his bluntness. 'Sir, Suresh knows Mr Tiwari well, and we hope to get his support,' I told him. He wasn't convinced. He reiterated that if we were serious about setting up a cement plant, we should consider Gujarat. He told us that he was flying to Ahmedabad that evening, and if we were to go with him, he would introduce us to everyone who mattered. 'Even if you don't know anyone in Gujarat, they will welcome you like a son-in-law,' he said.

Mr Pai then walked away to his meeting. Suresh and I were puzzled by his remark and suggestion. We had come to UP on the advice of Dr M.P. Jain, the managing director of Andhra Cements, one of South India's best-known cement companies in those days. I was then a cotton trader, and Suresh a distributor of petroleum products based out of Calcutta. We wanted to get into cement manufacturing, and Dr Jain, who was among the most respected professionals in the industry, was expected to join us as a partner.

He had told us about the availability of high-quality limestone mines in the Dehradun valley region of UP and how no one had exploited it as yet. The other reason he plumped for UP was that the state, despite its size, had only one small cement plant. Outside manufacturers met the rest of its cement demand.

We trusted Dr Jain's judgement on UP. Nevertheless, now that Mr Pai, who was among the most powerful bankers in the country, had proposed Gujarat, we decided that I should go with him to Ahmedabad out of courtesy and respect. The IDBI would be critical to our financing requirements when we reached that stage. I had never been to Ahmedabad; it would be a good adventure. I liked meeting new people and getting to know them.

However, at that moment, we were focused on our meeting with Mr Tiwari and his team. Unlike Mr Pai, we were still hopeful. Uttar Pradesh was one of India's most underdeveloped states, and we were proposing a significant new industrial investment there. Even if not the red carpet, we were at least hoping for a hearty and hospitable reception from Mr Tiwari. Besides, Suresh had known him for a long time.

When we reached Mr Tiwari's office, the reception was far from what we had expected. We were made to wait for hours as there was a queue of people waiting to see him. When we were finally ushered into his presence, all he did was shake our hands, give a polite smile, and ask us to handover our proposal to a secretary standing nearby. That was it. No conversation, no questions. The meeting was over in about two minutes.

What we saw was a live example of why UP had failed to attract industrial investment even in those days.

To say that we were disappointed would be an understatement. To my mind, our dream of setting up a cement plant in UP ended there. Seeing Mr Tiwari's indifferent response, I had no expectations from the state government. Disheartened and dejected, we left straight for the airport. Suresh was taking a flight back to Calcutta, while I had to meet Mr Pai and travel on his chartered plane to Ahmedabad.

I had no major expectations from this trip to the Gujarat capital. I saw it only as a minor detour on my way back to Bombay. I was going only because Mr Pai had invited me. We had a pleasant conversation about my cement ambition on the flight, and, as always, Mr Pai was very encouraging. It was dusk when we landed in Ahmedabad. As the small plane taxied to a stop, I could see a few people waiting on the tarmac. Those were the days when people could walk to the aircraft to receive their guests.

Mr Pai told me that Mr H.K. Khan, the chairman of Gujarat Industrial Investment Corporation (GIIC), had personally come to the airport to greet us. When we walked down the plane ladder, Mr Khan offered a bouquet to Mr Pai, and he, in turn, introduced me, saying, 'This is Mr Sekhsaria from Bombay. He wants to set up a cement plant in UP. I am trying to convince him to make this investment in Gujarat.' Mr Khan accompanied us in the car as we drove to Ahmedabad's Cama Hotel, where we were staying. As the chairman of GIIC, Mr Khan was the principal government bureaucrat in charge of the industrial development of the state. He thanked Mr Pai profusely for bringing me to Gujarat. Mr Pai said that he was scheduled to meet Chief Minister Mr Madhav Singh Solanki at 10 a.m. the next day and that he would inform him about my presence in Ahmedabad and my desire to set up a cement plant.

At the Cama Hotel, we decided to have a cup of tea with Mr Khan before retiring to our respective rooms. 'Khan, how will you make the cement plant possible for Mr Sekhsaria?' Mr Pai asked him as we waited at the coffee shop. 'Sir, you need not worry. Tomorrow after you meet the chief minister, I will make sure that his office issues a press statement saying Mr Pai has brought Mr Sekhsaria to Gujarat to set up a cement plant, and we welcome the possibility of this investment,' Mr Khan said. 'Once this announcement is made, Mr Sekhsaria will come to my office at GIIC, and we will work out a plan of action.' It was only an hour after we landed in Ahmedabad, but the super-efficient Gujarat government bureaucracy was already moving quickly.

The next day, as planned, Mr Pai met the chief minister at 10 a.m., and by noon a press statement was issued by the chief minister's office saying precisely what Mr Khan had told us. It felt like a regular drill that had been perfected by the Gujarat government officials. And as promised, Mr Khan's secretary called to say that he was expecting me at his office at 4 p.m. It all seemed to be going too fast for me. I had not had the time to think about this move to Gujarat nor consult Suresh. It felt as if between Mr Pai and Mr Khan, the decision had been made for us.

Mr Khan was warm and welcoming. He gave me the kind of reception I had hoped for from Mr Tiwari's office. Mr Khan ushered me into his cabin and made me comfortable by asking everyone else to leave. He offered me a cup of tea, and we made some small talk. It was almost as if he was meeting a long-lost friend. I spent half an hour with him. He assured me that it was his job to support and guide young people like me, who were keen on investing in Gujarat, even if they had no prior knowledge or experience. He said he would put his officials on the job, and they would prepare a note on the way forward. It would be sent to me within a few weeks.

On the flight back to Bombay that evening, I couldn't help but wonder how dramatically things had changed in the space of a single day. We had prepared for months to meet Mr Tiwari. His indifference and our fateful meeting with Mr Pai in a hotel lobby had changed all that.

My knowledge about cement was next to nothing. I had never seen a cement plant in my life. I had no idea about limestone deposits or the cement industry in Gujarat. And I had never negotiated an industrial agreement. Yet, in the next few weeks, I would need to be ready for a substantive meeting with Gujarat government officials.

Dr Jain had steered me towards setting up a cement plant in Uttar Pradesh with the promise that he would quit his job and join us as the founding managing director of our company, once we laid the groundwork in terms of location and regulatory permissions. His initial enthusiasm and assurance were why Suresh and his younger brother Vinod had come on board as co-promoters of the project.

My connection with the Neotia brothers was through my sister. She was the widow of their eldest brother, the late Bimal Kumar Poddar. I looked up to Suresh as an elder brother and often sought his advice and guidance. Suresh and Vinod were among the largest distributors of kerosene and other commodities in eastern India and several north Indian states like UP and Bihar. Suresh had a great flair for networking, especially with government people, in Delhi and the states where his companies operated. I thought of it as an asset that would come in handy on our cement project.

The plan was for Mr Jain to manage the project under the overall guidance of Suresh. At the same time, I would be the principal investor and sleeping partner. My dream was to be an industrialist, but without getting involved in the nitty-gritty of running a company. I led a comfortable life in Bombay as a successful cotton trader. I was still in my early thirties, made good money, worked only a few hours a day, and that too for only nine months of the cotton season, and often holidayed in India and abroad with my family. It was a comfortable work-life balance that I had earned, and I was loath to change it. My hope was that I would be able to step back after we had all the permissions and financing in place.

On my arrival in Bombay, I phoned Suresh to convey what had transpired in Ahmedabad. We realized that we had landed ourselves in a bit of a difficult situation. The Gujarat government was convinced that we had made the decision to invest in their state. But we had not given up on UP entirely as yet. Gujarat was a small state but was already home to several reputed cement manufacturers. UP, on the other hand, was a massive market with not a single large cement plant.

I called Dr Jain to apprise him of what had happened since our trip to Lucknow. He seemed happy with the progress but sounded less enthusiastic about joining us any time soon. He had told us earlier that he would not be available for the initial meetings because of his position as the managing director of Andhra Cements and would join full-time once the location and permissions were finalized.

The Gujarat government did not believe in wasting time. In less than a week, I received a formal letter from GIIC inviting us to come to Ahmedabad for more detailed discussions on the contours of a deal. Not only were they willing to help us with the land for the plant and the limestone mines, but they also wanted to invest in the project. It was much more than what I had originally expected.

When I called Suresh to give him the good news, he didn't seem as enthusiastic about Gujarat as he was about UP. He said that I should take Vinod with me for the next meeting, since negotiating a deal like this was not his cup of tea. I was not sure what had happened. My guess was that he was not as comfortable about Gujarat, because UP was a more familiar territory where he had an existing business operation.

I then spoke to Vinod. He was as clueless about cement as I was. He suggested that we take Mr P. Kariappa, an experienced professional who ran Macmet Limited, an engineering company owned by the Neotias, to Ahmedabad to present a professional facade to the GIIC team.

As we landed in Ahmedabad for the meeting, my big fear was that we would be called out for our lack of knowledge about the cement industry.

However, the GIIC officials were as indulgent towards us as Mr Khan was during my first visit. Instead of quizzing or assessing our capabilities and financial worth, they made an hour-long presentation on why we should invest in Gujarat, how they have assisted other companies and the success of their joint sector projects.

They laid out the details of the assistance that the Gujarat government and GIIC would provide us. Their investment in the project would be equal to the amount of money we invested. They would be an equal partner and take all the risks that we were taking. Additionally, we would be offered several tax concessions and incentives. We were bowled over by their eagerness to have this project come up in their state. I had heard about states welcoming investors with open arms. Still, the Gujarat government had taken it to a different level.

It was an offer we could not refuse. I had doubts whether the UP government would match it, especially after what we had gone through. Without consulting Suresh or Dr Jain, Vinod and I gave our consent to Mr Khan for the joint sector plan and thanked him for his help. Happy with our positive response, he requested us to go with him to Gandhinagar, the state capital, which is about a half-hour from Ahmedabad, to meet the state Industries Secretary N.Sivagnanam, a 1952-batch IAS officer, who oversaw the state's industrial development. This meeting signalled that our cement venture was now a reality and would come up in Gujarat as a joint sector project.

We thought at least Mr Sivagnanam would ask us tough questions to test our knowledge and capability. But he didn't. He was as welcoming as the rest. Mr Khan introduced us, saying, 'Sir, these are the businessmen who have come on Mr Pai's recommendation to put up a cement plant in Gujarat. They are happy to enter into a joint sector agreement with us.' It was almost as if we were doing the Gujarat government a favour by setting up our project in the state. Mr Sivagnanam offered us tea and biscuits and thanked us for choosing Gujarat as our investment destination.

Fifteen days after my second Ahmedabad trip, GIIC sent us the draft MOU for the joint sector project. A draft of the shareholders' agreement came a few weeks later, with a request for a date when Mr Khan could come down to Bombay to sign the final deal.

I am a firm believer in the invisible hand of destiny. And when I look back, I can see how it manoeuvred us towards Gujarat. Our meeting with Mr Pai in Lucknow, our fruitful interactions with Mr Khan and his officials, and their decision to make this a joint sector project despite our lack of knowledge and experience in cement and manufacturing. It was like a gift from God.

The UP idea was now a distant dream. Three months later, we were told by someone in the state government that there was no way we would have got the necessary permission to mine limestone in the Dehradun valley as it fell in an ecologically sensitive area. That is why, even four decades later, there are no cement plants in the area. Either Dr Jain was as ill-informed as us, or he knew about the ecological constraints but was pushing us to see if the government would make an exception. That was not to be.

Fate and destiny had brought me closer home to Gujarat. It was the beginning of the Ambuja story.

1

Destiny's Child

Chirawa to Bombay • The adoption story • From Marwari Vidyalaya to Hill Grange, Elphinstone College and University Department of Chemical Technology

Who knew we would do so much so quickly? I still wonder sometimes. How did we, a bunch of relative newcomers, build India's most successful cement company in a little over a decade? We started production at our first plant in 1986 and by 1996 we had plants in four states—Gujarat, Himachal Pradesh, Maharashtra and Punjab. Gujarat Ambuja was not the biggest, but it certainly was amongst the most profitable, most efficient, greenest and most investor-friendly cement companies globally.

How did we do this? As the founder, did I possess any exceptional abilities or skills? I do not think so. I was a chemical engineer who ran the family's cotton-trading firm while dreaming about becoming an industrialist. Did I have extraordinarily qualified people working with me? Not at all. My colleagues were regular middle-class professionals with technical degrees from India's small-town universities, who achieved extraordinary results through hard work, single-minded focus, imagination and creativity.

I had no ambitious plan in mind when I started work on Ambuja. It was the early 1980s, I had recently turned thirty and it was meant to be a step up from my cotton-trading operations. There was nothing in my family's past or in mine that foretold the future the way it unfolded. Ours was the familiar story of a Marwari business family from the Shekhawati region of Rajasthan, which had achieved moderate success across generations as traders and commission agents.

The Sekhsarias—like the Poddars, Singhanias and Jhunjhunwalas—are part of the business-minded Agarwal sub-clan of the Marwari community. Along with the Maheshwaris (which includes the likes of the Birlas and Bangurs, among others) and the Oswal Jains, the Agarwals are among the most significant business communities in Rajasthan. The Agarwals are traditionally known for their aggressive approach to business and penchant for taking risks, while the Maheshwaris are considered more conservative.

The Marwaris, as is well known, have a unique talent for trading and business, a talent that they have cultivated and put to use assiduously over the centuries. An intangible factor sometimes referred to as *baniya buddhi* or the 'trader's mindset', has ensured them success wherever they have gone. From running local businesses, to trading with camel caravans that travelled to India from Central Asia and beyond, to funding rulers throughout north India across reigns and kingdoms, the itinerant Marwari traders, moneylenders, financiers and bankers have been involved in every money-related activity throughout the history of modern India.

The arrival of the railways in the latter part of the nineteenth century made things easier for the peripatetic community, as travel became less painful and faster. This created a new class of Marwaris who based themselves in their hometowns and villages in Shekhawati, but followed the circular migration route—spending extensive periods doing business elsewhere in the country—returning to their families and homes every few months. My family belongs to this category of traders.

We, the Sekhsarias (also spelt Seksaria by some), are believed to have taken our name from the town of Sekhsar in present-day Bikaner district of Rajasthan, much like the Singhanias who come from Singhana, the Jhunjhunwalas from Jhunjhunu and the Jaipurias from Jaipur. Several generations ago, the Sekhsarias left Sekhsar for good, probably because of persistent drought conditions. They moved east to settle in the more prosperous Shekhawati region. One branch seems to have travelled 200 kilometres southeast to Nawalgarh, Shekhawati's most prosperous town in those days. At the same time, our ancestors moved 200 kilometres northeast to set up base in the trading town of Chirawa.

Chirawa and Nawalgarh (today towns in modern-day Jhunjhunu district of Rajasthan) have for some reason historically produced the largest concentration of prominent Marwari business families. The Dalmias, for example, are from Chirawa itself, while the Birlas are from Pilani, a distance of 17 kilometres. Nawalgarh, which produced the Goenkas, Khaitans, Poddars, Kedias, Ganeriwalas and Murarkas, is only 60 kilometres away. The Singhanias, Bajajs, Mittals, Ruias and Sarafs hail from other nearby towns and villages.

A walk around Chirawa gives one some idea of how prosperous it must have been in the nineteenth and early twentieth centuries. The streets are still lined with magnificent old-time havelis of merchant families built during that period. Most are in ruins since the descendants of the original families have abandoned them. A few, like mine, have been lovingly restored and are occupied at least a few times a year. Ornately carved hanging *jharoka* window-frames, carved doors, beautiful frescoes on walls and ceilings and remnants of imposing chandeliers distinguish these palatial havelis that were once owned by the rich.

Our spacious but relatively simple early twentieth-century haveli is indicative of our moderate wealth in that era. My forefathers were brokers and commission agents who dealt in commodities, including cotton, bullion and oil. The haveli, built by my great-grandfather, was designed in the style of Shekhawati architecture prevalent at the time, with two storeys and two courtyards—the forecourt or the mardana (men's courtyard) and the enclosed rear courtyard or the zenana (where women were sequestered, away from men)—hemmed in by bedrooms on both floors. Our haveli is strikingly bereft of the ornate embellishments of other havelis in the vicinity. There are no *jharokas*, frescoes, chandeliers, or elaborately carved doors.

The haveli was still home to our extended family when I was born on a pleasant August day in 1950, delivered by a midwife in a tiny windowless room by the inner courtyard. I was the third of five brothers in a house filled with uncles and cousins. I was born at a time when the family was debating the vital decision of shifting to Bombay for good, since the family trading business was based there. Most male members of the family spent a large part of the year in the coastal city, coming back to Chirawa only for a few months.

For over a century, Bombay had been the country's biggest cotton trading and textile manufacturing centre. Our family procured cotton from farmers and their brokers in and around Punjab, Haryana and Rajasthan. Still, the big trade deals, including those for export, were concluded in Bombay where the cotton exchange was located. In an earlier era, my forefathers would spend a few months in the city selling their cotton, before returning to Chirawa.

Over the years, better train connections made travel to Bombay simpler and faster, while improved communication facilities made contacts with our up-country suppliers easier. Slowly, an increasing number of our operations began shifting from Chirawa to Bombay. By the time I was born, the men in my family were spending as much as ten months in the city.

In doing so, they were only following the illustrious footsteps of Mr Govindram Seksaria, the first known person from the Sekhsaria clan to make it big in a large city. He was no relative of ours, but his rags-to-riches story is a legend among Marwaris. A descendant of the Nawalgarh Seksarias, he was born into a humble family in 1888. He made his way to Bombay at a young age in the early part of the last century. Using his skill at enterprise and speculation, he quickly rose to become the biggest cotton trader in the country, with memberships in the two biggest cotton exchanges in the world—Liverpool and New York.

The legend about him in the Marwari community is that he would bring trunks full of cash to his residence in Marine Drive in south Bombay. He later set up several textile mills and dabbled in various businesses, including sugar, bullion, minerals, printing, banking and even funding motion pictures. He died in 1946 at the age of fifty-eight. His stature was such that the cotton market and the stock market stayed shut that day as a mark of respect.

He is now largely forgotten. Besides a few educational institutions, his lasting legacy until recently was the Bank of Rajasthan that he set up in Udaipur in 1943. At one time, it was among the largest banks in the state, with close to 300 branches. It was merged with ICICI Bank in 2010. The only reminder of his fame in the city where he once held sway is Seksaria House, an art deco building on Marine Drive named after him. Further north, towards the Chowpatty end of Marine Drive, as one turns right to Babulnath, there is yet another Sekhsaria House that abuts the main road on the left. This five-storey building, constructed in the 1930s, was once owned and occupied by my great-grandfather Basantlalji Sekhsaria and his two brothers, Gorakhramji and Dwarkadasji, when they first set up base in Bombay. The proximity of the two properties is deceptive if one were to compare the fortunes of the families that owned them.

My forefathers led a comfortable life, but not one filled with luxuries. In the social hierarchy of the Marwari business community, we were at best on the third rung. Families like the Birlas, Singhanias, Bangurs, Dalmias, Somanis, Goenkas, Sarafs, Poddars, Khaitans and a few dozen others who had transformed themselves from traders to industrialists in the early part of the last century, were at the top.

The second rung was made up of affluent traders and speculators, like Mr Govindram Seksaria, who lived in opulent havelis and mansions and drove fancy cars even in those days. On the third rung were people like my family, comfortably upper middle-class, with a lifestyle at the margins of luxury. They sent their children to vernacular-medium schools. They shuttled between their villages and larger cities like Bombay and Calcutta, where they were based. And on the lowest rung were the owners of small businesses, shopkeepers and professionals who worked for those in the top three rungs.

Some of our families were related by marriage to those in the two upper rungs, but we were never on backslapping terms. The only time we met them was at weddings and social functions. We were expected to stand up in respect when they walked into the room. The conversation never went beyond a simple greeting and health enquiries. The hierarchies were clearly defined.

By the time I was born, the men in our family—including my grandfather Banarsilalji, his brother Satyanarayanji, my father Nagarmalji, uncle Makhanlalji and some of the older cousins—were spending most of their time in Bombay on business every year. The city had become more of a home to them than Chirawa. It was inevitable then that the rest of the family would shift as well. The final decision to move was made in 1953, when I had just turned three, after which Chirawa became only a holiday destination for us. In the first few years, we went back a few times every year. Then the frequency reduced until it became an occasional journey made by family elders.

Though business was the main reason for the shift, an additional factor was education. Slowly but surely, it had dawned on the family that proper schooling and possibly college, was necessary for the next generation of children if they were to take the business ahead. Education had not been a big priority for the family until then. None of the elders had studied beyond school. My father had studied only up to class seven. In those days, the belief in places like Chirawa was that children learnt faster on the job than in school. As a result, the town, despite its immense wealth, had no good schools. Even in the 1950s, kids were taught under large banyan trees. A college education was a distant dream.

Sometime in the 1940s, my great-grandfather split from his family to set up his own business. He moved his family to a third Sekhsaria House in south Bombay's Prarthana Samaj area. The area had been named after the nearby headquarters of a Hindu reformist movement popular in western India in the nineteenth and early twentieth centuries. Prarthana Samaj was a solidly middle-class area at that time. It was home to Gujarati and Marwari business families like ours because of its proximity to Kalbadevi, Bombay's central wholesale commodity trading district. Our two-storey office building was located at Kalbadevi, a few minutes away from the iconic Bombay Cotton Exchange set up in the 1930s.

With five of us brothers and four cousins, it was a happy place to grow up. The joint family was spread over several floors, but all the kids slept together. We all went to the nearby Marwari Vidyalaya High School. One of the oldest educational institutions in Bombay, it was set up by Marwari philanthropists in 1912 to cater to the needs of middle-class members of the community migrating to the city in large numbers. Though it has since transformed into a respected English-medium school, in those days the medium of education was strictly Hindi. English education was only for the elite. No one in my family spoke English.

Academics was not Marwari Vidyalaya's strong suit in those days. The parents who sent their kids to the school did not insist on it and the school did not oblige either. Teaching was geared towards somehow getting the kids to imbibe the basics to join the family business as soon as possible. For my family, though, it was a big jump from the school classes held under the banyan trees in Chirawa.

My grandfather was a donor to the school, so he was given the privilege of deciding which class each of his grandchildren—my brothers and cousins and I—should be admitted. The concept of structured schooling, where children started school at the scientifically determined age of five or six, was not known to him then. He used an arbitrary age criterion and at age five I was enrolled in class five. My brothers and cousins were dealt with in a similar fashion. The idea, as I said earlier, was to get the kids through school as soon as possible so that they could join the family business.

The only thing I remember of Marwari Vidyalaya from the several months I spent there was the fun and games and some bullying. Discipline was weak; the students did whatever they wanted. I have no memory of learning anything and have no friends from those days. Holiday weekends were spent at our family's office building in Kalbadevi. This place had the same look and feel of the *baithak* (sitting) room back in the Chirawa haveli, with everyone sitting on mattresses on the floor and working, while we ran around and played.

I was five, in my first year at school and in the midst of a happy childhood, when fate and destiny intervened to change my life forever.

The story begins with my grandfather Banarsilalji, the family patriarch. He had two sons and nine grandsons, but was worried about his younger brother Satyanarayanji. Twenty-five years younger than my grandfather and touching forty, Satyanarayanji had still not produced a male heir. As is well known, in those days, sons were more desired in Indian families than daughters. This was particularly important for Marwari business families like ours. Sons were essential to help the father in the family business and then to take it over and finally to look after the parents in their old age. Daughters, on the other hand, were married off at a noticeably young age and sent to their husband's home.

Satyanarayanji's daughter Bimla, whom I would later fondly call Bai, was born when Satyanarayanji was twenty. She had been married at a young age into the Calcutta-based Poddar family. After Bai's birth, Satyanarayanji's wife had suffered four miscarriages in the effort to conceive another child. The doctor had warned them about the risk to her life if they tried again. Weakened by tuberculosis (TB), Satyanarayanji himself was not in the best of health.

Concerned about what would happen to his brother, my grandfather called him home one Sunday and said, 'You are not in good health and have no male heir. I have nine grandsons and you need to adopt one of them as your son.' His wish, of course, was a command for every family member, including his younger brother. Later I learnt that Bai had a big hand in my grandfather devising this plan and in convincing her father to adopt a son.

Her father's deteriorating health led Bai to worry about who would look after him in his old age. Satyanarayanji told her his choice would be to adopt one of her sons. However, by then she had already undergone a miscarriage. And even if she had more children, Bai told him her husband and in-laws would not allow her to give away her first two sons for adoption and the chances of her having a third son were very slim. The only way out was for him to adopt a boy from another family.

Adopting a male child to secure the family line and fortune had been common practice among Marwaris for hundreds of years. It was a practical solution to a problem that had blighted the Indian subcontinent since time immemorial: the high rate of infant and child mortality. For many Marwari families, this created problems in taking forward the family business and hence the recourse to the custom of adoption. For obvious reasons, a vast majority of these adoptions happened within closely knit families, the most common of which involved uncles legally adopting nephews as their sons and heirs.

Fortunately in those days, most people lived in large joint families with lots of children, which mitigated the trauma of separation for both the child and the biological parents. Where adoption was not possible within the immediate family, the net would be cast wider into the extended family. Very rarely would it stretch to orphanages or child shelters.

Within my immediate family, several men were adopted—Bai's husband had been adopted as a child, as had my wife's brother and her uncle. And if one goes back into the history of Indian business, several prominent Marwaris—such as Mr Baldeo Das Birla, founder of the

Birla empire and father of Mr G.D. Birla; Mr Jamnalal Bajaj, founder of the Bajaj empire and grandfather of Mr Rahul Bajaj; Mr Lakshmi Narain Birla, the eldest son of Mr G.D. Birla, father of Mr S.K. Birla and grandfather of Mr Siddharth Birla—were all adoptees. This list of industrialists would not be complete were I to omit a very prominent non-Marwari—Mr Naval Tata who, for several decades, ran the Tata group with his cousin Mr J.R.D. Tata. An orphan distantly related to the Tatas, young Naval Tata had been formally adopted from a Parsi orphanage at the age of thirteen. He is the father of Mr Ratan Tata.

Grand-uncle Satyanarayanji was therefore given a free hand to pick the child he wanted. Though he was part of the family business, he no longer lived in our family home, Sekhsaria House. A few years earlier, he had shifted with his wife and daughter to a rented flat at Bhagwati Bhavan on Carmichael Road after a tiff between the women in the family in the Sekhsaria household. Carmichael Road, which is now among Bombay's more exclusive neighbourhoods, was in those days a wooded outpost where not many people wanted to live.

Satyanarayanji did not take much time to make his choice. A day later, he came back to tell my grandfather that he wanted to adopt me. It was my destiny that he chose me; after all, there were nine of us. Why else would he pick me and not one of my brothers or cousins?

I do recall that a habit of mine, which he had grown to like, had made me his favoured grand-nephew. As was the routine when we were young (and I was five at this time), all of us would be taken to the family trading office in Kalbadevi on Sundays and holidays for entertainment. The seating there was in the *baithak* style, with mattresses covered by crisp white sheets, topped by bolsters, one each for everyone who worked there. I did one thing every time we went there. I always gravitated towards Satyanarayanji and sat on his lap. While others would greet him or would bow with folded hands and do pranam before moving on, I felt a certain closeness to him and he liked that. I do not know what made me do that, but I think the mutual fondness and attachment contributed to his decision.

After my father was told about the decision, he informed my mother. She, in turn, conveyed the news to me, telling me that I would be going to a new home which would be better than ours. I do not recall her being too emotional about it. I was probably too young to understand what it all meant, or to fathom the enormity of that decision. I do not remember being upset or concerned about being separated from my parents, brothers or cousins, or even the fact that I was leaving them for good. Instead, I recall being ecstatic and strutting around like a peacock for a few days on being the chosen one. It was as if I had scored over my brothers and cousins to win the first prize in a competition.

On my grandfather's instructions, an astrologer was called to ascertain the most auspicious day for me to go to my new home. On the appointed day, a small prayer ceremony was performed at home, after which my mother did my tilak, gave me some *mishri* (rock sugar) and a one-rupee coin in a pouch as a *shagun* (an auspicious blessing). She had packed a small bag with my clothes; now she hugged me and told me to be a good boy. Our family priest then took me to Carmichael Road to my new home, new parents and new life. No one wept or said that they would miss me. It was an occasion bereft of any melodrama.

~

I took to my new home like a duck to water. In the early days, I felt like I was on top of the world. My older sister (Satyanarayanji's daughter) had long been married and lived in Calcutta, so I was the only child in a large house and was doted on by my new parents. Anything and everything I wanted or asked for—new clothes, new bags, whatever I wanted to eat, plenty of ice creams and sweets—was bought immediately to make me happy. It was a far cry from my old home, where the nine of us vied with each other for attention.

I did miss my old house sometimes, the easy camaraderie with my brothers and cousins, the game of cricket after school and, most importantly, the barrack-like sleeping arrangement where all the kids slept together. I still met my brothers and cousins at school, but I do not remember being traumatized or moping over not going back to my old home. Maybe all the love showered on me by my adoptive parents more than compensated for the loss I may have felt. Perhaps I was too young to understand the consequences of my sudden life-changing situation.

Or probably it was because Marwari families over generations have developed a natural skill for managing adopted kids, minimizing their trauma and helping them adjust to their new environment. One of the smarter things my family did in the first few years was to deliberately avoid frequent get-togethers with my brothers and cousins lest I feel homesick or become nostalgic about my biological family. Though we would meet at family functions, regular meetings were discouraged. My adoptive parents spared no effort in making me happy. Their world revolved around me. They liked nothing better than my calling them 'Ma' and 'Babuji'.

I was still at my old school for a few months after moving in with my new family. Discipline, as I have said earlier, was not a strong point at Marwari Vidyalaya and the bullies had a field day. One day, while playing, one of them pushed me with such force that I hit my head against a bench and got a big bleeding gash that had to be stitched up. All hell broke loose as soon as Ma heard about it. She told Babuji I would not be permitted to go back because I could have died that day and she would have lost her son.

I was happy that I was allowed to stay home for fifteen days so the wound could heal. My parents used this time to admit me to a new school. My mother's insistence on this changed my life forever. No one anticipated the trauma I would go through in adjusting to an English-medium school.

No one in my family had gone to an English-medium school and I was the first to make this tiny piece of family history. And I must fully credit my highly progressive sister for it. Though Bai was living in her marital home in Calcutta, she kept an eagle eye on everything at home in Bombay, including my progress at school and our parents' health. She had barely finished school before getting married, but was encouraged by her in-laws to work towards a BA degree via home tutoring. She was very education-minded and insisted that I be put in an English-medium school.

My father sought and got admission for me at a school that was closest to home. Hill Grange High School was founded and run by the redoubtable Mrs Sophy Kelly, a London-trained Jewish educationist and socialite famous for her proximity to local and national politicians including Jawaharlal Nehru. Founded in 1939, it was among the best schools in south Bombay.

I joined the school in 1957 and my memories of it veer between euphoria and dread. Euphoria because I was leaving behind a school where no one, other than the bullies who roamed free, bothered about what I did. I was now going to what looked like a proper school—a beautiful property spread over four acres, off Peddar Road. It had plenty of open space for games and even had an open-air auditorium.

However, I dreaded the fact that I was switching to an English-medium school. No one at home spoke English. It was a completely alien language. To compound matters, I was only six but was admitted to class three by my father, instead of to class one or two like other kids of my age. He had, in fact, sought to admit me in class five, the class I attended at Marwari Vidyalaya. But the school insisted on admitting me to class three because I was shifting from Hindi-medium to English. Mrs Kelly promised my father that I would be given a double promotion to class five if I did well.

After a difficult first few days, my father hired my class teacher at school, as my private tutor. She would come home after school to teach me. She was gentle, patient and understanding. It made a big difference to my life at school. The students were distinctly friendlier and I was a bit more relaxed. I slowly got used to the new language and did well enough in the final exams to be promoted to class five, but this promotion turned out to be real hell for me at that age.

Since my parents did not speak English, there was no help there. Class five brought new subjects like history, geography and science that I found largely incomprehensible. My father again ensured I had a teacher from school tutoring me at home (though this time it was not my class teacher), but I could not cope. Class three had been relatively easy. Despite the best efforts of the teachers at school and my tutor at home, it was a mighty struggle. Class five was the worst year of my entire academic life.

What I did not realize was that I was too young for the class five-syllabus at Hill Grange; I thought instead that I lacked the mental capacity to learn. Since my private tutor was not my new class teacher, I concluded that I had no one to protect me at school from bullies. Making friends with classmates who mostly conversed in English was challenging; I was totally by myself and miserable. Being the youngest, I was also physically the smallest and could not excel in any competitive sport against my older and bigger classmates. I was always among the extras—and all of this, for a while, created a deep inferiority complex in me.

Eventually, time proved to be the best healer. As the months passed, I started getting better in my studies and my social interactions. I began speaking English and started making new friends. Class six was better and by the time I was in class seven all my angst had disappeared and I was feeling normal once again. I started ranking among the best students in the class and my new friends began coming home to play. By the time I was in class eight, I had propelled myself to the top of the class.

~

When I look back, I feel I did not suffer any lasting damage from the tribulations and distress of my early years at school, only because of the love and affection of my parents at home—they made no academic demands of me and their love was unconditional. I was happiest at home, though I was an only child in a large house.

The biggest issue that adoptive families like mine had to wrestle with, was what to do in case of an unhappy adoption. There was an instance in our building where a family had adopted four siblings and had to send three back to the biological parents; only one chose to stay on. Luckily for my parents, I do not remember ever wanting to go back. Though I did meet my brothers and cousins occasionally, returning for good was something that never crossed my mind. I was well into adulthood and working by the time I re-established a more enduring relationship with my brothers.

Besides my father and mother, what helped in my happy solitary life was my passion for reading comics. I devoured Batman, Superman and Tarzan comics, spending a significant amount of time at a typical Bombay-style lending library located in a building called Kamal Mahal near my home. All my comics and books were rented from here. It was my favourite go-to place throughout my schooldays.

I was so in love with my new home that Ma and Babuji worried I was spending too much time indoors and encouraged me to go out and play with the kids in the building. Our second-floor flat was squeezed between two apartments. These were owned by the two sons of the legendary industrialist, philanthropist and disciple of Mahatma Gandhi, Mr Jamnalal Bajaj. His equally famous sons, Mr Kamalnayan Bajaj and Mr Ramkrishna Bajaj occupied the third and first floors along with their families. That included five sons.

Mr Rahul Bajaj, the elder of the two sons of Kamalnayanji was twelve years older than me. However, his younger brother Shishir and the sons of Ramkrishnaji—Shekhar, Madhur and Niraj—were roughly my age and we became best friends and playmates. I was painfully shy and diffident, but the Bajaj boys and the elders could not have been more understanding and welcoming despite their wealth, status and reputation. I spent a vast amount of time at their house. They treated me more like a family member than a neighbour.

Even at that age, I was able to comprehend the difference between their standard of living and ours. Their well-appointed homes were filled with pictures of family members with Mahatma Gandhi and other prominent political leaders. The children attended the elite schools of

Bombay and went on to prestigious universities abroad. Kamalnayanji was educated at Cambridge, while his son Rahul went to Harvard. They drove fancy cars and took holidays abroad. In comparison, our flat was an ordinary one. We owned an old Dodge and spent our holidays in India.

The Bajajs, like us, had started as traders in Shekhawati. Sometime in the early part of the last century, they had transformed themselves into successful industrialists. I consider myself lucky to have grown up in proximity to such an illustrious family. I am sure I imbibed a lot from them and from what I heard about them. Rahul *bhaiya*, with his education, his early success with Bajaj Scooters and even his good looks and charismatic nature, was an early inspiration for me.

In the 1940s and '50s, Bombay's Carmichael Road—where I have now lived for nearly seventy years—was not the affluent and fancy neighbourhood that it is today. Ours was a rented flat. Babuji had moved here after it became unbearable for Ma to live in our joint family set-up at Sekhsaria House in the Prarthana Samaj area. Babuji could not afford to rent in areas like Marine Drive, Dhobi Talao, Opera House and Malabar Hill where the rich lived in those days. Carmichael Road was the next best option. In the joint family, he had to always manage with a small room, so when the opportunity came to move out, he decided to rent a larger place. His prized possession was an old Dodge car, which my sister told me he had opted for instead of his share of the family property when he separated. The value of the Dodge was higher than the share he was offered.

Babuji was already into his forties when I was adopted. He was a gentle soul who rarely ever reprimanded me, even when I was young. An introvert with very few friends, he spent most of his time with the family. Family was everything to him. We did everything together—eat, play cards, go to the movies. He was a profoundly religious man and did his pooja every day, a routine that I still maintain. He had studied only up to class seven but was a man of strong values, ethics, integrity and honesty. Compassion was another one of his exceptional qualities. I never saw him being unreasonable with anybody, including those he helped financially. He never made them feel obliged for the help he provided. Being religious, he would spend two months every year in spiritual contemplation at a family bungalow we had built in Vrindavan.

Much later in life, I found out something more. One day in the late 1970s or early '80s, I found my wife Nalini packing cash worth a few lakhs into my father's bag. I was too overawed to ask him what he did with the money. Nilu told me that he took that much cash every time he went to Vrindavan and gave it out as alms to the needy. Similarly, he would distribute 100 bags of wheat to the poor every time he went to our hometown Chirawa. The bags were sent to their homes only at night. He did not want people to know about the charity he was doing. These were the values and principles that I witnessed first-hand (and hopefully imbibed) from my father quite early in life.

He was also a great storyteller, a terrific raconteur. Most of what I learnt about life comes from the many stories that he told me during my childhood. These were mostly tales from religious epics and mythology, which he recited with a flourish and never tired of repeating. Every story had a moral, which he made sure to emphasize. Consciously and unconsciously, these morals helped build my ethical self and my character. I have always lived by the simple philosophy that he taught me: you must be honest, do your job, be fair and compassionate to everyone and leave the rest to God.

The earliest lessons that he taught me when I started working were about how to earn money. With our capital of around ₹30 lakh in the family firm, he earned around ₹5 lakh a year. It was quite possible in those days to make more money in Bombay by lending out the same amount of capital at interest to speculators interested in investing in the stock market. This was called *vyaaj-badla*. When I pointed this out to him, he told me, 'You have to understand that even if I earn 10 per cent less, I am providing for the livelihood of the dozens of people who work for us. It is not only about making money but also about looking after your employees.'

Vyaaj-badla was okay in his book as long as you employed surplus capital for the short term, where you could make a bit more money than what the banks provided; but not as a primary source of living. For the same reason, he was against making a living out of the interest earned on one's inheritance, or earning by renting out property. 'The only money that is worth making is the money made from hard work,' was something that he always told me. My thinking about setting up a large enterprise and employing lots of people was probably subconsciously shaped by my father's philosophy about life and work.

As with women in most Marwari households during that time, my mother was a barely literate housewife whose life mostly revolved around me. When I disobeyed or upset her, she would say that I was misbehaving because she was not my birth mother. This would hurt me. And as I grew older, I became increasingly conscious of my centrality in their lives and tried my best to be the good son they wanted me to be.

My sister was my best friend. She would fly down to Bombay at the drop of a hat to meet our parents and me. To me she was like a fairy godmother. She did all the things that my parents could not and would not do for me. She took me for coffee and meals to the best restaurants and taught me how to eat with a knife and fork. My parents rarely ate in restaurants because, like a lot of older adults at that time, they were not comfortable eating what they called 'hotel *ka khana*'.

The happiest days of my childhood were the summer holidays. My father would rent a house in a hill station like Ooty where we would all go, sometimes for up to three months. We never stayed in hotels. The whole family would gather, including Bai, who would come from Calcutta. We would take all the house help, including the cook and the driver with us. Everybody had great fun playing cards, going for long walks and enjoying the surroundings. We also travelled to Kashmir, Nainital and Shimla, but Ooty was our favourite.

These were my best years. After the troubles of the initial years, I had slowly begun settling down in school. By the time I reached the eighth, I had started topping the class. I think I was subconsciously driven by the desire to raise the status of my family. In our daily lives, we were surrounded by wealthy and successful people and I was constantly reminded of our relative inadequacies. This was compounded by the occasional stories I heard about my father's subtle and not-so-subtle humiliations at community gatherings, sometimes because of his girth (he was in poor health and overweight) but mostly because of our comparatively not-so-high status.

As I have said earlier, we were at best a family of moderately successful traders. We were looked down upon by those who were wealthier and more successful, especially at community gatherings. My father would talk about being dismissed with a polite hello or even ignored at religious functions. On several occasions, I overheard him talking to my mother about these hurtful experiences. I believe all these incidents contributed to my single-mindedness to succeed at everything I did, even at a young age and gain respect for my family.

When I was about to enter class nine, our school decided to bring about a significant change in the curriculum by introducing the Indian School Certificate (ISC) examination as an alternative to the existing Secondary School Certificate (SSC) examination system. Only the cream of students, who did well academically, made the selection. I was one of the thirty selected. The next year, in class ten, this batch further shrunk to just seven students and I was chosen once again. We were recognized as smart and studious, the best of the best at Hill Grange.

It raised our stock in school and helped boost my confidence in my abilities. Fellow students now looked up to me and sought me out for help in their studies. I finished at the top of the class in the final board examination, with distinctions in physics, chemistry and mathematics. It was profoundly satisfying, especially considering where I had started.

I passed out of Hill Grange High School in December 1964. By then two of my elder brothers were in college, so it was understood that I would follow them. As an ISC student, I was allowed to skip the first year of college that SSC students had to go through and enter the second year for Inter (or Intermediate) Science. This meant that I saved yet another year and would not even be fifteen on entering college, while the others would be at least seventeen or eighteen.

My brothers had gone to Jai Hind and St. Xavier's, two of the more reputed colleges in south Bombay. Having topped my school in the tough ISC examination, admission to St. Xavier's, then considered the best college in Bombay, was a shoo-in. However, it had the reputation of being a place for fun, where 'socials' were popular and the students were far too fashionable for my family's liking. My father vetoed the idea of me going there. I was disappointed but did not want to cross him. The choice now was between Elphinstone, rated the second-best college in the city and Jai Hind. I opted for the former because I was given admission immediately, while the latter wanted me to wait for a few days.

Just as in school, the first few weeks at Elphinstone were a struggle. I found the Inter (Science) subjects extremely tough. I also had to switch from half pants to full pants, which was not to my liking. I had never worn full pants in school and I did not own a pair until I went to college. This switch was a big deal for me and so was the college lifestyle, as it was for many. The sheltered and regimented life at school had not prepared us for the unfettered freedom of college.

I went crazy with a new-found sense of liberation when I was told that attendance was not mandatory. Elphinstone was a reputed liberal arts college with students who were extremely good at debates and public speaking. I lacked the confidence and ability to do either. Still, I liked attending these events, viewing the participating students with a mix of awe and envy.

Luckily, I was good at making friends and in no time a bunch of us hung out together all the time. We rarely attended class. Most of our time was spent at the canteen or outside college. One of the few times that I did attend class, the professor threw me out for being a nuisance and disturbing her. She also told me not to attend her class again and I never went back. I was such a fixture in the canteen that some started calling me a 'canteen cockroach'.

Contrary to my conservative upbringing, I had started smoking and drinking quite early in life. I had already had my first drink in my senior year at school, on a trip to Nepal. As for smoking, I never bought cigarettes myself out of fear of my parents. But I could always rely on my friends for a steady supply.

The friends I made at Elphinstone and later at the University Department of Chemical Technology (UDCT), also in Bombay, were always out to have fun. They were a cosmopolitan mix; none of them came from my Marwari community. Two were burly Sikhs, who came to my rescue whenever I was teased or made fun of for my size. One of them, Parminder Singh, an army officer's son, has remained a lifelong friend. Thanks to the generous allowance my father gave me, my group and I rarely missed an opportunity to have fun.

When not in the canteen, we would hang out at the many restaurants around the college. South Bombay was a very vibrant neighbourhood even in those days, tailor-made for college students looking to have a good time. It was the fag end of what local historians describe as Bombay's jazz age. The long strip of road running alongside Churchgate station—with Marine Drive at one end and Flora Fountain and beyond at the other—was lined with restaurants that would turn into nightclubs in the evening, with names like Talk of The Town, Bistro Napoli, The Other Room, Bombelli's, Berry's, Venice, The Little Hut, Bistro, Volga and many more. Since half a dozen of Bombay's best colleges were located within walking distance, the restaurants would host special afternoon events for students with 'jam sessions' that featured live bands and dancing.

Jazz music gradually gave way to rock and roll and one of the young men responsible for this shift in Bombay was a Bangalore-born singer by the name of Biddu Appaiah, famous as Biddu. (Bangalore was renamed Bengaluru in 2014.) He had afternoon sessions at the Venice restaurant in Astoria Hotel near Churchgate station, where we were regulars. He would go on to pioneer the disco scene in Europe in the 1970s, with songs like 'Kung Fu Fighting' and 'I Love to Love' and later the Indi-pop scene in India in the 1980s.

The year I joined college, 1965, proved to be historically significant as well. The long-running strife between India and Pakistan culminated in the second major war between the two countries through August and September. We were still too young to understand its ramifications. Civil Defence sirens frequently wailed during the day, while blackouts were the order of the night. After the disruption of a few weeks, things slowly returned to normal and we resumed our daily routine, making the best of the situation.

Strangely enough, this was when I discovered spirituality! I do not remember how, but one day I ended up attending a lecture on the Bhagavad Gita and Hindu philosophy by spiritual leader Swami Chinmayananda. The Chinmaya Mission had become famous across the country by then. I was quite mesmerized by the talk. My father had taught me bits of the Gita at home but listening to it in English, as expounded by the charismatic swami gave me a more in-depth understanding of it. I became a regular at his lectures whenever he came to Bombay. The Gita and its teachings have been an essential part of my life ever since.

As far as my college studies were concerned, I drifted along aimlessly. I had neither any focus in life, nor was I particularly ambitious about the future. I attended a few classes and study days were few and far between. The only time I was committed to studying was during tests and examinations. However, when the results of the final exam were announced, I was in for a pleasant surprise. My marks were good enough for me to be placed among the top five students in our class. I was astonished and so were my friends. It pleased my father no end. Maybe I was fortunate to have got only those questions whose answers I knew. Or perhaps it was my destiny.

Even before the results had come out, it was quite clear from family conversations that I had to move on from Elphinstone and do an engineering degree like my brothers before me. It was not something that excited me, but I went along with it because my brothers had done it. They familiarized me with the hierarchy of the engineering colleges in Bombay. The Indian Institute of Technology (IIT) was ruled out because my family would not allow me to stay in a hostel. I had to be a day-scholar, commuting to college from home every day. All my options thus had to be Bombay-based, while I myself stayed home-based.

The choices were UDCT, a world-renowned chemical engineering college; Victoria Jubilee Technical Institute (VJTI), now known as Veermata Jijabai Technological Institute, which was well known for its mechanical, electrical and civil engineering departments; and Sardar Patel College of Engineering, a relatively new institute set up by the Bharatiya Vidya Bhavan in Andheri. I applied to each before my final exams at Elphinstone.

I was for some reason sure that I would be headed to Sardar Patel, because it was relatively easy to get in for low-scoring students. But I surprised myself by scoring well enough to be admitted to UDCT, the toughest of all colleges to get into, on the list (IIT having already been ruled out). Founded in 1933, UDCT was located in Matunga. Its faculty over the years has earned the reputation of being among the best in the country. Its alumni roster includes some of India's best-known chemical engineers and scientists, including Raghunath Mashelkar and Man Mohan Sharma and a veritable who's who of India's chemical, petrochemical and pharma industries—names like Mukesh Ambani of Reliance Industries, Keki Gharda of Gharda Chemicals, Ashwin Dani of

Asian Paints, K. Anji Reddy of Dr Reddy's Laboratories and Madhukar Parekh of Pidilite.

After an eventful year at Elphinstone, where fun and games were my primary preoccupation, I was now headed to the third and final phase of my formal education. But unlike others who were admitted to UDCT, I had no earnest desire to study chemical engineering. I was going there at the suggestion of my brothers. It was then the best engineering college in Bombay and I always wanted the best for myself. I became aware much later that the college offered a BSc Tech. degree in textile technology, which, if I had taken, would have been closer to our family's line of business.

I was not yet sixteen and as in school and at Elphinstone, I was younger than most others in my class. However at UDCT, for some reason, I did not feel the effects of the age gap. I instantly felt at home. Unlike Elphinstone, I liked attending classes here. Maybe I had matured. I was quick to make friends here too, just as I had at Elphinstone. My father's generosity also helped. Happy with my performance at Elphinstone, he had increased my daily allowance and gifted me an Ambassador car which I drove to college every day. I was one of the few students at UDCT who enjoyed this privilege. When lectures started getting monotonous, we would bunk college and go back to my old haunts in south Bombay, places like Napoli and Volga, for jam sessions.

Unlike my classmates, I knew I was never going to end up working as a chemical engineer, so I never really fell in love with the subject. What I did imbibe were qualities such as a scientific temper and a sense of logic, reasoning and enquiry. I particularly enjoyed the analytical approach to problem-solving. These were the biggest takeaways from my four years of engineering. I still revel in looking at a problem from various angles before arriving at a solution. Subjects like logic, economics and social behaviour were amongst my favourites.

The best part of UDCT was the distinguished faculty that made our lectures worth attending. One of them who stood out for me was Professor Man Mohan Sharma, whose classes I never missed. A chemical engineer with a PhD from Cambridge, he was a rising star at UDCT where he was appointed a professor at the age of twenty-seven. I was spellbound by the way he conducted his classes, his presentations and the way he talked. He was like the Amitabh Bachchan of chemical engineering. Not surprisingly, he went on to become the director of UDCT and the first Indian engineer to be made a Fellow of the Royal Society. He was awarded the Padma Vibhushan in 2001.

Despite all the fun and games, I managed to finish in the top 25 per cent of students in my first year and moved up into the top 10 per cent in the second year. By the third year, I had mastered the subjects and topped the university. I did the same in my final year as well. I was ecstatic; so were my parents. It was the most significant moment of my life until then. I had come a long way since my Marwari Vidyalaya days, fifteen years ago. Professor Sharma was disappointed that I was not keen to pursue a master's degree or join some reputed chemical company through campus placement. I had decided to stay back in Bombay and start my own business. 'You've wasted a seat, a seat that could have benefited someone else,' he told me.

I disagreed with his assessment. My four years at UDCT were extremely productive and I benefited from them tremendously. Four rigorous years in a chemical engineering college prepare you for more than running a chemical plant. They help you learn to think logically and laterally, understand intricate processes and solve complex problems.

The examples of Asian Paints chairman Ashwin Dani, who was at UDCT before me and Mukesh Ambani, who was four years my junior, prove this point. So do the successes of the likes of Raghuram Rajan and Nandan Nilekani, both of whom are electrical engineers from IIT. What I learnt at UDCT had a significant role to play in everything that I did thereafter in life, from the transformation of our family's cotton-trading business to the setting up of Gujarat Ambuja and its success over the years.

In other ways too, UDCT was an eye-opener for me. I saw first-hand and for the first time, the struggle of poor students who were classmates of mine, from towns across India. I learnt how difficult life was for them and the conditions they lived in at the hostel on campus. I had led a very sheltered life and this was a good learning experience about the world outside. It gave me a unique appreciation of the privileges that I had grown up with and the realization that I should be grateful to God for all my successes.

The UDCT years also gave me three of my closest friends in life. Unlike me, they all moved to the United States of America (henceforth the US) after graduation for further studies, work and finally, retirement—T.C. Venkat worked with Sony and now lives in San Diego; Abhay Mehta worked with Aramco in Saudi Arabia before retiring to Denver; and Kris Murdia, who still works with Fluor Corporation and lives in Los Angeles. A few years ago, all of us went on a holiday to Goa and after that to Las Vegas. Likewise, I meet my close friend Parminder Singh from my Elphinstone days at least twice a year, in Bombay or in Dubai, where he now lives.

It was also UDCT that helped me find a mentor in Mr T.V. Chidambaram, the legendary registrar of Bombay University in its glory days of the 1960s and '70s. Bombay University in those days was one of India's great centres of learning, with some of the best faculties in the country. The vice-chancellors were illustrious men like Dr John Matthai and Justice P.B. Gajendragadkar. They gave the university vision and direction, while the day-to-day running was in the hands of equally powerful registrars such as Mr Chidambaram. He was a self-made man who started life as a stenographer and worked his way up. He was the father of T.C. Venkat who became a close friend after we met in our second year at UDCT. We spent a lot of time in each other's homes. Because of my gregarious nature, I became close to his parents as well.

Venkat went through a difficult phase when he failed to clear his exams and had to repeat the second year. Mr Chidambaram was having a tough time communicating with him and his younger brother. He suspected that his sons were indulging in undesirable activities. I, on the other hand, probably came across as more mature and that is why he asked me to help Venkat out of the terrible mess he was in, which I did. It brought us even closer. Venkat went on to do his master's in chemical engineering in the US and had a successful corporate career.

Mr Chidambaram thought of me as a son and I used to spend quite a bit of time at their house even after Venkat left for the US. I saw first-hand the grace with which Mr Chidambaram handled the pressure of his job. Running Bombay University, with its over 1,00,000 students and dozens of colleges spread across the city, was a massive enterprise in those days. Watching him work was a master class in management. His integrity, professionalism and ability to keep himself and the university above politics taught me a lot.

He was always ready to discuss with and counsel anybody who came to him with a problem. From office assistants to the CM, no one left his office or home without their issues being resolved. He expected nothing in return. It was not surprising that Bombay University was considered among the best run in India till the time he was in office. His retirement coincided with the beginning of the decline of the university's strong reputation built over more than 100 years by men like him.

Mr Chidambaram took pride in my academic achievements. After I passed out of UDCT with impressive credentials, he wrote to the CM requesting that I be made a 'Justice of the Peace', a prestigious honour granted by the government to private citizens in those days, which gave them certain rights and privileges to help people. I got the appointment within a week of his recommendation. I was not yet twenty and was probably the youngest ever 'Justice of the Peace' in the city!

As a frequent visitor to his house in those days, I sought Mr Chidambaram's advice very often, even after I joined my family's cotton business. When I was looking for a new banking relationship, he took out his phone book and called all the senior bankers he knew. He helped me in a variety of other ways as well. When he was retiring from Bombay University, I asked him where he was going to stay. He told me he had bought a small flat in Matunga with his savings. I felt a man of his stature deserved better, particularly after having lived in a large house in south

Bombay during his time as registrar. I asked him to move into the three-bedroom flat I owned on Nepean Sea Road. That was the least I could do for him. He died there not long ago. His ninety-three-year-old wife still lives in the flat with their younger son.

As I mentioned above, when I left UDCT, Professor Sharma had chided me for wasting a seat. He was referring to the fact that I was not keen on further studies. That was a period in the country's history when opportunities were limited. A vast majority of professionally qualified students from universities like IIT and UDCT, including my closest friends, were going abroad for their master's, followed by a high-paying job in multinational corporations (MNCs) in the US or Europe. Those were the early days of the great Indian brain drain.

Professor Sharma was shocked when I told him that I had no such plan. It was not a decision that I arrived at impulsively or reluctantly. I had planned my career path even before I entered college. Whatever my degree, my eventual destination was my family business. Though this surprised Professor Sharma, it would not have startled anyone in our Marwari community. Our minds are wired to work for ourselves. The idea of working for others was almost an alien concept even then.

The thought of going abroad did cross my mind occasionally, particularly in the final year as I watched my friends go through their admission processes to international universities. If the circumstances were different, I would have opted for an MBA and not a master's in engineering. I was not interested in doing any more research in chemical engineering and a management degree would have helped me in my business. However, this was only a passing thought and not something that I considered seriously.

There was no question of me leaving my parents and going anywhere. It was what my parents wanted and it was something that I wholeheartedly wanted too. I never even broached the idea of going abroad. My father would have been shattered if I had told him that I was going away for two or three years. Times were different then. Remember that I was not even allowed to take the IIT entrance examination, because if I got in I would have to stay on campus in a hostel.

I never felt any resentment towards my parents for the decision I made. Not for a moment did I think that I was doing it for them. My sense of duty towards them was unconditional. A year earlier I had, on their urging, happily got engaged to my future wife Nalini. Ma and Babuji were getting old and they wanted me married as soon as I finished college and, of course, have children.

I was nineteen and in my final year at college. Even by the standards of the 1960s, I was too young to be married. Nilu was hardly fifteen and lived with her parents on Marine Drive. I was so shy about the whole thing that I kept it a secret from even my closest friends. I got married in January 1971, within seven months of graduating from UDCT. I would have been married four months earlier, but for a tragedy in the family when my sister's husband died unexpectedly.

Nilu got in the family way almost immediately and our son Pulkit was born in December 1971, within ten months of our wedding. His birth carries many memories for me. I still remember the evening when I had to drive Nilu to Elizabeth's Nursing Home on Malabar Hill in pitch darkness. We were in the middle of the third Indo-Pak war (from 3 to 16 December 1971), and Bombay was under a complete blackout over fears of a night-time air raid. The streetlights were switched off, our windows at home were sealed with black paper to prevent light from seeping out and the car's headlights were perforce blacked out. There was an eerie silence on the streets and the only light was from the stars above. Luckily for us, everything went smoothly. I was just twenty-one, still trying to figure out what to do with my life.

By a strange quirk of fate, my college phase was wedged between the two major wars that India and Pakistan fought in 1965 and '71. Our illustrious neighbour Mr Kamalnayan Bajaj was a three-term Congress MP, but we never discussed politics at home. It was not something that interested my father. I did keep track of the momentous changes in the country in those five years—Lal Bahadur Shastri's Jai Jawan Jai Kisan movement; his death in Tashkent; Mrs Indira Gandhi's rise to power; her leftward tilt; the nationalization of banks; the split in the Congress; the abolition of the privy purse; the Gold (Control) Act; the Garibi Hatao movement; the wars with Pakistan; and the eventual creation of Bangladesh.

I had also grown to like the courage and methods of an up-and-coming Bombay trade union leader-turned-politician George Fernandes, who had just started making his presence felt. I had chanced upon his speech one evening at Chowpatty beach. My admiration for him grew when he dealt a politically fatal blow to the then powerful Union minister and so-called 'king of Bombay' S.K. Patil, in the 1967-parliamentary election from the Bombay South constituency. Patil, who was known for his cosy relations with prominent Bombay industrialists, never recovered from that defeat. At the same time, Fernandes was thrust on the national stage almost immediately.

I got to know him well later in life and my respect only increased. He was a clean, idealistic politician and a diehard socialist. Unlike others of his ilk whom I knew, he never asked for money, directly or indirectly. I used to visit him at his home in Bombay and was always impressed by his simple lifestyle. He was always warm and welcoming.

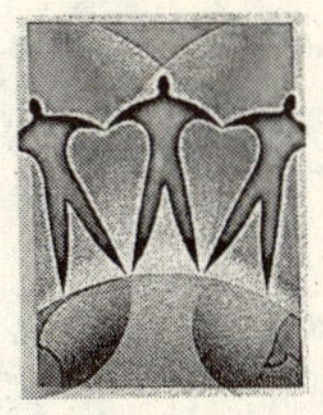

2

The Making of a Trader

Modernizing the family cotton business • Export success • Foray into construction, chemicals, pharmaceuticals and more

The early 1970s were the worst of times if you were a young man starting out. The war of 1971, the Bangladesh refugee crisis and frequent monsoon failures had ruined the economy. High food prices, rupee devaluation and rocketing unemployment had ravaged the economy. The margins on our cotton business had reduced to a level where my father was reluctant even to ask me to join him and his cousins. 'You didn't become an engineer to become a trader,' he would tell me.

Coming from a Marwari business background, the thought of looking for a job, even with the fanciest of salaries, was anathema. Had I wanted, I could have easily taken up a job during campus recruitment when the best of Indian chemical companies descended on UDCT, because of the high quality of chemists and engineers it produces. I hoped to start my own business, preferably in chemicals, since that was my specialization. I had no clue how to go about this. I knew that raising capital would not be easy. My father's share in the family's cotton-trading business was worth less than ₹15 lakh.

I started meeting people within my family and others I knew for advice—extended family members, friends and social acquaintances in similar businesses. I even met my neighbours, the Bajajs, since they were running several companies across the country. Two things happened as a result. A family friend I respected told me bluntly, 'You cannot set up a business from scratch where your family has no connection or working knowledge. You should first join your family business and then do everything else later. You do not have much capital, so join the family cotton business, use your skills to make it more profitable and then look to do other things you are passionate about on the side.'

When I told him that there was no future in cotton, he said, 'This is where your skills will come into play. Your challenge will be to revive the business in a bad environment.' It was a piece of advice that made a significant impact on me, something that has remained with me all my life.

In July or August 1970, roughly around the same time that I met the gentleman quoted above, I attended a seminar at the Taj Mahal Hotel in Bombay on how to start a small business, something which I thought would help me. It was a two-day affair attended by around 100 people and I remember paying a few hundred rupees to register, a princely sum in those days. On the sidelines of the seminar, I met a young man in the same boat as me. Inder Somani's family ran companies like Digvijay Cement and West Coast Paper. We exchanged numbers and got to know each other well over the next few months.

Like me, Inder was just out of college. We would meet up once a week and exchange notes. One day when we were walking on Marine Drive, we ran into a friend of his, Deepak Ratansi. He was the son of Mr Ratansi Muljee, the owner of Finlay, Gold Mohur and Swan, three leading textile mills in Bombay and was a year or two elder to me.

Later that evening, we met up with Deepak for coffee post-dinner, where I got to know that he had just started working with his father at Finlay. When I told him that my family was in the cotton-trading business, he graciously offered to introduce me to his father. It piqued my interest because I knew my family had not been able to make an entry into the hugely competitive Bombay textile mills market despite being cotton traders in the city for nearly two generations.

Besides exporting cotton to Japan, which we had been doing for many years, most of our operations were based out of Punjab, Rajasthan and Haryana, where we bought locally grown cotton from the suppliers and sold it to nearby textile mills as commission agents. We had never been able to make inroads directly into the mills of two of India's biggest textile cities, Ahmedabad and Bombay. I sensed Deepak's offer as an opportunity to change this history.

Deepak was the youngest of four brothers and his father's favourite. When he told Mr Ratansi about me and my Marwari background and how I was also just out of college, he readily agreed to meet me. Mr Ratansi had originally been a commission agent for the Bombay-based textile arm of the Calcutta-headquartered, colonial-era Scottish management agency, James Finlay & Co. When the company decided to exit India in the mid-1960s, its Calcutta-based tea operation was sold to the Tatas while Mr Ratansi bought its three Bombay-based textile mills for a paltry sum of ₹80 lakh, which he paid over five years. I went to see him in the hope that as the owner of some of Bombay's most prestigious mills, he would allow us to supply him cotton.

Mr Ratansi was an impressive-looking man clad fully in white. After exchanging pleasantries in his office, he asked what he could do for me. I gave him an account of our family's lengthy trading background. I told him that I would be grateful if he gave me a chance to supply him cotton because we had never worked with a Bombay mill before. He was sceptical initially, saying that Finlay used only imported cotton for its fabrics. I said that was not a problem. 'Please give me an order for 100 bales and assess my ability to service it.' He agreed to give me a chance and wrote down the details of the quality of cotton that he wanted, on a sheet of paper.

When I told my father and my other family members about the deal, they could hardly believe that a reputed mill in Bombay had placed an order with us. With the help of my father, I got the cotton bales of the required quality from a local broker. I delivered it to Finlay well within the stipulated time. Mr Ratansi was happy with the quality of the cotton, the price and my service. And I made a good profit on the deal, the first in my life.

I then began meeting Mr Ratansi regularly and he gave me more orders. Every day, around 4 p.m., suppliers like me were required to meet him for orders. He would meet us individually, discuss the price that day on the cotton exchange and the demand-supply situation, after which the order would be placed, if at all that day. Depending on the price, he would either buy the cotton requirement for a few weeks or a few months. If it was for a more extended period, the supplier was expected to warehouse the cotton and bear the cost, which would be reimbursed when the mill picked up the supply.

I would land up at his office in the evening and first spend some time with my friend Deepak, who worked with his father. Mr Ratansi would then call me and discuss what was happening in the market and then place the order. I quickly mastered his buying process. I worked hard and provided him with the best of service. He, in turn, began trusting me more and raised my quota every month. Within two years, I became the biggest supplier of cotton to Finlay, responsible for more than half of its requirements.

As time passed, my business expanded to include the group's other mills, Gold Mohur and Swan. In the first year, I must have supplied 5,000 to 7,000 bales; in the second year, the figure more than doubled to 15,000 bales and I never looked back thereafter. The group was known in Bombay for the high quality of its fabrics and bought the best-quality Egyptian and Sudanese cotton. My mantra even then was to be very efficient and timely in our supply and to keep our costs down to a minimum. Their fabric sold at a premium, so they paid the best price for the cotton. My profits virtually doubled every year.

For me, the success was even sweeter because, in the parochial world of Bombay's textile mills, Gujarati mill owners invariably worked with only Gujarati cotton brokers. At least at Finlay, I was the first Marwari to breach this wall. In the early years, there was even an incident that solidified my relationship with Mr Ratansi.

He was going away to Kashmir for his annual family vacation. He asked me to buy his regular quota of cotton while he was away. No sooner had I purchased his requirement at the instructed price than rates started shooting up on account of some changes in the international market. Having studied the market carefully over months, I had a hunch that the prices would shoot up further. I felt it would result in a massive loss for Mr Ratansi. I quickly bought more cotton for him over the next few days, though he had not instructed me to do so. My understanding was that even if he did not buy it from me, I would be able to sell it in the open market and make a much bigger profit.

My hunch proved to be right and by the time Mr Ratansi came back prices had more than doubled. He was distraught and called for me immediately. He asked me whether I had bought the cotton that he had ordered; I said I had and that I knew it would last him only a few weeks. He said he would suffer a significant loss if the prices did not come down. That is when I revealed what I had done on his behalf. He was bewildered. 'Why would you give it to me at last month's price when the price has more than doubled now?' he asked me incredulously.

I told him I had bought it for him and not to make any extra profit. In the cut-throat world of cotton trading where profit was the primary motive, it was unlikely that anyone would have said this to him. He refused my offer, saying that I deserved to keep the gains because of my sharp thinking. In his calculation, I was offering to forgo ₹50 lakh. 'Traders pray and dream about this kind of windfall. You are foolish to make this offer,' he declared. I reminded him that I was an agent and was entitled to only my regular commission.

I insisted that Mr Ratansi take the cotton at the price I had paid. Instead of short-term profit, I was looking to build a long-term business relationship with him, I said. He couldn't believe that anyone in his right mind would forgo a windfall profit of this kind. As for me, I was not acting out of character. My father, who believed in ethics and integrity, would have wanted me to do this. I have always believed that honesty and ethics pay a much higher dividend in the long run.

Mr Ratansi had another problem. He told me that he did not have the money in hand to take delivery of the entire quantity of cotton that I had bought for him. I told him not to worry and that I would finance it. By then, I had developed good relations with the banks.

The news of what I had done for Mr Ratansi soon spread across the cotton and textile community in Bombay. My stock went up in the fraternity and I got a call from a fellow broker saying Mr Yogendra Mafatlal wanted to see me. I was more than flattered by this call. At that time, the undivided Mafatlal family owned some of India's most successful textile mills including Mafatlal Industries, Matulya Mills and Standard Mills. At their peak in the 1960s and the '70s, they were among the wealthiest and most successful business houses in Bombay. To get a call from them was undoubtedly any cotton broker's dream.

Mr Yogendra Mafatlal was the younger brother of the group patriarch, Mr Arvind Mafatlal. As I rode up the lift at Mafatlal House, their Nariman Point headquarters, I was nothing short of ecstatic. Mr Yogendra Mafatlal greeted me warmly, asked about my background and demanded that I give him a full rundown on what happened with Finlay. He said I had done something unthinkable in Bombay's world of cotton trading and asked me about our family cotton business.

I told him that our strength was in Punjab cotton that we had been selling for decades. I requested him to buy our cotton, which was among the best in India. He asked for some samples to be sent across for testing, which I did. In no time, I became a regular supplier to the Mafatlal group mills, again the first Marwari to break what was till then a monopoly of Gujarati brokers.

Mr Yogendra Mafatlal instructed me to call him at 9 a.m. every day to brief him on the situation in the cotton market, based on which he would make his purchase decisions. Gradually I got to know the other members of the Mafatlal family as well, including Mr Arvind Mafatlal and his son Padmanabh.

My growing business relationship with the Mafatlals helped enhance my reputation in the market. I started getting calls from other mill owners and soon I was in business with more than half a dozen of the biggest textile mills in the city, including those owned by the Goenkas and the Kanorias. And the best part was that I was still in my early twenties! Even mill owners who never did business with me, like Mr Mohanlal Piramal who owned Piramal Mills, would often call me for consultation and general chit-chat.

I think they were impressed by the fact that I was an engineer from a reputed college but chose to be a cotton trader. Unlike with other brokers, they could discuss subjects like the state of the economy with me and the subsequent fluctuations in the cotton prices. At the risk of sounding immodest, even at that young age I had the ability to establish my credibility at the very first meeting with most people I met. My youth was no bar at all for people to take me seriously.

Besides timely service and quality, the other big trump card in getting business from the Bombay mills in those days was the finance facility that I offered them for long-term purchase of cotton. I had established a large banking facility for myself, which helped me fund the warehousing of the cotton bought by clients. It gave me a significant advantage over my competitors who, like my own family members, were still reluctant to use financing from banks to expand their business.

The general view in those days was that banks hated financing local traders, which was partly right. Traders, in turn, were reluctant to deal with banks because of this attitude. When I joined our business, we had a cash credit limit of only ₹30 lakh at our bank. I asked my father and uncles about it and they said they had never approached the bank to raise the credit limit because they were not sure if the bank would agree. They were worried that the bank would cancel even the existing facility. My family preferred to fund their trades themselves, which meant that we could not do any big deals.

I found this attitude self-defeating. We were model clients of the bank, had never defaulted, had no pending dues, were always on time with our interest and principal repayments and were consistently profitable. I found my family's fear of approaching the bank very irrational and I decided to do something about it.

Our account in those days was with the main branch of the Bank of India (BoI) on Mahatma Gandhi Road in south Bombay. I decided to talk to them myself. No sooner had I enquired about raising our drawing limit than the concerned officer launched into a tirade, 'You people are useless; you have the facility, but never send us a balance sheet, income tax return statement or even a profit and loss statement.'

He added in a tone of exasperation, 'I don't even get a stock statement. We do not know where the stock is.' He pulled out a statement, looked at me and said, 'It says here that you have 3,000 bales in Punjab; I don't know which godown, if I want to cross-check.'

I pacified him by saying that I would make sure all the statements were sent to him immediately. At the end of the tirade, as my father had predicted, he said he was going to cancel our credit limit. I decided that I had to be firm with him. 'Have I ever defaulted on my payments?' I asked him. He said no.

'Have I even once overdrawn on my limit?' He said no.

'We have never issued a bounced cheque either,' I said. 'Not providing information on time cannot be the grounds for cancelling anyone's facility.'

He said it was better to talk to his senior.

His senior was Mr G.N. Ranade who sat at the main office of the bank at Flora Fountain's iconic BoI building. He was the cash credit manager for the Bombay region, which made him the sanctioning authority for any loans issued in the city. He seemed amiable and warm as he welcomed me into his office. He asked me about my background.

When I mentioned UDCT, he said it was the finest engineering college in India but was surprised that I had joined my father's business after graduation. I said I had to do it because my father was old and not very well. 'Let me compliment you, young man,' he said, 'your thinking is right, you must first look after your family and your father.'

I was relieved that the meeting had started on the right note. Mr Ranade was impressed by my credentials and the fact that we had always made money and had never defaulted on our banking obligations. He promised to increase our credit limit if I submitted all the required documents regularly. I promised to do that and requested him to guide me in banking as I was new to it. He was more than happy and eager to do this. 'You can have a cup of tea with me any day between 2 and 2.30 in the afternoon,' he told me.

Once I had submitted all the documents, he issued the order for a significant increase in our credit limit. I began meeting him quite often. He was generous with his time and knowledge. He introduced me to the people in his office who handled hundi payments. Long used by Indian traders as a financial instrument to extend credit, the hundi was still immensely popular in those days.

The BoI's hundi department also used to collect credit intelligence from the markets about borrowers of the bank. I got to know the two officers who managed this department. Whenever I went to see Mr Ranade, I would also spend time with them, absorbing all the information and knowledge I could on the goings-on in markets like grain and bullion. I picked up a lot of my banking knowledge from Mr Ranade and the understanding of other markets from my new friends in the hundi department.

I used the enhanced bank credit facility mostly to help fund the warehousing facility that I provided mill owners for their long-term purchase of cotton. I would put down 25 per cent of the required capital and the banks would give the rest. The great thing about this was that I ended up making money out of these financial arrangements. We used to charge the client 2.5 per cent per month, which came to 30 per cent annually. My annual interest payment to the bank totalled around 15 per cent. After paying about another 1 per cent as warehouse rent and expenses, the rest was my profit. The warehousing business turned out to be a hugely profitable operation. My earnings at one point were as much as 60 per cent of the investment.

With time, my warm relationship with BoI extended to Mr Ranade's boss, Mr R.S. Balsekar, Bombay region's general manager. He was the officer who signed off on all my loans and this relationship proved to be useful during a national strike when all banking operations had come to a standstill. I had a consignment of cotton waiting at the docks, for which I had to pay an import duty of ₹50 lakh. I had money in my account, but I could not access it because of the strike. As a result, I was being forced to pay demurrage, the expensive penalty that ports charge for not clearing imported consignments within the stipulated time.

I went to Mr Balsekar, who was working through the strike and told him about my plight. I requested him to help me withdraw my money. These were pre-computer days and he had no way to confirm if I had the necessary funds in my account. He did not even ask for my passbook when he pulled his drawer open and took out a Reserve Bank of India (RBI) chequebook. He wrote out a cheque for the required amount. I was stunned by what he had done, the trust he had reposed in me. An RBI cheque is among the safest financial instruments and is used only rarely. He had never done this before, he told me. Fortunately, the strike ended after two days and things went back to normal. I felt a sense of pride in my ability to build relationships where people went out of their way to help me.

By the mid-1970s, the exponential growth in my business meant that I was personally contributing to as much as 90 per cent of our family business turnover and most of its profit. I was still in my midtwenties, but I had already taken over the leadership role in my family. While people shy away from such a role, I enjoyed it immensely. My uncles, brothers and cousins, including those much older than me, looked up to me to make critical decisions. I did not shy away.

I was reasonably well-off now. I had a wonderful life with my wife and two young children. My daughter Padmini was born in 1975. I worked only from 11 a.m. to 6 p.m. on most days, was a member of some of south Bombay's best clubs and took frequent holidays within India and abroad. I loved cars and had been driving one since I was sixteen. Now I could afford imported cars like a Toyota. I used to buy new cars quite often from the State Trading Corporation (STC), the government organization that was the only authorized agency for the sale of foreign vehicles.

I loved staying in the best of hotels while on holiday or business. Once while in London, I met Mr Padmanabh Mafatlal and took him out for drinks and dinner to a very fancy place. One of the things he asked me was how a cotton trader like me could afford such a lifestyle. And then when we went back to my hotel, he was even more surprised because I was staying at the high-end Four Seasons, while he was at a much cheaper hotel! I liked to live well.

~

After thriving for more than a century, by the mid-1970s the textile mills in the organized sector all around the country began facing a significant headwind. Things only got worse with every passing year. A combination of problems including the prolonged economic slowdown, competition from the surging power loom sector across the country that was churning out cheaper textiles, illegal imports from China, Japan and Korea and the rise of Dr Datta Samant, a physician-turned-labour leader and his brand of aggressive trade unionism, progressively destroyed the industry in less than a decade.

Finlay, which had kick-started my career, was among the earliest to face problems. It went from being a very profitable mill to making losses in a matter of a few years. I could see the immediate impact of this downturn in the form of delayed payments. When I first started working with them, I would get my payment the day after the delivery of the contracted cotton. It then became three days and after some time, seven days. It was a matter of concern. After about three months, the delay increased to fifteen days and then thirty days. I had a policy of 'no credit' to clients and it had served me well. Things were not looking good with Finlay.

I continued doing business with Mr Ratansi only because of sentimental reasons. By 1975, however, I was worried as my dues had risen to more than ₹1 crore, which was my profit for two years. While I was stressing about this, help came in the form of another bank manager. I first met Mr B.K. Vora when he was the deputy general manager of Punjab National Bank (PNB) in Bombay. As my business grew, I needed more lines of credit, so I expanded my portfolio of banks to include PNB, which was close to our office in Kalbadevi.

Within months of our meeting, Mr Vora became the general manager of the bank and not long after that was appointed as the chairman of Dena Bank. The position of general manager of a bank like PNB was in those days equivalent to the chairmanship of a small bank like Dena. Though I had no working relationship with Dena Bank, I kept in touch with Mr Vora and met him often when he was in the city.

Luckily for me, Dena Bank was the principal banker to Mr Ratansi and the Finlay group. One Sunday when Mr Vora was in Bombay, I went to see him at his guest house in Sterling Apartments on Peddar Road. During our conversation, I told him about my pending payments with Finlay. I was particularly concerned because the mill was incurring huge losses and the prospect of recovering my money was increasingly looking bleak. He thought about it for a while and told me to come to his office at Horniman Circle at 10 a.m. the next day.

I went, not knowing what to expect. When I arrived, to my surprise Mr Ratansi was also waiting to see him. I was convinced that Mr Ratansi had somehow got to know about my conversation with Mr Vora and was probably upset about it. He looked as tense as I was. I greeted him formally while we waited. Mr Vora summoned us into his cabin together, made us sit next to each other and asked Mr Ratansi, 'Does Narotam supply cotton to you?'

Mr Ratansi replied in the affirmative.

'Are you happy with him?'

He again said yes and added, 'He supplies 50 per cent of my requirement of premium cotton and he is like my son.'

Mr Vora then said, 'I also treat Narotam like my son, but I would like to find a solution to the problem he is facing regarding the unpaid dues of Finlay.'

Mr Ratansi replied that the simple solution would be for Dena Bank to give him a loan, since his proposal was already pending with the bank. 'You sanction my loan and I will pay him,' he told Mr Vora.

It looked like a quick fix to my problem, but Mr Vora did not buy it. 'I can't sanction a loan like that,' he said.

'Then how will I pay him if I am making losses? Everyone knows that the textile industry is in big trouble,' Mr Ratansi responded.

Mr Vora asked him if he had any textile stock that could be given to me in place of my dues. Mr Ratansi said that he could not give away finished textiles, but could give me fents and rags worth the amount of the loan. Fents and rags are leftover fabric that is either damaged or is of a non-standard size. Any material that is less than 90 centimetres in length is defined as fent, while rags are even smaller. Textile mills collect and sell them periodically. Commonly known as cut-piece fabric, these are always in high demand across the country because they are cheap and are used to make children's clothes and women's blouses and tops.

Mr Ratansi said he had about ₹1.5 crore worth of fents and rags sitting in his godown, which he could give me. Mr Vora asked me if I was prepared to take them. I impulsively said yes, though I had no idea what we would do with them. Mr Vora then told Mr Ratansi to take me to the Finlay office and work out the deal. We decided to meet the next day.

When I went back home and asked my father if he had any idea about the market for fents and rags, he said he was clueless. I told him that this was the only way I could recover my money from Finlay and that even if we made a loss of ₹15 to 20 lakh, it was better than losing ₹1 crore.

'How will you sell it?' he wanted to know. I had no immediate answer and told him that I was going to ask others.

Besides our office in Kalbadevi, in those days we also had an office at Tamarind Lane, next to the Bombay Stock Exchange (BSE). In the next building was the office of a textile mill called Raja Bahadur Motilal Poona Mills. I used to know a textile broker who worked there. The next day I asked him if he had any idea about fents and rags, particularly the ones from Finlay. He said he dealt in them and that those sold by Finlay were among the best in the Bombay market and fetched a high price. I told him about the stock I would be getting and he immediately offered to buy it.

On my father's advice I set up a new division named Radheshyam Textiles as part of our trading company. I picked up the fents and rags from Finlay under its name. Mr Ratansi was more than happy to part with them and clear my dues. The quality of my stock was so good that the broker helped me dispose of the complete stock and in the process I also made a small profit, instead of the anticipated loss. I never dealt in fents and rags again but used Radheshyam Textiles as the base for the export of finished textiles, a new business that I had started. Though I continued to work with Finlay, I progressively reduced my supply to them. I did not want more problems for myself or to embarrass Mr Ratansi any further. Instead, I stepped up our export of cotton and textiles.

~

For more than two generations, my family business had been conducted out of a two-storey office building that we owned in Kalbadevi. It was our first office, set up when Kalbadevi was the premier trading district for cotton, and in an area dominated by the building that housed the cotton exchange. India's biggest cotton and textile traders had their offices here, as did many textile mills.

Gujaratis and Marwaris like us dominated the trade, working out of traditional *pedi-gadhi* style offices where everyone sat on the floor on wall-to-wall mattresses covered by crisp white sheets, strewn with bolsters to lean against. Low desks held the traditional red ledgers referred to as *bahi-khata* and our transactions and accounts were recorded in these. Cash was stored in an iron safe in a corner. A small adjacent room had mattresses laid out for the elderly family members to take an afternoon nap.

My family was still working out of our Kalbadevi office when I joined the business in 1970. But I, with my engineering degree and a more modern sensibility, was reluctant to work out of that office. I could not imagine sitting cross-legged on a mattress and working the whole day. It was not the kind of place where one could invite a friend or business associate for a meeting. I decided to work from our relatively more modern Tamarind Lane office at Fort, where the export and stock-trading division was based. I shared a table with my cousin, who was working as an understudy to the export manager.

However, I outgrew the Tamarind Lane office relatively quickly as well. The gleaming new high-rises that were coming up at Nariman Point, Bombay's newest office district at the southern end of Marine Drive, had caught my fancy. The first of the glass-and-steel skyscrapers—the Air India building, Express Towers and Mafatlal House—were already up. This was the smart new face of Indian business and I wanted to be part of a new generation of businessmen working there. Within a year of starting to trade, I had made enough money to afford office space in one of these buildings. When I told my father that I was looking at Nariman Point, he did not think it was a good idea. 'Look at Ballard Estate or Fort; you will get properties at half the price,' he told me. But I was adamant.

A cotton broker put me in touch with a member of the Mittal family who had started work on a building named Mittal Chambers, not far from Express Towers. I went to meet him and told him I was looking for a 1,000 square-feet office. He said he had a few on the sixth and seventh floors. From my experience of visiting the BoI office at Express Towers, a higher floor would mean a long wait for the lift. I asked him how many lifts his building would have. He said four. Express Towers had six and still had long queues.

I told him I would prefer something on the first or second floor, because I did not want to use the lift. He probably thought I was stupid, because in those early days of the skyscraper experience in Bombay, everyone wanted to be on a higher floor. Unfortunately, he told me, the lower floors only had larger spaces, 5,000 square feet or more. I did not want such a large space. In that case, he said, there was nothing he could do. He was offering it at ₹125 per square foot, which I quickly calculated would come to ₹6.25 lakh.

Since the building was still under construction, I asked him how much I would have to pay upfront. He said 90 per cent, in a tone that was dismissive. I think he was trying to get rid of me because at twenty-two I looked too young to buy a property that size. To show him I was serious, I told him I would take the space right away and he would have his cheque of ₹5.5 lakh in a few hours. 'My person will collect the agreement tomorrow,' I told him. He looked surprised.

I came home and told my father what I had done.

He said, 'You've gone crazy. What are you going to do with 5,000 square feet?'

I told him not to worry, I would sell it when the price went up, or we could rent out the extra space. To me, it was like a trading transaction. A few days later, the agreement came to me and it had a clause which said that I had to pay ₹1.25 per square foot as perpetual rent per month to the Government of Maharashtra for the property. My father was even more upset. He told me I would have got the best of properties on rent elsewhere in south Bombay for much less.

It took two years for the building to be ready and for me to move there. It proved to be lucky for me, as my business prospered. I converted a large corner of the office into a traditional-style office area with a floor mattress and bolsters and moved my entire family business there as well. It was the office where I started the many companies that I set up over the years, including Gujarat Ambuja in the early 1980s. For a long time, Corporation Bank's foreign exchange division was our tenant in one part of the property. Our cotton-trading operation is still run from there, nearly fifty years later.

My first diversification in the early 1970s was into bulk drugs and pharma. It was a logical extension since I had spent four of the best years of my life studying chemical engineering. And it was the first area of business that I had explored after college before serendipitously landing the Finlay deal. Soon after my initial success in cotton trading, I had invested ₹10 lakh in setting up a chemical-trading business under the name of Sekhsaria Chemicals. It proved to be profitable quite early.

Around the same time, an old college acquaintance of mine by the name of Dr S.K. Agarwal, who had stayed on at UDCT to do his master's and PhD, came to see me. He said he had an idea to set up a bulk drug unit to manufacture a chemical called oxyphenbutazone, a much-in-demand ingredient used in painkillers such as Ibuprofen. He said he had figured out a way of synthesizing it at a low cost. I asked him what this would entail as a business. He said he would need to build a small laboratory to synthesize the compound and a manufacturing unit with 20 litre glass flasks, which would later be scaled up to 10,000 litre glass-lined vessels.

'What about people?' I asked. He said the head of the Chemistry department at UDCT had agreed to come on board, in addition to which he had found a few PhD candidates who were willing to join.

I thought of it as a workable idea with good export potential. If it were a simple compound involving a large-scale chemical process, the manufacturing cost difference between India and the US would be negligible. But in the case of a complex molecule, like the one Dr Agarwal was suggesting, it would require dozens of qualified chemists to supervise the processes. This would prove to be expensive in the US but cheaper in India. I gave Dr Agarwal the go-ahead and thus was born my first manufacturing facility, under the aegis of Sekhsaria Chemicals.

It took about a year to set up the laboratory in the northern Bombay suburb of Dombivli and another year to set up our first factory in the same plot at Dombivli. By now, Dr Agarwal had been joined by two other PhDs, Dr Nandkumar Chodankar and his wife Dr Laxmi Chodankar, who was the sister of a friend of mine. Eventually, the team grew to around forty people. Production started in small batches in 1974. Suhrid Geigy, a Baroda-based formulations maker, was our leading consumer.

Every Sunday morning I would pick up Dr Agarwal who lived in Bandra and make the ninety-minute journey to Dombivli and Ambernath by car to monitor the progress. Unlike my experience with cotton trading, we had a tough time breaking even. We just about broke even after five years and it took a few more years to scale up the operation to industrial size. And then there was the massive effort that went into getting certification from the Food & Drug Administration (FDA), which took time.

It was nearly a decade before we were able to export the products to the US and European markets. A unit that we set up to make formulations turned out to be a disaster. To compensate for that, I had to put up another bulk drugs unit at an adjacent site.

After Dr Agarwal left the company, it was run by the Chodankars. Like Dr Agarwal, they were good scientists but lacked business and marketing sense or experience. By the mid-1980s, I was busy with Gujarat Ambuja and was unable to devote more than an hour a week to the company. As a result, the company plodded along. It took three decades for the turnover to touch ₹100 crore.

In 2005 when the Chodankars told me that they wanted to retire, I did not want to run the company either. I asked them to find me a buyer which they did. I sold the company for ₹130 crore and gave the Chodankars a part of the profit. By my reckoning, I had invested around ₹45 to 50 crore in the company over the years. Today, I think I made a mistake by selling the facility. I should have brought in new management and given it a second chance to grow faster.

I made a similar mistake with two other pharma companies that I helped start in quick succession in the early 1980s. I had excess cash sitting in the bank, the value of which was being eroded by inflation and high taxes. It was one of my motivations to start work on Gujarat Ambuja. At the same time, I felt it would be good to cast my net wider and look at something else. The hope was that at least one of these projects would prove to be a big winner. Gujarat Ambuja was still on the drawing board at that time.

In 1982, when Mr D.N. Chaturvedi, then chief financial officer (CFO) of pharma giant Searle India, came to me through Dr Agarwal, saying he was looking to quit and had plans to set up a formulation marketing company, I decided to back him. He said he would get the manufacturing done by a third party, which I thought was a good idea. That led to the setting up of my second pharma company, Syncare Limited.

Similarly, a year later in 1983, I met Dr V.A. Padval at a party. He was the MD of Burroughs Wellcome and an old acquaintance of mine. He mentioned that he was retiring, so I asked him to do something with me. He came back with a plan to set up a formulation company on the lines of Syncare. He brought along his colleague Dr R.S. Wahie, the marketing director of Burroughs Wellcome, as his partner. Since I did not want any clash between two senior industry professionals, I set up a new company called Blue Shield for them.

Both these companies developed great formulation products, but they never really took off. Despite their best intentions and hard work, the professionals lacked the marketing and distribution expertise to set up and run a pharma company from the bottom-up. I discovered that the medical representatives they had hired to market the products to doctors, collected their salary from us but mostly sold the products of other companies. I realized later that both Mr Chaturvedi and Dr Padval were way past their prime and hence lacked the fire in their belly to make the ventures work. I must have invested close to ₹10 crore collectively in the companies. But neither of them ever made a profit. I sold Blue Shield in 1989 and recovered my investment, but made a loss of ₹3 crore when I sold Syncare in 1991.

Pharma was not my only diversification in the 1970s; I also made a brief detour into construction. A family acquaintance by the name of Chittaranjan Shah, who owned the then famous Satyam, Shivam, Sachinam cinema theatres at Worli in Bombay, came with a proposal to make me an investment partner in a new housing project he was starting in Juhu. Chuffed by my success in selling cotton, I readily agreed even though I had no idea about the business.

A few years earlier, my elder brother Surendra, who was working in Calcutta with our uncle, had moved back to Bombay saying he did not like it there. Since he wanted to work with me, I asked him to look after the construction business and made him a working partner. We bought a plot in Malad and began the construction of a residential building there. Later we invested in a third plot in Juhu, which we purchased from Great Eastern.

It was around this time, in June 1975, that Prime Minister Indira Gandhi declared her infamous Emergency. One of her main targets was the black money generated by real estate. As a result, there was a significant slowdown in construction activities across major cities in the country. The government imposed a ban on people buying more than one flat in large cities like Bombay, which led to buyers backing off and affected us tremendously.

Though we finished construction on both our properties, we could not sell any of the flats because people were reluctant to buy. It was only after the Emergency was lifted two years later that we were able to sell the flats. As for the Great Eastern plot, we could not do anything with it, because getting permission was cumbersome in those days. We sold it subsequently. We barely covered our costs in all the transactions and I decided it was not a business I understood or liked.

Another foray of mine in the 1970s that turned out to be far more successful was into the business of supplying cotton waste. This idea came to me while I was in London where I was told about Bunzl & Biach, a firm that specialized in recycling paper and waste cotton into pulp, used in the making of durable paper for printing of currencies and stamp paper. I thought of this as a useful business extension since we were already into cotton. I asked for an appointment, met one of their directors and asked him if I could be one of their suppliers.

He said that the company already had enough suppliers and was not looking for anyone new. I requested him to buy 100 bales from me on trial. 'I assure you that it will be better than anything that you are buying right now in terms of both quality and price. You name the quality and the price and I will make good the offer,' I told him.

'What if I ask you to supply at half the price,' he said, 'and ask for a quality that would be impossible for you to match at that price?'

I told him, 'As an experienced professional, I don't expect you to misuse my fair offer. I am asking you to specify the quality you want and a fair price. I am not even bargaining.'

He was impressed by my confidence and gave me an order for 100 bales. I fulfilled the order in terms of quality and within the delivery deadline. He was happy. When I met him after three months, he declared that I must have made a loss.

'No sir,' I replied, 'I made a profit. I put in extra work and got the best quality at a good price from my supplier. A business should be a win-win situation for both parties. I am not in this business to make a loss. If you make me a regular supplier, I will make my price even more competitive.' That impressed him and he made me a long-term supplier. It turned out to be a very lucrative venture for me for many years.

Yet another time, in the mid-1970s, I made a killing on the silver market. For cotton traders like us, the business period lasts for about nine months every year—from the time we invest in buying cotton to the time we sell it and recoup the investment along with the profit. We start investing in the purchase of cotton from November to April. All the cotton is delivered to the mills by July or August, when we recoup the investment with the profit. The cycle starts once again in November.

In one of those good years, I had about ₹50 lakh lying in our bank. To make extra returns on this money during the three months of the year that it sat idle in the bank, we, like many other business people, gave it out as a loan in the *vyaaj-badla* market. This was an informal short-term financing system on the BSE where people like us, with extra cash, would fund stock market speculators for their carry-forward deals. Though moderately risky, the earnings in *vyaaj-badla* were much better than bank fixed deposits. The Securities and Exchange Board of India (SEBI) subsequently banned it in the mid-1990s.

The same year I suggested to my father that we buy silver. I had read in the papers that the price was expected to go up because the Texas-based billionaire Hunt brothers—Nelson Bunker Hunt, Lamar Hunt and William Herbert Hunt—who had made their fortune in oil, were starting to corner silver from around the world including India, the world's biggest supplier of silver. Silver, like gold, was a safe asset which Indians had invested in from time immemorial. I found a broker to sell me silver and a bank vault to keep it in. As expected, the price more than doubled in three months and I made a windfall profit when I cashed out.

Of course, it was not a happy ending for the Hunt brothers. By the first quarter of 1980, they had bought a third of the world's silver supply, pushing up the prices by 700 per cent in a year. The price came crashing down on Thursday, 27 March 1980, when the regulators changed the rules on silver speculation to dissuade hoarding. The Hunt brothers saw much of their wealth evaporate and the day is still remembered as Silver Thursday in bullion markets around the world.

In January 1980, three years after an angry electorate ousted her, Mrs Gandhi came roaring back to power in a surprisingly strong showing in the Lok Sabha elections. A few months later, the commerce ministry issued a notification banning the export of cotton. The arbitrary manner in which it was done and the sheer irrationality of it, caught cotton exporters like me off guard.

Usually, bans are preceded by discussions, debates and consultations with interested parties. None of that had happened this time. And importantly, the ban covered even the export contracts that had already been signed and registered with the government. This meant that most cotton exporters like me were in dire straits, certain of making significant losses because we had already committed to supplying large quantities to international buyers.

We quickly found out the reason behind this suspicious ban. A new exporter from Chandigarh had devised a hare-brained scheme, in league with a Liverpool cotton agent by the name of Meredith Jones & Co, to make windfall profits that year from Japanese exports.

Japan in those days used to import large quantities of a cotton variety called Bengal Desi from India. Grown in northern states such as Punjab, Haryana and Rajasthan, this cotton is used in making cotton mattresses and pillows because of its high air permeability even in a compressed state. There is a high demand for this cotton in Japan, where it is used to make futons, the traditional floor mattresses. Japan at that time used to import as much as 1,50,000 tonnes of Bengal Desi from various Indian exporters like me every year.

That year the Chandigarh exporter told the owner of Meredith Jones that he would corner bales worth close to $10 million early in the season and send them to Japan where they should store it in a warehouse. Once the cotton reached Japan, he would use his political connections to get the Indian government to ban the export of cotton. When that happened—and no one else would be able to export cotton—the price of the warehoused cotton in Japan would shoot up and Meredith Jones would make a massive profit by selling it.

Things went as per plan. The Chandigarh exporter got Meredith Jones to fund his purchases here and the moment the cotton reached Japan, the Indian commerce ministry issued a notification stating that all cotton exports were to be banned in the interest of Indian handloom weavers.

In the past, when such bans were imposed, the government would at least exempt the already contracted exports that were registered with the textile commissioner. This time, understandably, no such exemptions were allowed. Each of us was thus stuck with a vast inventory of cotton bought in anticipation of export.

I was stuck with 10,000 bales, which I could not export. The only option was to sell them in the local market at a loss, as the prices had already crashed on account of excess supply. All of us exporters went and met the concerned minister in a group to protest the ban, but he was unmoved. Everyone went back to their respective cities after this failed mission. I did not want to give up on principle. I felt wronged and decided to use other ways to influence the government. I parked myself in Delhi in the hope of meeting the commerce minister one-on-one and convincing him.

After about two weeks of speaking to various people, I managed to get a brief meeting with the same minister. He heard me out patiently as I explained the unfairness of the ban, but was non-committal on what he would do. 'I will do something,' was all he said.

It was an open-ended statement. When nothing happened for a few days, I started frequenting his office again and spending time with his personal assistant (PA). The PA took pity on me, heard me out and told me that the minister would not do anything. He informed me that since he had himself initiated the ban two months earlier, it was unlikely he would rescind it personally. Someone else would have to do it. The PA told me that he would talk about it with one of the minister's trusted special assistants.

I was not privy to what happened internally. A few days later, the ministry issued a single-line note saying something on the lines of, 'because of market developments we are reverting to the position held three months ago'. The ban was lifted immediately, without much fanfare. After spending two months in Delhi, I had achieved my goal. My perseverance had borne fruit. Fellow exporters called to congratulate me. Everyone managed to fulfil their export commitments. We also made a joint decision not to deal with Meredith Jones & Co again.

A similar drama unfolded in Japan as well. News travelled about what the Chandigarh exporter and Meredith Jones had done. The big Tokyo importers were so vexed that they collectively took the decision not to touch the 20,000 bales belonging to Meredith Jones that lay in the warehouse and never to do business with them in Japan.

The cotton lay there for a year; no one was prepared to touch it, not even Meredith Jones's Tokyo representative, who was afraid he himself might be blacklisted. The company did not know what to do. In desperation, they sought help from Mr George Walter, a reputed cotton dealer based out of Hamburg with contacts in India and Japan. We shared a common agent in Japan. George called the Japanese agent first to find out if anything could be done. He replied that the only person who might be able to intervene in the matter was Narotam Sekhsaria in Bombay, who had got the Indian ban lifted. George then phoned me and we had a friendly conversation.

He asked me if I would be open to meeting Mr Nigel Jones, the man who ran Meredith Jones. 'He is quite desperate to settle the issue and cut his losses,' he said. I did not know what I could do for Nigel Jones, but I impulsively agreed to meet him in the privacy of a hotel room. I did not want to be seen in public with him, lest any of my fellow exporters spot us together. After all, he was blacklisted in India as well.

He called immediately and I asked him to come to Bombay. He booked himself into the Oberoi at Nariman Point and phoned after checking into the hotel. I asked a friend of mine to book a suite in his name at the same hotel and decided to use that room for the meeting and summoned Nigel to my suite. A tall, thin, handsome man, he looked anxious and distraught. He told me he would go bankrupt if he was unable to sell the cotton lying in the Japanese warehouse. He said he was misled by the Chandigarh exporter and had made a big blunder. He almost went down on his knees asking for help.

I told him I did not have the mandate from the Indian merchants or Japanese importers to talk to him or negotiate on their behalf. What he had done was unpardonable and had caused problems both in India and Japan. He said he was prepared to do anything to resolve the issue. On a whim, I asked him if he was ready to pay an amount as compensation to the Indian merchants. Without batting an eyelid, he said yes.

I asked him if he was prepared to sell the warehoused cotton to the Japanese importers at a 10 per cent discounted price, as compensation for what he had done. He agreed immediately to this as well. He said he would also write apology notes to both Japanese and Indian parties involved, expressing deep remorse and regret at what he had done. Having got all these assurances, I told him I would try and talk to my fellow exporters and seek their opinion on the matter. I was his only hope, he told me.

I left the hotel and walked across to my office in the nearby Mittal Chambers. I decided to first talk to the owners of Khimji Visram & Sons, the most prominent cotton merchant in India at that time and the biggest exporter to Japan. Their office was above mine. I arrived there unannounced and asked to see the owner. He happened to be there and I was ushered into his cabin immediately. I told him that I had been contacted by the Meredith Jones people to find out if the issue of their blacklisting in India and Japan could be resolved.

He expressed his helplessness, saying the damage they had done was considerable. 'Luckily for us, we didn't suffer any losses because the Japanese were nice to us and increased the quantum of their import and offered us a better price. We made up our losses because they stood by us and we should do the same. Unless the Japanese lift their ban, it is not right for us to lift the ban,' he added. He suggested that the only way the Japanese would relent, was if Meredith Jones offered to sell the warehoused cotton at a 4 or 5 per cent discount on the market price.

I asked him, 'What about us?', to which he replied, 'We have recovered our money, so we don't need anything from Meredith Jones, but they will have to promise that they will never trade in Bengal Desi.'

I told him that I would ask for a rather large amount as compensation for us, along with an apology letter. He looked incredulous, 'Don't be stupid. Ask him for a reasonable amount, which can be divided among all the exporters.'

I asked him if the others would agree. He called a few other exporters, all of whom were fine with settling the issue with a small compensation. I went back to Nigel and told him that the other Indian exporters had agreed to whatever I had suggested. He was over the moon. But there were two things still outstanding. We did not know if the Japanese would agree to the plan, because we had not spoken to them yet. Secondly, the agreed compensation had to be paid before he left India.

He said he was confident that if the Indians lifted his ban, the Japanese would do the same. He then picked up the phone and asked the hotel operator to book a call to his office in Liverpool. He asked for my bank account details. When the call came through, he told his office to transfer the amount into my account immediately.

The money was in my bank account within twenty-four hours. I went back to Khimji Visram and told him that though he wanted only a small amount, I had got the exporters much more. He couldn't believe it and called the other traders to give them the good news. In return, I told him to talk to their Japanese agents and clients. They were also surprised that I had got Nigel to offer a 10 per cent discount to the Japanese buyers. The Japanese got back after a few hours saying that the matter could be resolved if he sent an apology letter.

Back at the hotel, I told Nigel to telex the apology letter to five senior people in the Japanese cotton importers association, along with the promise of a 10 per cent discount if they bought the warehoused cotton. He also had to pledge that he would not trade in Japan after that ever again. The matter was resolved to everyone's satisfaction the next day and Meredith Jones managed to sell its cotton to the Japanese.

Nigel called me from London to thank me once again. 'I am indebted to you for life,' he told me. 'My 100-year-old firm and I would have gone bankrupt if it wasn't for what you have done.' He asked me if there was anything he could do for me. I told him he could buy me lunch the next time I visited Liverpool.

Not long after that, I was in London for a holiday. I took a train to Liverpool where Nigel received me at the station. He seemed overjoyed that I was finally visiting him. He took me to his office, did a town hall meeting with his employees and introduced me to everyone in the office as the man who saved Meredith Jones from bankruptcy. That evening, he invited me to dine with his family. In the course of our conversation, he asked me if I could be his agent in India. I reminded him that he was blacklisted as far as Bengal Desi cotton was concerned.

He said he wanted to create a market for other varieties. I told him I did not want to be a commission agent. He then offered me a fifty-fifty profit-sharing partnership. I agreed to the deal after I was allowed to charge another 1 per cent for expenses. It turned out to be a lucrative partnership for me. The money I made from the cotton I exported on behalf of Meredith Jones paid for my share of Gujarat Ambuja and the pharma ventures. The relationship lasted for a few years, by which time I was deeply involved in setting up Ambuja.

When I was in London again, I visited Nigel and found that much had changed in his company. New partners had taken over and they were not enthusiastic about our arrangement. I told Nigel that our partnership had run its course and that it was time we went our separate ways. He agreed and we parted in good faith. A few years later, I learnt that he was forced to leave the company and was having family problems. I offered him financial help; he declined saying he did not need it.

My association with Meredith Jones was highly profitable. It also opened the doors of business with numerous other international trading firms. It helped build my reputation among the cotton trading community across the country.

By the early 1980s, just a decade after we had started, we were among the biggest cotton-trading operations in India, with a turnover exceeding ₹100 crore. Most people who mattered in the cotton industry knew me or had at least heard my name. It was not surprising then that one day in the middle of the cotton-trading season in 1982, I got a call from the secretary of the Department of Cooperation in the Maharashtra government, Mr R.C. Sinha. He said he wanted to see me urgently. I rushed to Mantralaya to meet him.

He had just moved to Bombay from Delhi and seemed like a dynamic officer. The department he was heading controlled sugar factories, cooperative marketing federations and cooperative banks, among others. It was among the most powerful ministries in the state government. The new CM, Mr Babasaheb Bhosale, had kept this ministerial portfolio with himself and had hand-picked Mr Sinha to run it. Mr Sinha's problem had to do with the excess cotton bought by the Maharashtra State Co-operative Cotton Grower's Marketing Federation Limited.

Commonly known as the 'Cotton Federation', it was the government arm that bought cotton from farmers across the state every year at a predetermined fixed price under the Monopoly Cotton Procurement Scheme. The cotton was then auctioned off to textile mills across the country. The crop had been particularly good that year, not only in Maharashtra but also in the neighbouring states and the Cotton Federation's purchases topped 40 lakh bales, far more than usual.

Since the Cotton Federation lacked a proper warehousing facility for the storage of cotton bales in such large numbers, Mr Sinha wanted help in selling the excess cotton in the international market, because selling locally would depress the prices leading to losses for the government. Mr Sinha said that he had heard about me from people in the market and he needed my help to sell the excess cotton.

Through my international contacts, I was aware that the Romanian government was in the market for bulk purchase and that they were talking to the Chinese government. I told Mr Sinha about this and he jumped at the opportunity. Selling to Romania made sense from his perspective because it was a communist country and it would be a state-to-state deal rather than a private one. Besides, in those days, India had a rupee trade agreement with the Soviet Union and East European countries, which allowed both countries to trade in local currency. That would make life simpler for the Romanians as they would not have to pay in dollars.

I asked Mr Sinha to give me a few days to contact officials in Bucharest. When I spoke to the Romanians, they were more than eager and wanted to fly down immediately. Mr Sinha was also keen to close the deal as soon as possible. He told me he wanted a price that he would reveal on the day of the deal, which would be based on the international cotton price on that day. Since the government had a policy of not paying commission to cotton brokers like me, he told me that it would have to be added on to the final sale price which would be paid for by the Romanians.

The Romanians agreed to the contours of the deal. They came down to Bombay for the final discussion and contract signing. Mr Sinha got Chief Minister Bhosale to sign off on the transaction, because he feared that if the local price went up the next day (which was bound to happen because of market dynamics), he would be blamed by the Opposition for selling the cotton at a lower price.

The deal was signed by a deputy minister in the Romanian government who had flown down with the team. The Cotton Federation issued a contract in the name of the Romanians and they established a letter of credit with the State Bank of India (SBI). Arrangements were made to ship the cotton immediately. The plan was that the payment would be made simultaneously with the cotton being loaded into the cargo vessels at Bombay port. Everything seemed to be going well initially, with the Romanians transferring the first instalment of 10 per cent of the payment. Then, as the ships were being loaded in the dock, the payments stopped.

Mr Sinha tried calling the officials in Bucharest but did not get any response for a few days. He called me, but I could not do anything either. I told him that the only way out was for us to go to Bucharest to sort things out with the Romanians face to face. I offered to accompany him. He got the government's permission to travel.

When we arrived in the Romanian capital, we were surprised by the ministerial reception we got at the airport. We were picked up from the plane and provided a full security entourage. For some reason, they had mistaken Mr Sinha's designation of secretary, Government of Maharashtra, as being equivalent to that of a minister, like in the US cabinet, hence the grand reception. We decided to play along.

When we arrived at the Hilton Hotel, they said that they did not accept the Romanian leu that Mr Sinha was carrying. They wanted to be paid in dollars. It was the pre-credit card era and he suggested that we look for a smaller hotel that would accept the local currency. I was carrying dollars, so I told him that it would not look good if an Indian minister stayed in anything less than a Hilton and I offered to pay.

We were told by our ambassador in Bucharest to be careful of the bugs and listening devices planted by the country's intelligence services. We planned for me to refer to Mr Sinha as His Excellency at the meeting, to keep up with the Romanian impression that he was a minister. We decided that he would speak in Hindi and I would be his English translator. That would give us time to think and respond to what the Romanians were saying. The ambassador had told us that the Romanian bureaucrats had no sense of humour, so we should eschew any jokes to break the ice.

We knew that the Romanian government had ₹12 crore lying in SBI's Delhi branch. We planned to tell them that the Government of India had the legal right to confiscate the money if the payment was not made immediately. We kept the tone of the meeting extremely serious and business-like. Besides speaking in Hindi, Mr Sinha spent time lighting his pipe every time he had to respond to a question.

He told them that the Romanian cargo ships with the cotton were still in the docks at Bombay and that he would legally detain them if the money was not paid on time. It would result in the Romanian credit rating in the international market going for a toss because of a payment default. He said he was aware of the Romanian money lying in SBI and that the Government of India could legally impound it. He made it clear in no uncertain terms that the payment had to be made immediately.

The threat worked and the Romanians transferred the payment to the Cotton Federation's account overnight. Our trip was a success. As soon as the news of the transaction was made public, the price of cotton shot up in the Bombay market and the Cotton Federation was able to sell the remaining 30 lakh bales at a good profit.

The incident helped to solidify my reputation in the cotton market. More importantly, I gained a lifelong friend in Mr R.C. Sinha, who went on to become one of India's most celebrated IAS officers. I had a small role to play in two of his biggest successes in Bombay: the revival of New Bombay as a city in the early 1990s and the Bombay–Pune Expressway project a decade later. I also helped him plan what became the Bandra–Worli Sea Link project, in which he was involved in the early stages.

My passion for befriending knowledgeable people from whom I could imbibe wisdom and insight proved to be an asset all through my career. Mr Chidambaram, Mr Ratansi, Mr Arvind and Mr Yogendra Mafatlal and Mr R.C. Sinha are among those whose acquaintance benefited me at various times in my career. Another big name in this group was Mr N.N. Pai, who was the chairman of Corporation Bank when I first met him. It was because of him that I met the two people who steered me towards setting up Gujarat Ambuja.

Originally from Nileshwararam in Kerala's Kasaragod district, Narayan Pai was the little-known CFO of a Bombay-based machinery manufacturer, Batliboi & Co, when he was requested by fellow community members to help Corporation Bank, a small bank they owned which had run into trouble. It was the oldest of four—Syndicate Bank, Vijaya Bank and Canara Bank being the other three—founded in the Mangalore (renamed Mangaluru in 2014) area in the early part of the last century. Mr Pai helped nurse the bank to good health and took over as the chairman in 1975 when he was fifty-three.

I first met Mr Pai on the evening of 16 January 1978. I remember the date vividly because history was made on that day by then Prime Minister Morarji Desai, when he demonetized ₹1,000 notes. This had been done for the first time since Independence. The ostensible reason was to drive out the black money that was funding elections. People were given only a day to exchange their high-value notes at the bank branches. Corporation Bank was one of our bankers and for a while they had been our tenants in one part of our office at Mittal Chambers at Nariman Point. The main branch that handled foreign-trade transactions now had its headquarters next to our office, on the same floor.

When I walked across to exchange the few ₹1,000 notes that I had, the branch had unfortunately closed for the day. Since it was past banking hours, the people there told me that the only person who could help me was the chairman. Luckily, Mr Pai was still in his office on the sixth floor of the same building. I was a bit nervous about whether he would entertain me, but decided to try, nevertheless. I walked into the office and requested to see him. I was surprised that he called me in immediately. Soft-spoken and pleasant, he asked me to sit down. After I told him my problem, he called the branch manager and asked him to get my notes exchanged. I was more than grateful.

He then asked me to stay on for a cup of tea. We had a good conversation about a variety of business-related issues, including the demonetization. He was non-judgemental and seemed keen to listen than to lecture. I found this refreshing from someone in his position. He promised to meet me again when he was in Bombay. Thus, began a friendship that lasted until he passed away in 2008.

Mr Pai was based in Mangalore, where Corporation Bank still maintained its headquarters. When he was in Bombay, he often made it a point to call me. He was always eager to find out what was happening in the city. We became good friends and he often used me as a source for Bombay's business news.

In 1980, Mr Pai was thrust into the limelight when Prime Minister Indira Gandhi initiated the second round of bank nationalization and the government took over Corporation Bank, along with six smaller banks. A few months later came the headline news that Mr R.K. Talwar had resigned as chairman of IDBI. It was not an unexpected move. The legendary banker had a similar experience in 1975, during Mrs Gandhi's earlier tenure as PM, when he had to quit abruptly as the chairman of SBI.

Mr Morarji Desai's government that followed had rehabilitated Mr Talwar by making him the chairman of IDBI. But with Mrs Gandhi back in power, Mr Talwar decided to quit. What was surprising though was the announcement of the relatively unknown Mr Pai as his successor. I was thrilled that someone I knew was taking over such a prestigious banking position. I called up Suresh Neotia, to whom I spoke quite often and gave him the good news.

Suresh and his brother Vinod were close to me because Bai, my sister, was the widow of their eldest brother Bimal Kumar Poddar. Suresh was fourteen years older and I used to call him *bhaiya*. He was among the most knowledgeable and well-connected members of my extended family. I used him as a sounding board for new ideas and consulted him quite often. Suresh told me I should throw a party in Mr Pai's honour in Bombay to celebrate and make it an occasion where he could meet some of the city's leading businessmen. He knew that I met Mr Pai quite often in Bombay and that he did not know too many people in the city. 'Who should I invite?' I asked Suresh. 'My trader friends?'

'No,' he replied, 'the industrialists and mill owners.' I asked him why they would come.

'They will not come for you,' he said, 'but they will come for Mr Pai because nobody knows him and he has just been appointed chairman of IDBI.'

This had not crossed my mind and seemed like a great idea. Mr Pai was not an outgoing person and this party would provide him with an opportunity to meet Bombay's business luminaries. It would also reinforce my relationship with him and help raise my profile in Bombay's business circles. When I phoned to ask him if I could throw a welcome party for him, he was more than open to the idea. The party was held at the Gateway Room of Taj Mahal Hotel.

About seventy-five people turned up. Considering that I was still a small-time cotton trader, it was an impressive guest list. There were no Tatas or Birlas, but the mill owners showed up in large numbers. The Piramals, Thackerseys, Mafatlals, Ruias, Kanorias and many others came, as did many bankers, including some of Mr Pai's new colleagues from IDBI. The evening went off very well.

Mr Pai was happy and I got to network with a significant number of who's who of the Bombay business world. Since Mr Pai was now back in Bombay, I began meeting him once a week after office hours for a cup of tea. I had no specific agenda or business interest with IDBI. Still, I enjoyed these meetings because I got to learn a lot about development finance, banking, industry and much more. I would talk to him about my business and dealings with bankers and I always found his advice valuable. I would spend time with his senior staff members, many of whom I got to know very well. Since I was not seeking any loan, they knew I had no agenda, so they were quite open in their discussions.

Six months after he took over, Mr Pai asked me to become a member of the Western Committee of IDBI, which I gladly accepted. The bank had a zonal committee for each of the four geographical regions of the country. It was a loan-review board for the region, made up of experts from outside and senior IDBI executives and presided over by the chairman. Its job was to review and advise IDBI in the sanctioning of loans up to ₹50 lakh for companies in their respective regions. The request for bigger loans would go to IDBI's main board.

The other outside members on this committee were Dr N.A. Kalyani of Kalyani Forge and a Bombay management consultant. It was a three-year tenure and we met once a month in the IDBI boardroom. A few days before the meeting, we would all be sent a docket with the details of the companies that had requested loans. There would be at least twenty-five to thirty companies to discuss each time. I took this job very seriously, going through each proposal carefully and studying the company and the industry.

The proposals covered a broad spectrum of industries, such as steel, mini-cement and dyestuff, chemicals, textile and many others. The detailed analysis done by the IDBI managers taught me a lot about project financing and the state of various industries. It was on this committee that I learnt about the cement industry from close quarters. It was the first time I came across the name of GIIC, the Gujarat government institution that played a crucial role in the creation of Gujarat Ambuja.

Mr Pai was a remarkably simple man, business-friendly, comfortable to talk to and warm towards everyone. He was very impressionable, as a result of which quite a few unworthy loans got sanctioned under his watch, despite advice to the contrary from his senior staff members. It was likely that many of the sanctions were done under pressure from his bosses in Delhi.

In 1982, in a move that was as unexpected as his appointment, Mr Pai resigned from his position. He was the chairman for a little over two years. It is likely that he was asked to leave for not obliging someone high-up in Delhi. He never talked about his resignation and went into quiet retirement. My relationship with him remained unaffected. I met him very often after his retirement as well and his son who is a chartered accountant, served on the board of one of my companies.

3

Gujarat Ambuja's Unlikely Origins

The idea of cement • Neotias as co-promoters • The GIIC partnership • From Mahuva to Kodinar

Mr Pai's decision to appoint me on the Western Committee proved to be a pivotal moment in my career. After the news became public, I was approached by many mid-level industrialists seeking help with their loans, which I used to pass on to the concerned officials at IDBI. One of them was Dr M.P. Jain, the MD of Andhra Cements Limited, a company controlled by the Jains, owners of *The Times of India*. The company had plants in Andhra Pradesh's Guntur region. Dr Jain, who was no relative of the owners, was considered to be among the top cement industry professionals in those days.

Sometime around 1980 or '81, Dr Jain, who was based in Delhi, came to see me through a common acquaintance for help in getting some provisions of an Andhra Cements loan modified by IDBI. I passed on the request to the IDBI cement department. Following this, he would come to see me every time he was in Bombay. I got to know him well over time. When he found out that I was looking to invest in new ventures, he was the first one who told me about cement. He spoke about its future potential, its centrality in India's growth story and its impending total decontrol, all of which made it an attractive investment opportunity. I knew truly little about the industry beyond what I had read in the loan proposals at our IDBI's Western Committee meetings.

After I showed more interest in investing in cement, Dr Jain got excited. And over time he became persistent that I should set up a cement company. I asked him whether he was willing to join me as a partner. He said he was open to the idea and hinted that he was ready to quit Andhra Cements to run the company. With Dr Jain as a partner, the idea sounded workable, something for me to chew over. It was a big career move where the funds involved would be several times higher than what I had invested in my pharma and chemical ventures. The idea of investing in a cement plant came at a time when many compelling reasons were pulling me towards getting into manufacturing.

I had been a successful cotton trader for over a decade. By the early 1980s, I had made more money than I had ever imagined. But something was missing in my life, a void that I felt quite often. I wanted the recognition and respect that was accorded to industrialists in our community, but denied to traders like me. Traders, however successful, were classified with brokers and middlemen as low-level commission agents. They were never seen as wealth or asset creators; this was an honour reserved for industrialists. Respect, esteem and admiration were always reserved for those who had successfully set up large manufacturing companies. After being a trader for more than a decade, I longed for that kind of respect.

It was the era of Prime Minister Indira Gandhi's extreme socialism. Banks and textile mills were still being nationalized and people who made large profits were punished mercilessly with high taxes. The marginal tax rate was 60 per cent. With the surcharges, I was paying as much as 70 per cent tax on my trading profit. To top that was the high inflation that ate away a large portion of whatever was left after taxes. Unlike manufacturing companies, we traders got no tax breaks like investment allowances and depreciation. The industrialists had it better than traders. It was another reason I felt that it was time to move into manufacturing.

The more I thought about it, Dr Jain's idea of partnering with me in setting up a cement company seemed like a good starting point to get into manufacturing. The plan in my mind was that I would invest and he would run the company. That way, I would have the manufacturing enterprise I eagerly wanted and still be able to continue with the comfortable lifestyle I was used to at that time. As a trader, I did not have the stress of running a large establishment with lots of employees. Our cotton business was well established by now and I spent only a few hours on it every day. The rest of my day was spent with family or in my other interests like the work of the IDBI Western Committee and meeting people I had befriended in various areas of business and banking. It was a way of life I had got used to over the years and I was loath to change it.

As the discussion got serious, I decided to get more partners involved. Unlike my chemical and pharma forays, the investment in cement was expected to be considerably higher, so I felt the need for co-promoters to share the risk. Who better than Suresh Neotia? He was, as I have said earlier, my sounding board and confidant on business matters and I felt he was the kind of person who would be interested. When I asked Suresh, he was more than happy to join hands and promised to play an active role as did his younger brother Vinod Neotia who was his business partner. We decided to give Dr Jain a generous 10 per cent stake as sweat equity for agreeing to run the company. The rest of the capital was to be divided between the Neotias and me.

With the investment plan in place by early 1982, the Neotias and I met Dr Jain formally to indicate our willingness to join hands with him to set up the cement project. We told him about our sweat equity offer as well. He sounded excited and said that he would join us once the groundwork on the project was complete; till then he would guide us from the sidelines. Neither the Neotias nor I knew much about cement. I had never seen a cement plant. In that sense, we were entirely dependent on Dr Jain for guidance. He was, after all, a cement technologist and one of the most experienced professionals in the industry.

The starting point for a cement plant was to find the right location. It had to be close to the mines from which limestone, the primary raw material, would be extracted. It also had to be close to the market where cement was sold. The farther it was from the limestone mines and the market for the finished product, the higher the cost of transportation, which in turn would raise the price of the cement, making it less competitive in the market.

Limestone is a sedimentary rock formed over millions of years from the compressed remains of fish, corals, shells and other sea organisms. The presence of limestone mines in any place is an indicator that the sea has retreated from the area millions of years ago. Limestone mines are found in most states in India, except for a handful like Punjab, Kerala, West Bengal and some north-eastern states. Good quality limestone results in high quality cement.

Dr Jain's first suggestion was that we should explore the possibility of setting up our plant in western Uttar Pradesh, close to the Dehradun valley, which was known to have very high-quality limestone deposits. No one had set up a cement plant in the area yet. Despite being the largest state in the country, Uttar Pradesh did not have a single cement plant, except for a small obsolete plant of the Uttar Pradesh State Cement Corporation. The state's consumption needs were met almost entirely by cement bought from outside. It made perfect business sense to set up our plant there.

Since the suggestion came from Dr Jain, Suresh and I did not feel the need to question its reasoning. I could have discussed the matter with Mr Pai at IDBI, but I did not want to mix personal business with my work on IDBI's Western Committee. I kept the two at arm's length. I did not seek Mr Pai's help, nor did I tell him about my plans.

Dr Jain told us that the first task was to seek blessings and help from the Union government and the state government. The former was responsible for issuing the manufacturing licence, while the latter allocated land for the limestone quarries and the plant. The person to meet, we decided, was Mr Narayan Dutt Tiwari, then among the most powerful politicians in Uttar Pradesh and the state chief minister till 1977. As the Union minister of industry in Mrs Gandhi's government, Mr Tiwari was now the deciding authority on issuing the manufacturing licence. As former CM, he still retained considerable influence in Uttar Pradesh. Suresh had met him earlier and managed to get us an appointment for a meeting with him in Lucknow sometime in June 1982.

The original plan was for all three of us to go to Lucknow. Dr Jain, however, backed out for reasons mentioned earlier. It fell on Suresh and me to make the journey and the initial contact with Mr Tiwari and the state government. The visit and what happened after that, including the chance meeting in Lucknow with Mr Pai of IDBI, has been described in the Prologue of the book, so I will skip the details here.

To recap, we were sitting in the lobby of the Clarks Hotel in Lucknow before proceeding to the meeting with Mr Tiwari when we ran into Mr Pai. After hearing about the purpose of our visit, he said that we should invest in Gujarat instead of Uttar Pradesh and if I flew back with him to Ahmedabad that evening, he would introduce me to all the officials concerned. Our meeting with Mr Tiwari turned out to be a damp squib and I took Mr Pai's advice and travelled with him to Ahmedabad the same evening. There he introduced me to the legendary IAS officer Mr H.K. Khan, the CMD of GIIC, the leading industrial development arm of the state government.

It was my destiny that I ran into Mr Pai in the lobby of a Lucknow hotel and that he introduced me to Mr Khan the same evening. Mr Khan was a visionary who was part of the team that in the previous two decades had turned Gujarat from an agrarian state with a few textile mills, to a powerhouse in chemicals and fertilizers. Over the next decade, they would push the state into a leadership position in areas like petrochemicals, petroleum, pharmaceuticals and energy.

Mr Khan stood out among industrial development-minded bureaucrats, because he passionately believed in creating industrialists out of small entrepreneurs rather than just supporting established industrialists. Years later, he would cite the example of two new entrepreneurs that he had taken a risk on and who went on to become successful industrialists—Narotam Sekhsaria and Karsanbhai Patel.

He was right. We were nothing before he took us under his wing. Karsanbhai used to make Nirma washing powder in his backyard and sell it door to door on his cycle, while I was just a cotton trader. In an interview published just before he passed away, Mr Khan said, 'For me, the high-water mark was the exciting days in the 1980s, when one can say that the industrial revolution took shape in Gujarat.'

I was lucky to have been one of the people he mentored as part of this revolution. He had pioneered the concept of single-window clearance for entrepreneurs at GIIC and we were among the earliest beneficiaries. It helped expedite approvals to the extent that we were able to finalize our agreement with GIIC within weeks, rather than months and years as was the practice in the rest of the country in those days.

Our original plan for Uttar Pradesh and Gujarat too, was to get the state government to provide us with the necessary infrastructure, including land and power, for setting up a cement plant. Mr Khan went one step further. Without us even asking for it, he turned our proposal into a joint-sector project with GIIC! It was an unexpected decision. He hardly knew the Neotias or me. We were small-time businessmen with no public reputation.

Mr Khan was gracious enough to be our chairman in the first few years. He provided us with much-needed guidance as we navigated through all the early teething problems. He also played an essential role in the success of our Initial Public Offering (IPO) in 1985. He was one of those great men who played a significant role in moulding our destiny. I feel proud of the fact that GIIC still lists Ambuja Cement on their website as one of their biggest success stories. I am glad to have played a small role in his move to Delhi as the Union petroleum secretary in the late 1980s, from where he helped reset the country's energy policy in the early days of economic liberalization.

Once Mr Khan decided to back us and turn our project into a joint venture with GIIC as a partner, things moved fast. Besides the Neotias, I got a school friend of mine, Suresh Mulani, as the third financial promoter from our side. He was a London-based non-resident Indian (NRI) who had made his money through trading in Nigeria. Those were the days when NRIs were first allowed to invest in the country and their presence on a company's board helped enhance its reputation. My thinking was that Suresh Mulani's presence would help us in our negotiation for finance with banks, as well as during our IPO a few years down the line.

The project cost for the proposed 7,00,000-tonne cement plant was assessed at ₹80 crore, divided into ₹20 crore of equity and ₹60 crore of debt in the form of loans from development finance institutions led by IDBI. Of the ₹20 crore equity, the three individual promoters—the Neotias (₹1.25 crore), Suresh Mulani (₹1.25 crore) and I (₹2.5 crore)—were to invest a total of ₹5 crore, with GIIC contributing an equal amount of ₹5 crore. The rest of the capital was to come from a public issue or IPO slated three years later. The eventual shareholding was supposed to be GIIC 26 per cent, promoters 25 per cent and the public 49 per cent.

Our contribution was only 6.25 per cent of the project cost. The debt to equity ratio was 3:1. The control of the company could easily be taken over as our equity holding was quite low. We as promoters held just 25 per cent of the equity. Finance people would refer to it as a 'highly leveraged' or 'highly geared company'. The pressure on me to make it work was even higher now. Failure would have meant that we would be swimming in a sea of debt for the rest of our lives.

The burden of this risk came at a time when it was increasingly becoming clear that Dr Jain was not interested in joining us. I am not sure why he developed cold feet despite his initial enthusiasm. He likely had a rethink on whether he wanted to take a risk with a bunch of newcomers. It is also likely that he wanted to wait and see how far we would be successful in setting up the project before making a decision.

Dr Jain's reluctance was a significant disappointment for me. It meant that I would have to take the project forward myself. My plans for being only a passive investor had now fallen apart. It was becoming evident that I would have to play a much bigger role in running the company than I had initially envisaged. I was left with no choice. I couldn't have abandoned the project at this late stage. That would have been disastrous for my reputation because I had been fronting this all along, with the banks, GIIC and the Gujarat government. I had to educate myself on cement as fast as possible now and roll up my sleeves and be the person in charge. This project was my baby and I would have to nurture it to the best of my ability.

As I took on the challenge, I felt that the confidence I had developed over the previous decade, running my profitable cotton business, networking with a number of successful mill owners and serving on the Western Committee of IDBI, was not enough to fight my nervousness. The line separating self-confidence from self-doubt was indeed fragile. The consolation was that Dr Jain offered his services as an informal adviser for the project. He would travel to Bombay once every fortnight and provide me with the necessary guidance. His industry-wide contacts came in particularly handy during the earliest recruitments that we did in the company.

Once I mentally committed myself to run the company, I embraced my responsibility with the same passion with which I had approached cotton trading. The earliest life-changing decision I made was to give up cotton trading for good. I felt I should not be running two businesses at the same time. The new project would require my full attention. I discontinued my practice of making the rounds of the offices of textile mill owners, something that I had relished doing. I handed over the reins of the operation to my brothers and cousins, though I still worked from the same Mittal Chambers office at Nariman Point and was available for advice.

The good part was that 1982 was a great year to get into cement for a newcomer like me. Mrs Gandhi's government had finally decided to initiate the long-pending reform of decontrolling cement, albeit only partially. For the first time in several decades, cement manufacturers were allowed to sell cement in the open market after meeting the levy obligation of supplying 66.6 per cent of the production to government agencies. I thought of it as an auspicious beginning. Little did I realize that it would also lure dozens of new entrepreneurs like me from across the country to get into the cement business. By the end of the 1980s, the installed capacity for cement in the country would more than double to 61 million tonnes. It brought with it a whole range of new problems, which I will discuss later.

Though the government had partially decontrolled cement sales that year, the licence raj in terms of setting up new plants was still firmly in place. We needed a licence from the industry ministry to set up our plant. It was a process that could have taken more than a few months, considering the various layers of permissions that were involved. The GIIC advised us to buy an existing unused licence from someone they knew in Gujarat. They put us in touch with a gentleman by the name of Mr Bhagwandas Mehta, who had procured a licence three years earlier with the idea of setting up a 5,00,000-tonne annual capacity cement plant in the state. The licence was in the name of a company called Ambuja Cement. We bought the company from Mr Mehta, completing the formalities by November 1982.

I was in two minds on whether we should change the name of the company. When I told my father about it, he reminded me that Ambuja was another name for Goddess Lakshmi. 'Why do you want to change the name? Destiny has brought it to you,' he told me. It was a good piece of advice. We later added 'Gujarat' to the name to indicate our partnership with GIIC, calling ourselves Gujarat Ambuja.

Much later, my friend Ravi Gupta, MD of Trikaya Advertising and the man who created brand Ambuja, would say to me, 'Ideally, we should call the company "Giant Cement Company", from which we derive our "giant strength" identity.' I had to remind him that Ambuja was a very traditional and auspicious Indian name.

Ambuja Cement's original licence was for setting up the manufacturing unit in Sabarkantha, an underdeveloped district in northern Gujarat on the border with Rajasthan. We hired the engineering consultancy firm Dastur & Co to prepare a feasibility report on the location. Their finding was that a cement unit there would be unviable owing to the lack of infrastructure. The area with the limestone mines lacked infrastructure like roads and bridges.

The Gujarat government then advised us to shift the manufacturing site to Mahuva, a small coastal town in Bhavnagar district on the west coast of southern Saurashtra, an area which, according to the surveys of the Geological Survey of India, was rich in limestone. Mahuva was a notified backward area, which allowed us more concessions. It was close to the sea and the railway junction was not far. We liked the place and immediately commissioned the geological services department of India's largest cement company—Associated Cement Companies (ACC)—to survey limestone in and around the villages of Mahuva town, as the ACC's geological services department undertook work for other companies as well. Simultaneously, I began building our team.

Recruiting was not easy for a small company like ours started by a bunch of newcomers. There was no reason any seasoned CEO would want to join us. Nevertheless, in November, Dr Jain helped me hire the first employee of Gujarat Ambuja—Mr Bhaskar Shovakar, an ambitious commercial manager at Lakshmi Cements, part of the JK group. He was a tall, handsome, charming Bengali with a pleasant personality. He spoke impeccable English and exuded the confidence of someone who could handle a large project. Mr Shovakar was aspiring to be a chief executive, but it would have taken him at least ten to fifteen years at JK to get there. I not only made him the CEO at Ambuja, but also inducted him into the board of directors.

It must be mentioned here that I deliberately stayed away from super-achievers and professionals with fancy degrees from high-profile universities in India and abroad, whilst recruiting. Attrition was a big problem in cement companies as executives changed jobs frequently in search of better earnings and designations. I planned to build a team of hard-working professionals from ordinary Indian universities who were prepared to give their best in an environment that encouraged them to think creatively and dream big.

Mr Shovakar's first big task was to draft our first term loan application to a consortium of financial institutions (FIs) fronted by IDBI and including ICICI, General Insurance Corporation of India (GIC), Unit Trust of India (UTI) and Industrial Finance Corporation of India (IFCI). Through his contacts at ICICI, he was able to get Mrs Chanda Kochhar, then an executive trainee at the bank, to spend time with us to complete the application. She spent more than ten days in our small boardroom working on this. I got to know her very well following this. We had a personal relationship even after she became the MD and CEO of ICICI Bank. I feel sorry for what she has had to go through in recent times.

A few weeks later, Mr Shovakar helped us recruit our second employee Mr Prakash B. Kulkarni, a mechanical engineer from Mysore University, who had been a colleague of his at the JK group. Mr Kulkarni was the chief engineer at Lakshmi Cements with expertise in project management. He had recently helped set up the company's new plant in Sirohi, Rajasthan. After having spent many years setting up projects in remote areas, he wanted to settle his family in Bombay for the sake of his children's education.

After Dr Jain interviewed him at the Taj Mahal Hotel in Bombay, I called Mr Kulkarni to our office. We spoke for about half an hour. I was not yet well versed about cement so I could not judge his technical competence. He came across as mild-mannered, self-effacing and unpretentious to a fault; a person I felt I could get along with easily. We offered him a job immediately at a salary higher than he was drawing at JK and helped him find a house in Bombay.

He committed to staying with us for at least five years but went on to work with the company for twenty-six years, retiring as a director. Over the years, he evolved to become one of the most respected technical people in the industry. He was a team-builder who inspired his team to newer heights with every project and a fearless innovator who pioneered many technical innovations. I never thought of him as an employee but as a partner. Together we built Ambuja into one of the finest cement companies in the world. He is as much a father of Ambuja as I am.

The third employee was Mr S.S. Bhandari, who joined as CFO. He was yet another pillar in the early Ambuja days. A chartered accountant with fifteen years of rich experience with the likes of Birla, Ruia and Reliance, he was the most experienced professional to join us. When I asked him what brought him to Ambuja, considering the glamour and stature of Reliance where he was working, he said he was attracted by the opportunity of working on a greenfield project which would enable him to grow professionally. Success in the project, he told me, would give him tremendous growth potential financially and professionally, as high risk and high returns go hand in hand.

Within days of joining, I assigned him the task of appointing a statutory auditor, something that had to be done immediately because our first accounts closing was only a few days away. After much research, he came up with the name of M/s Dalal & Shah. He was surprised that I accepted his suggestion without any reservation. Dalal & Shah turned out to be an excellent firm of auditors who worked with us for many years. That was my management style—recruit competent professionals, trust their judgement and back them wholeheartedly even if mistakes were made in some instances. More often than not, I discovered that people gave their best when they were unfettered by the fear of failure.

Mr Bhandari's innovative approach to finance was also crucial to our early fundraising efforts. At that time, only SBI would provide loans for manufacturing companies. When we approached them with our project, their attitude was one of condescension. 'Leave your papers here and we will look into it,' was what an official told us. We decided to approach my banker from the cotton-trading days, BoI. Not only were they grateful for the opportunity, but they also put together a consortium with Dena Bank and Bank of Baroda (BoB). For the first time in the history of corporate India, we raised a project loan from a consortium of three mainstream nationalized banks—BoI, Dena Bank and BoB.

At this point, Mr Bhandari broke further new ground by getting these banks to provide us with a loan beyond their threshold limit. Since this required RBI sanction, a process that could take more than six months, the finance team prepared an exhaustive proposal to make a case for speedy approval. The RBI gave us its sanction within two months. It might not seem like a big deal in present times, but in those days it was a significant achievement because raising finance for projects in the pre-liberalization era was a big challenge for new entrants. Our proposal was for many years used as a model proposal in the training colleges of BoI and Dena Bank.

Mr Bhandari's astute handling of the finance department, including the culture of transparency and ethics that he promoted, gave me the confidence to give him full autonomy to handle his department. His work was so thorough that I rarely got involved with banking matters after the first few years. It left me with plenty of free time to work on other parts of the operation.

Mr Bhandari also played a significant role in the early days in another area. A few months after he joined, we began hearing about problems with our land acquisition effort in Mahuva. Though it was the Gujarat government's responsibility to acquire and give us the land, I thought it would be helpful if we got involved to expedite the process.

I requested Mr Bhandari, the only senior person in my team who could read and write Gujarati, to help out. He said he had no experience in buying land or dealing with the government, but I assured him of my full support.

He worked extremely hard over the next few months, shuttling between Bombay, Ahmedabad and the villages around Mahuva, coordinating between government officials and locals in the land acquisition effort. Since infrastructure was deficient in and around Mahuva, the team would often have to sleep in small circuit houses in the town due to lack of hotel facilities. Though we eventually failed in finding land in Mahuva, Mr Bhandari's negotiation skills came in handy when we shifted the plant site to Kodinar (of which I will talk about more, later).

Mr Kulkarni, Mr Bhandari, Mr B.L. Taparia (who looked after the secretarial functions), Mr M.M. Hirpara (project engineer and Mr Kulkarni's deputy) and a few others helped build the foundation on which the Gujarat Ambuja edifice was created and nurtured. My hope when they joined was that each of them would last more than a few years with the company. Instead, to my pleasant surprise, most of them spent their entire careers with Gujarat Ambuja. The company's success is as much theirs as it is mine.

Some call it a stereotype, but I am a firm believer in the idea that most Marwaris possess an intangible asset that we call *baniya buddhi* or the trader's mindset. It is one of the main reasons for our success as businessmen over the centuries. *Baniya* refers to the trading or merchant class, while *buddhi* is a Sanskrit term with a variety of meanings associated with the mind, including intellect, thinking, wisdom and reasoning. In my interpretation, *baniya buddhi*, which every Marwari kid picks up early, is the *baniya* way of thinking about handling money and spending it. It is a trait that we have inherited from an unbroken line of forebears, all of whom were merchants and traders. It is this *baniya buddhi* that has always driven my thinking, both as a trader and now as a cement entrepreneur.

The first thing I did when we started work was to estimate the cost involved in setting up the plant and day-to-day operations after that. I found that cement manufacturing involves 40 per cent capital cost and 40 per cent energy cost. If we had to succeed as a company, we would have to be singularly focused on keeping these costs under control. Also, in Gujarat, we would be up against long-established competitors whose plant values would have been written down to a bare minimum, making their cement much cheaper. It meant setting up our plant to produce the best quality cement at the least possible cost in the shortest possible time. It was a corporate mantra that served us well over the years.

Our choice of the main plant supplier was down to two: Bombay-based Larsen & Toubro (L&T), which was a big player in the plant equipment business in collaboration with Danish giant FLSmidth & Co AS and German machinery giant Krupp Polysius AG through its Indian subsidiary Buckau Wolf India. The latter was a relative newcomer in the Indian market and was eager for new business.

Mr Shovakar was quite keen to handle the negotiations with L&T himself because he knew the people there. I met them a few times, but found them very arrogant and patronizing. Very much in contrast was the low-key approach of the Buckau Wolf MD, Mr Dara Damania, whom I had got to know well through the Neotias. I was also annoyed with Mr Shovakar about his reluctance to part with information on the progress of his discussions.

I was quite vocal about L&T's arrogance. Sensing an opportunity, Buckau Wolf dropped the price. In Mr Kulkarni's assessment, their plant was more robust, packed with more steel and weighed close to 1,700 tonnes. In comparison, the L&T–FLSmidth plant weighed 1,400 tonnes. It was evident that the Germans were offering a plant capable of producing much more cement than the rated capacity. With Krupp's storied technical reputation, it was unlikely that their plant would in any way be inferior to the Danish plant.

At the final stage of the discussion, I called both companies and asked them to give me their last offer in a sealed envelope. When I opened the bids, the Buckau Wolf quotation was far lower. I called Mr Shovakar and told him about my decision to go with the Germans. He asked me the reason and I showed him the price difference. He was not very happy. My feeling was that he had probably committed to his friends at L&T that they would get the order. But what I had done was in the best interest of the company.

It turned out to be a point of friction between Mr Shovakar and me. As far as L&T was concerned, the lackadaisical manner in which they executed a subsequent contract for the plant's process control system proved that I was right about not giving them the order for the main plant.

I went against the standard market practice when ordering the high-tension motor, a critical piece of plant equipment that was required to be ordered well in advance. It ended up saving us not only a substantial quantum of money but, more importantly, time as well. The conventional wisdom among cement companies till then was to buy the high-tension motor from Bharat Heavy Electricals Limited (BHEL), the monopoly manufacturer in the country at that time. When I approached BHEL, they told me that it would take a minimum of eighteen months for delivery. And as is the case with all monopolists, they were not prepared to make any exceptions to their schedule. I was not happy about this, nor was I pleased with their 'take it or leave it' attitude.

Luckily, the Thapar company, Crompton Greaves, was planning to get into the same business at that time. They heard about us from the market and their MD, Mr K.K. Nohria came and met me personally, saying that they were getting into making high-tension motors. He offered to supply it to us at half the price and within six months. This was music to my ears. I was shown their plant and I decided to take a risk and give them the order. After all, they were a very reputed company. It proved to be the right decision. Their equipment never gave us any problem and they kept to the promised schedule.

Around this time, I had my second and final run-in with Mr Shovakar. It happened on account of one of our executives who had come back from Mahuva and was briefing me on the progress of the land acquisition. Mr Shovakar was out for lunch, so I started the meeting without him. When he came back, he barged into my cabin, looking upset and demanded to know why I was talking to the executive without him being present. I reminded him that as the MD, I could meet anyone, any time.

'You cannot meet him without me,' he reiterated.

'What nonsense are you talking?!' I retorted.

He was now even more agitated. He claimed that since Gujarat Ambuja was a joint-sector project, he was responsible to the Gujarat government and IDBI for anything that happened in the company, so everything had to be routed through him. I was surprised by his assertion. I told him that if he thought he was responsible to the Gujarat government and that they had appointed him, he should resign immediately.

The confrontation was tense, something that I had not anticipated. Mr Shovakar was not ready to back down and gave me his resignation letter within minutes of the showdown. For me, it was a matter of principle. What happened was a clear indicator of our different styles of management. The 'my way or the highway' approach ran contrary to everything I stood for. My preference was for teamwork, cooperation and mutual consultation. Looking back, I am glad that it happened early in Mr Shovakar's stint with us.

Something similar had happened when I had signed the joint-sector agreement with GIIC a year earlier. An official there told me that they had a system of dual signatures for all cheques beyond a certain amount, one from the company's side and the other from GIIC. I told him, in that case, I would have two of my people sign the cheques. He said that was not acceptable; one signature had to be from GIIC's side. I told him it would be impossible to run a large project with this kind of a rule. His point was that this was the established system and we had to follow it, implying that we had no choice in the matter.

I was exasperated and told him GIIC could be the sole signatory in that case and should take responsibility for all payments. 'You either take full responsibility and be accountable or allow me to do my job. You can question me, or you do it and I will question you. You have to decide,' I told him. Not used to this kind of straight talk, he immediately backed off. I was told later that Gujarat Ambuja was the only company in their stable of joint ventures that was allowed to sign its own cheques at the project stage. For me, it always was a matter of principle. If something was not right in principle, I would not agree to it.

Mr Shovakar had put himself and me in a similar situation. Soon after the resignation drama in my cabin, I told Mr Kulkarni, who was in the office, about what had happened. It was vital for me to take him into confidence since he was the senior-most technical person and Mr Shovakar had recruited him. 'Will you be comfortable working here without Mr Shovakar?' I asked. 'Are you prepared to continue? Are you prepared to take responsibility? Will you handle everything that Mr Shovakar is handling?'

He was very calm and said that he had no problem continuing and that he would do everything to the best of his ability. Next, I went to Mr M.V. Basrur, a retired former chairman of the Railway Board whom we had employed as an adviser to help us with our railway linkage in Mahuva and who was present in the office that day. He was the most senior person around, so I asked him if I had done the right thing. He said yes. I asked him whether he was okay working with me. He said he was. That was all I needed.

I called the accounts people, asked them to settle Mr Shovakar's dues and give him whatever he wanted. I allowed him to retain his car, his house and a cabin in our office for as long as he wanted until he moved on to another job. I did not want him to be bitter about the time he had spent with us.

With Mr Shovakar gone, the responsibility for managing the entire show was now on my shoulders. And the first test of my ability to handle adversity came soon after this showdown.

For much of 1983, things had gone smoothly. The financing was mostly in place, the orders for the plant and other equipment had been placed and some of the parts had been shipped by the end of the year. Our plans to start plant construction at Mahuva was also ready and we had already hired two of the country's most reputed consultants—Bhagwati & Co for civil engineering and Chemtech India for mechanical engineering and project management.

In early 1984, we finally moved out of my old cotton-trading office in Nariman Point, to Gujarat Ambuja's own office at the nearby Maker Chambers III. The news from Mahuva though, was not very encouraging. The government, through GIIC, had taken on the responsibility of acquiring the required land for the project. The collector of Bhavnagar, who had been entrusted with the task, was finding it difficult to convince people to sell their land.

Setting up a cement factory requires more land than most industries, because of the limestone mines. Three separate parcels of land are needed—one for the plant and office buildings; the second for employees' housing located some distance away, because of the dust and other noxious emissions from the plant; and the third and the biggest parcel for the limestone mines. Our total requirement was determined at around 225 acres, of which 100 acres of government-owned wasteland had been transferred to us in the early stages of land acquisition.

The rest was to come from private owners, for which, as required by law, the collector of Bhavnagar issued the notification under Section 4 of the Land Acquisition Act, which expresses the government's intention to acquire the land. It was followed by the notification under Section 6, which empowers the government to acquire the land forcefully by paying the necessary compensation.

Land acquisition for the setting up of an industrial plant is never easy in India, even in the best of times. It is a process that usually takes a year or two, depending on the location and the type of land. Much depends on the negotiation and persuasion skills of the collector and the willingness of the landowners to give in. The negotiations stretch for months before they arrive at a compromise on the price that is reasonable and fair. We thought that the same thing was happening here and it was only a question of time before the villagers accepted what was being offered. We were dismayed that this was not the case. In Mahuva, other interests were at play.

I was advised by everyone to stay put in Bombay and not travel to Mahuva, lest the villagers see me and hike up the price. I told Mr Bhandari to go and camp in the area to see if we could help. I asked him to contact the villagers and their leaders directly. For the next few months, he and his small team shuttled between Bombay, Ahmedabad, Bhavnagar and Mahuva, talking to all the stakeholders, village landowners, local politicians and government officials. But the picture that emerged was not very encouraging. The villagers were refusing to part with their land, irrespective of the price being offered.

Mahuva is a sleepy little town with pleasant weather throughout the year. Interestingly, the best-known people from the area include Hindi cinema legend Asha Parekh, spiritual leader Morari Bapu and music director Himesh Reshammiya. The serene calmness of the area and the villages around, proved to be deceptive. The officials of the ACC's geological services department, whom we had contracted to survey the limestone potential of the area, had met with some resistance from the villagers in early 1983 and had told us about it. But we had not taken it seriously. It was now clear why they had been resisting.

There were at least three parties who felt threatened by our arrival in Mahuva. A local businessman, who owned a mini-cement plant nearby, thought our larger plant would wipe him out and he was instigating the villagers against selling their land. Then there was the local bootleg mafia which had makeshift hooch distilleries in some of the local villages. They were worried that our arrival would increase the police exposure in the area and put them under the scanner. They were also influencing the villagers.

Finally, there was a Bombay-based industrialist who was from Mahuva. He did charity work in the area and owned vast tracts of land in the vicinity. Though he had no plans to set up any operations, I was told that he did not want any large manufacturing units here. To top it all, the government land acquisition policy in those days was a big mess. The compensation was a pittance, a fraction of the actual worth of the land. There was hardly any thinking involved in the way the land was priced.

The government never considers the fact that forcing people to sell their land has life-altering implications. In most cases, it is the only physical asset they own and often has been part of the family for generations. There is always a sentimental value attached to it. No amount of money is good enough to compensate for this loss. It is an important criterion that needs to be factored in when calculating the value of land being acquired.

Then there is their loss of livelihood, which needs to be adequately compensated. It will guarantee that the landowners do not end up on the streets in a year or two after exhausting the money they got from the sale. It is common sense that one has to offer them a price that considers all these factors. Though no one would be happy about parting with their family heirloom, at least the government has to make sure that they are not bitter about it or feel cheated. It should be an offer they cannot refuse, because it is really worth their while; not because they are compelled. In a place like Mahuva especially, the compensation should have been large enough to overcome the propaganda unleashed by the various parties with vested interests.

Looking back, the situation in Mahuva was similar to what happened in Singur, West Bengal, twenty-five years later with Tata Motors. In both these places, the government promised land to the company without assessing the ground situation. In our case, when the villagers refused to sell the land, the Gujarat government tried to use the state machinery to acquire the land mandatorily. This led to protests and agitations, which soon spiralled out of hand. Some of the landowners even went to court against the government and us.

The issues came to a head on a hot evening in May 1984. An agitation by some villagers turned violent and the police had to resort to firing. Fortunately, it was only in the air and no one was injured. I was devastated when I heard the news. We had set out to do something beneficial for the people of Mahuva and it had ended in a tragedy. It felt as if my dreams were crumbling even before we laid the foundation for the plant. Something at the back of my mind told me that our Mahuva chapter was over for good.

Almost until the end, I was under the impression that much of the agitation was a negotiation tactic to get the best price for the land. Mahuva was, after all, a backward region with lots of poor people. It was not a very fertile area and much of the land that we were looking at was fallow, where people were hardly making anything. I failed to understand why villagers would object to the setting up of a large-scale manufacturing plant that would create hundreds of jobs, directly and indirectly. As per law, at least one person from every family selling land has to be mandatorily employed by the company. The police action proved that I was wholly mistaken in my assessment of how people thought in a situation of this kind and the sway local leaders and charismatic politicians had over them.

After the police firing—a turning point—we were too stunned to figure out a future course of action. It was early days, yet I had no clue about where we were headed and neither did any of my team members. They looked to me for answers. I had none. Those were some of my darkest days. Loans from the banks were already in our account and major portions of the payment for plant purchases had also been made.

Vendors had started shipping many of the plant components. We neither had a site to locate our plant, nor any idea about alternative locations. I was having nightmares about how I would pay off the loans if this situation continued for too long. The government, as usually happens in such cases, was in deep-freeze mode, numbed into inaction. My plans had gone off the rails at the first big hurdle. It was nearly two months before we finally saw the light at the end of our dark tunnel.

In August 1984, one of our senior executives Mr K.J. Trivedi, who had worked with Mr Bhandari on the land issue, came to my office to inform me about a chat he had had with a senior government official on a train journey in Gujarat. The official had told Mr Trivedi to forget Mahuva because the situation was never going to change there. It was better to start considering a new location. He suggested Kodinar, another coastal town, which also had good limestone deposits.

Kodinar is 130 kilometres west of Mahuva, close to the tourist sites like Gir National Park and the Somnath Temple. At that time, it was part of the Junagadh district, but is now in the Gir Somnath district.

I told Trivedi that I was aware of the area, but that too many people had already applied for a licence to put up cement plants there. The other problem was that the limestone estimates there, were much smaller than in Mahuva. However, he rightfully suggested that there was no harm in checking out the place, which I agreed was worth the effort. In the situation that we were in at that time, we had no choice but to explore every potential opportunity.

We dispatched our senior engineer, Mr Hirpara, to assess the limestone potential. He took along a freelance geologist and reported back that they had found rich deposits of quality limestone in and around Vadnagar village at a distance of 6 kilometres from Kodinar town. I immediately flew to Gandhinagar and met Mr Khan at GIIC and the chief secretary of the Gujarat government. They agreed it was a good idea to move to Kodinar. I then went to the industry secretary to apprise him of the new plan and he promised to expedite the necessary clearances.

The Gujarat government granted us the required permissions to shift to Kodinar in a record three days. And in 'public interest', our application was prioritized over others to enable us to start the land acquisition process immediately. They allowed us to shift the project to Kodinar *mutatis mutandis*, a legal term meaning 'as is where is', which permitted us to avail all the concessions, incentives and permissions in the new location that we had in Mahuva.

The Gujarat government's policy at that time ensured that the first large plant to come up in any backward district with an investment of over ₹20 crore, could claim extra incentives. We were granted these concessions in Mahuva, but there were already quite a few large industries in the Kodinar area and we were sceptical about getting them now. Once again, an exception was made for us. The government officials helped wrap up the shifting process at an unprecedented speed and we had a genuine soft-landing in Kodinar.

We still had to acquire land there however. I was determined to apply the lessons we had learnt in Mahuva. I told my people we would not go through the government this time but buy the land directly from the villagers, offering them whatever price they wanted. I told my team to meet Mr S.R. Rao, the district collector of Amreli and inform him of the new plan. Mr Rao couldn't have been more helpful. A few years later, he would gain nationwide fame for cleaning up Surat after a major plague outbreak.

Next, I sent three senior team members under Mr Bhandari to plan and execute the land acquisition. Our plan was straightforward—call all landowners for a meeting in one hall; ask them to come up with a per bigha price for different types of land that was acceptable to all the landowners; accept the price they wanted without any prolonged negotiations; and get them to sign on the deal the same day. We did not want to delay the process.

Once in Kodinar, the team did a great job. They employed an innovative measure to get a quick answer from the villagers. They divided them into three groups and a competition was set up to see which group would sign up first to sell their land. Whoever signed up first was to be given the first choice in the job selection at the plant. One member from each family that sold us land was entitled to be employed by us. It worked well.

The price that the Kodinar landowners quoted for their land was three to four times higher than what the government had offered in Mahuva. We agreed to the price they quoted and everyone signed up to sell the same day. Everyone was paid for their land the next day. The whole exercise went off without a hitch. We spent close to ₹5 crore to buy the land. In comparison, a competitor who had purchased a similar tract of land nearby had paid just ₹40 lakh not long before us. He was not happy with what we had done and complained to the district collector that we had spoiled the real estate market in the area.

As far as we were concerned, the adequate compensation assured that the villagers were not unhappy about parting with their land. Some of them had standing crop and requested us to allow time till the end of the harvest season, which we agreed to. We had completed the whole exercise without the involvement of the government or local administration. By October 1984, we had the land we wanted—103 acres for the plant in Vadnagar and around 250 acres for limestone in the surrounding villages. Things were now back on track.

I believe it was destiny that brought me to Kodinar. The tragic incident of the police firing in Mahuva had led us to a better site that was closer to a railway junction and not very far from the sea. Without the Mahuva disaster, we would have never reached Kodinar.

Without Kodinar, we wouldn't have pioneered organized sea transportation of cement in the country. We discovered it was the most practical and cost-effective way of shipping cement to Bombay, which would go on to become our biggest market.

The irony about Mahuva and its troubled tryst with cement manufacturers is worth talking about here. Not having learnt any lessons from our unfortunate experience, Nirma Cements made a valiant attempt to set up a cement factory there twenty-five years later, in 2008. It was to be several times bigger than our plant. The government allocated over 250 hectares of land across nine villages. The plant itself was supposed to cost ₹1,000 crore.

The conditions in Mahuva had undergone a radical transformation since the time we were there. The state government had spent over ₹200 crore in the 1990s to set up four giant reservoirs in the area. The water helped turn most of the fallow land in the area into fertile cultivable land. Once again, though for wholly different reasons, the farmers of Mahuva refused to give up their land. They took Nirma to the Supreme Court and won. The Ministry of Environment in 2011 cancelled the plant's environment clearance, forcing the company to shift its plant to Pali in Rajasthan.

Mahuva was never destined to have a cement plant.

4

Idea to Reality

Plant construction • Successful IPO • Start of commercial production • Management philosophy anchored in ethics and values

After all that had happened, it was with a mixed feeling of exhaustion, relief and nervousness that I arrived in Vadnagar for the first time on Dussehra day, Wednesday, 10 October 1984. We conducted the ground-breaking ceremony, the *bhoomi pooja*, for our plant and the complex which we would later name Ambujanagar. My exhaustion stemmed from the nightmare that was now behind us and relief from the fact that it was hopefully over—even if it had meant a delay of four months and moving to a new site 130 kilometres away. The nervousness stemmed from the thought of what lay ahead.

Getting to Kodinar was not very easy. A train journey from Bombay took more than thirty-six hours, so the only option was to fly to one of the three airports in the vicinity (Keshod, Bhavnagar or Rajkot) and from there proceed by road—a journey of anything between three and five hours. Those were the days before the advent of private airlines. Indian Airlines ruled the roost and there were only a few flights a week.

The communication system was even worse. It was the 1980s and rural telecom connectivity was poor. We did not get a phone connection at our construction site for almost a year. We used a primitive walkie-talkie for internal communication and every time someone had to get in touch with the Bombay office, they had to travel more than 15 kilometres to reach the nearest phone. And because regular long-distance trunk calls were challenging to get through on most occasions, we mostly used the more expensive 'lightning calls' that were usually reserved for senior government officials. The problems provide a vivid portrayal of how difficult it was in the 1980s and '90s for an entrepreneur to put up an industrial plant, even in a progressive state like Gujarat.

The first major decision I had to make was on where to build the factory township. Staff quarters of cement plants are usually built a minimum of 5 kilometres away, because of the emission and dust problems. I had neither the energy nor the inclination to put my team through another round of land acquisition. As a result, we decided to build staff quarters within the factory complex, a rare thing for any cement company.

Consciously and subconsciously, this forced us into investing in a world-class emission-and-dust-control system in all our plants. We created one of the greenest cement factory campuses in India, packed with trees and birds. Not only did this prove useful for the environment and our employees, but it also benefited our bottom line. Dust is one of the biggest reasons for frequent plant breakdowns in India. Remember, this was years before environmental laws concerning industrial emission were entirely codified and at least a year before the Union Ministry of Environment & Forest (MoEF) itself was set up.

The farmers who had sold us the land for the factory had requested for an extra month after the *bhoomi pooja* to harvest their standing kharif crop. The civil work started in November 1984. Our contractors were Gannon Dunkerley & Co and Buildmet, two of India's most reputed civil engineering companies. The order for the 100-tonne cement mill from Krupp Polysius of Germany and some other equipment had been placed before the Mahuva episode and it was already on its way. No delay was expected on that count.

If everything went as per plan, our target was to have the plant operational in eighteen months, as against the three years that was standard in India then. Mr Kulkarni, with his years of experience of installing cement plants, had set this deadline. As per our calculation, at an annual inflation rate of 10 per cent, we would save as much as ₹6 crore if we cut down the installation time by a year.

I had long been inspired by Mr Dhirubhai Ambani's example of setting up manufacturing plants in as short a time as possible. Like him, we were going to strike our own path and set our own standards, rather than follow the rules set by existing manufacturers. I never allowed myself to be constrained by the yardstick of the past, either in cotton trading or in setting up cement plants. In my book, everything that was deemed the conventional way of doing things, was up for questioning and review. Beyond the monetary savings, the shorter deadline helped set the tone for the future—it instilled a sense of mission, urgency, discipline and purpose in each one of us in our small team.

Of course, the speed of installation and cost-consciousness would not be at the expense of technology or quality of work. I was a believer in using the best of technologies, negotiating it down to the lowest possible price and getting the best people to run it. My determination to employ the best possible technology in Ambuja was reinforced when we visited Narmada Cement's new plant nearby, the only time I visited an Indian cement company other than my own. I had gone with Mr Kulkarni and Mr Bhandari and was shocked at the ankle-high dust we had to wade through in the plant. We were all caked in dust within a few minutes and made a hasty exit. On our way back I told my colleagues that if our plant were to look like this, I would rather not set it up.

As a result, we decided to invest in the most modern dust-and-pollution-control technology available at that time—a conventional electrostatic precipitator along with the more advanced reverse-air baghouse. The latter was new to India and consisted of cylindrical tubes or bags lined with high-temperature-resistant fabrics which trapped 99 per cent of the dust when gas from the kiln and the raw mill passed through it. For this equipment, we contracted American company Zurn & Co, a world leader in the technology, through their local partner Thermax.

Over the years, it helped us bring down our dust emission to as low as 50 milligrams per cubic metre as compared to the 50 to 100 milligrams regulatory norm in Europe and 150 to 200 milligrams in India. We later installed these in all our plants across the country. It is now specified as standard equipment by the Central Pollution Control Board (CPCB).

The dry process plant and the state-of-the-art pollution-control equipment would make us one of the most advanced cement manufacturing facilities in the country at that time. While we achieved the best with everything that was under our control, our major problem lay in areas where we had to deal with government agencies, particularly those dealing with electricity. The high-tension power lines, in our case, had to come from the state electricity board substation 33 kilometres away.

Despite Gujarat being among the most progressive industrial states and despite ours being a joint-sector project with the Gujarat government, it made no difference. We had to cajole and beg to get a power line to the factory site, which arrived after a delay of nearly eight months. To bridge this delay, we had to compress our commissioning time considerably. The issue was that we did not have money at that time to buy a captive power generator (which we eventually did in 1989), or else we would not have jumped through the unending hoops of the state electricity board for so long.

I never trusted state electricity boards after that and we budgeted for a captive power plant for every new cement plant we built after that. Our plant at Chandrapur in Maharashtra was the first in the country to be set up without any linkage to the local electricity grid, which at that time was hailed as a brave move.

The railways were a bit more efficient. They laid a new 5-kilometre track from Kodinar station to our plant well in time before production started. We were also allowed concessional freight charges based on a formula of the shortest possible distance from Kodinar to Ahmedabad via Amreli. The actual route was much longer because the trains were re-routed around the protected Gir forest area.

As luck would have it, the concession was withdrawn after a new general manager took office at Western Railway a few years later. He insisted on us paying for the longer route. It added a steep ₹200 per tonne of cement to our freight cost and was the trigger that led us to explore the possibility of transporting our cement to Bombay by sea. This idea became a reality a few years later when we pioneered the shipping of cement by sea across long distances in India. It was an instance where we turned a challenge into an opportunity.

~

The start of the civil work at Kodinar was the signal for me to get over my awkwardness and embrace the idea that I was now the full-time captain of the ship called Gujarat Ambuja that had just set sail and that there was no looking back. I had to roll up my sleeves and start getting my hands dirty on the factory floor as the leader. The departure of Mr Shovakar a few months earlier had removed the ambiguity about who was going to be running the company. I decided I would run the company as the MD on a full-time basis hereafter.

Having seen only one working cement plant in my life, I knew next to nothing about erecting a cement plant or running one. Luckily, I had Mr Kulkarni by my side as the technical head. Mr Shovakar's exit had thrust him into a leadership position. It turned out to be a blessing in disguise for both of us. It allowed his talent to flourish in a manner that made him one of the most respected technical professionals in the Indian cement industry over the years.

As for me, I got a working partner who believed in my mission implicitly and whom I trusted unequivocally. Our close working relationship would prove to be the critical engine of Gujarat Ambuja's success over the next two decades. He was the best deputy I could have hoped for, the expert facilitator and implementer of my ambitious and sometimes seemingly outlandish ideas, agendas and plans, big and small. He executed each of them to perfection, sometimes even better than I had imagined. In my long association with him, he never said no to anything that I wanted to be done. Genial and soft-spoken, he was unflappable even in the direst of circumstances and had an almost Zen-like approach to work.

Mr Kulkarni assembled a team of bright young engineers to work with him in Kodinar and Bombay; the average age was hardly thirty-two or thirty-three and that turned out to be a significant advantage. Their boundless energy, open-mindedness and ability to work hard were infectious. The baggage of past working methods did not bog them down. They were eager and open to embracing new ideas and came up with suggestions for improvements and changes that would benefit us in the long run. I myself was only thirty-four and my complete lack of experience in setting up cement plants in that sense proved to be advantageous.

When needed though, I made sure that we recruited the best of senior professionals. Mr Kulkarni, for example, had told me that he knew how to set up a plant but had no knowledge of operating one. 'I am not a manufacturing person,' he said. 'For operating the plant, we need an experienced manufacturing professional.' So we searched for a manufacturing expert and managed to locate and lure Mr G.C. Kotwal, who was once the head of manufacturing at one of the cement companies of the B.K. Birla group.

Between Mr Kotwal, Mr Kulkarni, Mr Bhandari, Mr Taparia and Mr P.C. Jain, who joined as the head of commercial operations, we had the core project team in place. Mr Kulkarni spent three weeks a month at Kodinar, while I was content with travelling there once a fortnight for a few days crammed with meetings and site visits. I lived out of a small little corner room in our recently constructed employees' hostel next to the plant and worked out of the conference room. With very few distractions in Kodinar, I was able to spend long hours at work. I had a set daily routine—breakfast at the hostel at 8 a.m., a walk around the plant to check progress at 9 a.m. and then straight to the conference room for meetings and reviews.

I had a review meeting in the boardroom every time I was in Kodinar and every plant manager, senior and junior, was required to participate. Every issue was discussed thoroughly and problems, if any, sorted out in full view of everyone. It ensured transparency and openness from top to bottom, which is the key to the smooth running of any organization. It eliminated the chances of people playing politics and talking behind one another's back. It helped create a work culture of camaraderie and cooperation, which I believe benefited the company tremendously.

The other decisive aspect of work culture we fostered from the very beginning was to empower everyone to think and act with as much autonomy as possible. I did not want yes-men, but men who would correct a wrong whenever they saw one and, importantly, men who were always thinking of making the operations more efficient and cost-effective.

Once the plant became operational, our engineers were allowed to make crucial investment decisions on plant modifications up to a certain level of investment without consulting the top management. My thinking was that if cost had to be controlled, it seemed absurd for engineers to check back with their seniors on every little decision. The time lost in consulting seniors would be far more expensive than the money lost due to any errors they would make. The freedom to make decisions came with the occasional risk of failure and I was okay with that. Failure, I have always believed, is valuable as an experience; it is the first step to eventual success.

I honestly believe that Ambuja was not built with cement or steel, but on trust, creative freedom and hard work. We trusted our managers and engineers to think creatively, using their knowledge and experience to come up with innovative ideas that would solve problems and benefit the company. My theory was that if you trusted someone fully, nine times out of ten, the person would not let you down. Let a manager set his own target, provide him the freedom and authority to do it in his own way and the work will become a mission.

There were two incidents during our construction phase that benefited from our decision to empower people. In the first instance, an alert engineer came and reported to us that one of his colleagues who was in charge of monitoring the construction of the raw-meal silo, was being wined and dined by a construction subcontractor. In exchange, the contractor had got away with using less steel than required for the foundation of the building. The silo is one of the biggest and heaviest structures in a cement plant and Mr Kulkarni was worried about the durability of the building. We were glad that the engineer was conscientious enough to inform Mr Kulkarni about the matter before it was too late. The culprit was sacked and the foundation was redone, albeit at a considerable cost.

The second incident concerned the 100-tonne cement mill shell from our German supplier Krupp Polysius, which was being transported from their local partner Buckau Wolf's Pune plant to Kodinar. On the way, the giant trailer truck had an accident near Dhule in northern Maharashtra. The mill fell into a ditch and was damaged on one side. When our team reached there to survey the scene, experts from Buckau Wolf told them that it would be best to take the mill back to their facility to fix the damage. The exercise would have taken an additional four months, one month to be transported to Pune, two months to repair it and another month for the trip back to Kodinar. It would have considerably delayed the erection and commissioning of the plant.

We knew the Buckau Wolf experts were playing it safe to avoid being blamed later if something went wrong. That is when Mr G.D. Bhosale, in charge of our mechanical engineering division, suggested that we do the repairs ourselves at our plant site. He said we should be able to do it in a few days. The team from Buckau Wolf tried their best to discourage us, saying that if we were not able to do a good job, then they would have to take it back to Pune which would mean a further delay. Mr Bhosale was confident about us fixing the damage ourselves and we decided to back him. We took the mill to Kodinar and, as promised, he fixed it in a week. The mill is still in operation after thirty years!

Other than these and a few other instances, vendor problems during our construction phase were few and far between. It had a lot to do with the harmonious relationship I sought to build with them as company policy from the beginning. I viewed them as vital partners in our road to success and prosperity. They needed to give their best, as much as our own company executives. I believe that an adversarial relationship with vendors benefits no one, neither them nor us.

To develop this bond, I put in place guidelines for our dealings with vendors and suppliers. First, in our price negotiations, it was important not to squeeze them dry, but to leave something on the table that made them happy. They would never walk away feeling discontented if they made a profit that was commensurate with their effort. Only this would incentivize them to give us their best. I learnt this from my father. Fairness is the key to sustaining long-term relationships with buyers and sellers and when you go beyond that and do something extra, they will also reciprocate. Most of all, they will not cheat you. Ninety per cent of people cheat you because they feel that they have not got a fair deal.

Secondly, while we had to be strict on quality and deadlines, we made sure they were paid before time as a matter of routine. This was important for their cash flow and created a stress-free working environment for them. This ran contrary to the prevailing practice among Indian companies where vendors routinely fought their way through a thicket of company bureaucracy over long periods, to get paid. It invariably led to them cutting corners and affected the quality of work.

I am proud of the fact that I never came across, or even heard about, a single vendor who cheated us during my time at Gujarat Ambuja. We never took a vendor to court or sought to enforce the liquidated damage clause in our contracts. Occasionally, we even helped our contractors with funds and extended deadlines when they were not able to meet their commitments for genuine reasons. It helped create a congenial and pleasant work atmosphere which proved vital in our race to meet our ambitious targets. In time, we came to be known as the best cement company to work with, because of which we were able to command the best terms and prices.

The other crucial component of my workplace policy concerned the moral dimension of doing business in India—the issue of corruption. As far as I was concerned, there was no dilemma on this count. An unwavering commitment to ethics and honesty was an essential part of the value system my parents instilled in me. It had been the guiding principle of every aspect of my life. And it was something that I made part of the work culture at Ambuja.

I remember a senior executive from my finance team coming to me when we were moving to our new office at Nariman Point. He said that we were getting the interior design work done by an architect known to us. It provided an excellent opportunity to generate some cash that could come in handy when needed later. My advice to him was that all our company transactions should be legal and transparent, without any shortcuts, even if we lost money. It sent a strong signal to everyone handling finance that all our dealings, big and small, should be above board.

Another time, when we were consistently running our plant at over 100 per cent capacity utilization, I recall a rival manufacturer telling me that once you have crossed the 100 per cent figure, it is easy to fiddle around with the numbers to avoid paying excise duty and other taxes on the excess production. Being new to the business, I was a little surprised when he said this was standard industry practice. I think he was disappointed when I told him that I did not believe in this style of doing business.

I always believed in leading from the front, setting an example of the principles and work practices I preached in the company. I deliberately stayed in the smallest room at our staff hostel whenever I was in Kodinar and refused to have a fancy office made for me, preferring to work long hours from the boardroom. I even gave up on my love for luxury foreign cars in favour of a simple white Premier Padmini, lest my colleagues think that I was extravagant with company money while preaching frugality to others.

I drove the same car well into the 1990s, even after we became financially prosperous. And it indeed became a bit of a problem for others. Newer and better cars were being launched in the market, but none of my senior colleagues could even think of upgrading simply because the boss was still driving a basic Premier Padmini!

Eventually, I realized I was being unfair to everyone and upgraded to a fancier set of wheels, which is when others started buying more modern and bigger cars. My personal commitment to a relatively frugal work-related lifestyle, I think, had a beneficial effect on everyone.

In mid-1985, I began work on our promised IPO. As per our agreement with our co-promoters—GIIC and the banks—we were to double our share capital to ₹14.65 crore by raising ₹7.15 crore through an IPO. A successful issue would mean that the investing public would own half our shares. The issue was planned for November and I have to admit that I started on a complacent note. I sought comfort in the thought that the issue was to be fully underwritten by the development banks we were already working with—IDBI, ICICI and IFCI. With that kind of backing, I was confident that our issue would sail through without any problems.

Besides raising capital, the IPO was going to be Gujarat Ambuja's public debut. For the first time, investors and media across the country would become aware of the Gujarat Ambuja name. We needed to put our best foot forward. Significantly though, the IPO market was not in a good state in those days, especially for cement companies. The stock market itself was in the dumps and, on top of that, cement companies were battling a combination of glut in supply and slowing demand. As a result, their share price was being beaten down even more than other companies on the stock market.

The IPOs of even established cement players were facing stiff resistance from investors. Modi Cement and Shree Cement of the Bangur group had a tough time getting subscribed. Rumours were rife that private financiers had to bail them out. The IPO of the Cement Corporation of Gujarat Limited (CCGL), part of the Mahendra Mehta group and a reputed name in Gujarat, received only 8 per cent subscription, which was abysmally low.

I realized that I was in a position that was much worse than theirs. My fellow partners, Suresh and Vinod Neotia and I were virtually unknown to the investment community; we had no background in manufacturing or cement; our project was still in the construction phase; and finally, we were only one among the 150 'mini-giant' companies that had been given a licence in recent years to set up cement plants. It was a perfect mix for a primary market disaster.

A failed IPO, or even one with an inadequate response, had the potential to ruin the name of the company before it even started production. I spoke to people about why some recent IPOs had fared poorly. Besides the market conditions, the consensus opinion was that promoters and owners had done very little to convince the investors of their company's long-term viability. But failure did not bother them. They were confident that the underwriters would bail them out, just as they had in the past.

Failure, however, was never an option for me. That was not how I lived my life or conducted myself as a businessman. I found out that most of these companies had treated IPO management as a mechanical process. They had left most of the work in the hands of their merchant banker. Their personal involvement was negligible. I did not want to repeat their mistakes. I went to meet my lawyer, friend and sometimes mentor, Mr M.L. Bhakta. He was and still is one of the country's leading business lawyers and a senior partner at a leading firm of solicitors, Kanga & Co.

He had guided me in my career for a long time. I told him, 'Bhakta *saab*, I have to launch an IPO in the coming months and I do not know how to go about it.'

Mr Bhakta, as always, was gentle and calm. 'Don't worry,' he said, 'you appoint a good merchant banker and he will guide you through the process.' He suggested his friend, Mr Nimesh Kampani.

Mr Kampani had left his family brokerage business to start out on his own. In less than two years, his firm JM Financial had become the most successful merchant banker in the country. He had successfully handled some of the biggest public issues of that time and he sat on the board of many leading companies. But I did not know him. Mr Bhakta offered to make the introduction. He asked his secretary to call Mr Kampani and when he came on the line, Mr Bhakta told him that he had to handle my IPO.

Mr Kampani immediately said yes and came over to my office soon after. We had a long chat. He told me about the Nagarjuna Fertilizers' issue that he had successfully handled recently. By the end of the conversation, I had decided to appoint JM Financial as our merchant banker. In my opinion, JM was in the process of building a brand for itself and would have more skin in the game. A failed issue would tarnish JM's reputation as well.

Nimeshbhai had several rounds of meetings with us where he coached us on the path ahead, on how to organize the roadshow and investor meets and on what to say and what not to say at these meetings. We discussed what could be our main talking points: our excellent track record as businessmen; the fact that we had GIIC, which had promoted some of the most successful companies in Gujarat, as our joint-venture partner; that our project implementation was far ahead of schedule as compared to similar greenfield projects; and that we had done it at a comparatively lower cost.

He also lectured us on the importance of servicing our investors once the issue got subscribed. He told us that most companies were negligent about this. Gujarat Ambuja, he said, should set a benchmark in the time taken to make the share allotment, dispatching share certificates, issuing refunds, listing the shares on the stock exchange and addressing investor complaints. Accordingly, we segregated our work into two parts—pre-issue preparation and post-issue response. We decided to request our chairman Mr Khan and other reputed board members like Mr Pai, who enjoyed great investor and industry goodwill and respect, to address our broker meetings and investor conferences.

An essential aspect of an IPO launch in those days was marketing and public relations (PR). For that, we hired another up-and-coming agency called Clea Advertising. Several established agencies had pitched for the business, but I liked the enthusiasm of the two young men who had recently set up Clea—Sunil Gautam and P. Venugopal. Though they had worked on IPO launches in their previous jobs, they had only handled one IPO since starting their company. I saw this perceived weakness as a strength; it would make them work harder to build their own reputation. To ensure that they were working for us full-time, I made them promise that they would not take on another IPO until ours was done.

Besides Bombay in Maharashtra, Gujarat was the biggest investor market for IPOs in those days. Sunil and Venugopal suggested that we create ads in Gujarati rather than using a Gujarati translation of English ads, which was the usual practice. In the Gujarati ads, we played up our Gujarat roots, our contribution to the state in locating our plant in Saurashtra, our partnership with the Gujarat government through GIIC, etc. It was a very effective strategy.

Our national advertising was equally effective. It was an eye-opener for me as to what good advertising could achieve; it became the template for the future Gujarat Ambuja advertising strategy. In contrast, our first broker conference in Bombay did not get off to a good start, mainly because I was not fully prepared for it. I had never been to an investor/broker conference, so I knew little about how to conduct it. Nimeshbhai had told me that I, as the promoter, was required to speak at the meeting. I am a shy public speaker at the best of times and had even enrolled at Bombay's Nazareth Public Speaking Academy in the hope of getting better, but ended up taking no classes because of my punishing schedule. When I told Nimeshbhai about this, he asked me not to worry as his people would be writing the speech and all I had to do was read it out.

Before the event was about to start, a JM executive handed me a two-page note that he said was my speech. There was very little time for me to gather my thoughts or change it. I read it out mechanically to the brokers. Although the audience heard me out in silence, I could make out that I was not connecting with them. There was nothing in the speech to excite anyone. I was disappointed in myself. It was not a speech that I would want to hear. It was boring and carried no conviction. All I ended up doing was talking about the size of the plant, its features, when it was likely to go on stream, etc. It was like reading an information brochure. It was my first public interaction with potential investors as the company MD and I had done poorly.

A similar conference of brokers was planned for the next day in Ahmedabad and I was determined to get it right this time. On the early morning flight from Bombay, I wrote the speech myself. In my interactions with the brokers in Bombay, I had heard their concerns and queries, which I decided would be the main subject of my talk. I concentrated on the four aspects of our project which I thought would help explain all their queries—why cement; the future of the cement industry in India; why we as promoters were investing in cement; and, why Gujarat?

I wrote that cement was a product which had no substitute. It had been around for 100 years and it would be around for another 100 years, if not more. A developing country like India would need to develop its infrastructure for the next fifty years and it still wouldn't be enough. India, with its growing population, would see accelerating demand for new housing in the coming decades as the standard of living improved. And as more and more poor people rose above the poverty line, housing would become as important as food and clothing. And cement would be critical to the building of homes, big or small.

The other thing about cement was that it was one of the few industries in the world where manufacturing technology had already matured. A cement plant would not become technically obsolete in ten, twenty or even thirty or forty years. There had hardly been any obsolescence in cement technology over the years. It was one of the main reasons I invested in cement and the same reason that some of India's most prominent business houses, including the Tatas, Birlas, L&T, Dalmias and Bangurs, invested in cement before me.

To the possible question of why Gujarat, well I could not have asked for a better state. Where else would I have found a government partner like GIIC that had set up three of India's most successful joint-sector projects—Gujarat State Fertilizers & Chemicals Limited (GSFC), Gujarat Narmada Valley Fertilizers & Chemicals Limited (GNFC) and Gujarat Alkalies and Chemicals Limited (GACL).

While I was new, my partner GIIC was very experienced and represented the Government of Gujarat. When the Gujarat government is your partner, you don't have to worry. Also, while new cement plants were coming up in Rajasthan, Madhya Pradesh and Karnataka, none were planned for Gujarat in the near future barring Ambuja. Gujarat had the most vibrant economy among all these states and hence would have the most demand. We would essentially have a captive market.

As for the future, every shareholder, big or small, would be an equal partner and I promised that Gujarat Ambuja would not be dishonest with anyone. We would work to the best of our ability to make investment worthwhile. The Birlas, Tatas and Modis had been successful in this business, so there was no reason we could not be. I had the business experience even if it was not in cement. I had a great product and I had a market. It was now up to me and my team to make it work.

I felt confident going into the Ahmedabad conference. Being better prepared, I was more at ease with my speech and the audience seemed far more responsive. I ended by saying, 'You may be putting in a small amount of money as your investment, but I have put my reputation and a large personal fortune on the line. If this company is not successful, then

I have no future.' The speech got a tremendous ovation. Nimeshbhai was the first to congratulate me. I could feel the upbeat mood in the room during the question-and-answer session and later in the informal chats with the investors after the conference.

What helped in Ahmedabad was the buzz created by GIIC and the Gujarat government officers. We had worked closely with them over the previous two years and they were aware of our commitment and hard work. I was sure that many of the Ahmedabad brokers would have spoken to some of these officers for information on us and would have got good feedback. The optimism and momentum created by the Ahmedabad conference carried us through the rest of the roadshow. I followed up with visits to Delhi and Madras (renamed Chennai in 1996), while my team went to small towns around the country.

Dubai too was on my agenda. The Gulf state even then was a significant source of NRI investment into Indian stock markets. On my request our chairman Mr Khan also travelled with me. I thought his name and fame would attract a significant section of well-heeled Indians and they did. After the investor conference, we had a special dinner for prominent invitees. Because of Mr Khan's presence, we had a good turnout.

I still remember the speech he made. He said this was a unique project being set up by a combination of the three best business-minded communities in India—the Gujaratis (represented by GIIC), the Marwaris (represented by me) and the Sindhis (represented by Mr Suresh Mulani). The chances of this project failing were next to nil. That went down well with the audience and set the tone for the evening. He then followed up by addressing the most common problem of NRI investors those days, a sixty-day delay in the allotment and refunding of investor money. I promised I would do it in fifteen days for NRIs, which we did.

The guests committed to investing sizeable amounts in the issue, with promises ranging from ₹10 to 50 lakh, and some even talking about figures in crores. I was impressed because they all looked like seasoned and prosperous investors. After dinner, I asked Mr Khan for his assessment of the evening. 'Don't be fooled by these people; these promises are made only for my benefit,' he said. 'I will be surprised if even a handful of them keep their promise.' This turned out to be true.

The overwhelming response was from professionals and regular salaried men and women, the kind who had turned up at the open investor conference. To my delight, most of them seemed to have made up their mind about investing in our IPO. Their questions were about the minimum shares that would be allotted to them if the issue were to be oversubscribed. I promised that each of them would get at least 100 shares.

It would be remiss of me not to mention that I was nervous as the date of the IPO approached. And finally, when it did—on Monday, 18 November 1985—my fears proved to be ill-founded. The early news from merchant bankers was that the response was much better than expected. It got even better over the next two days and we were able to close on the earliest closing day, 21 November. The IPO was oversubscribed seven times. It was a success beyond our wildest expectations. All our hard work had proved to be worthwhile. No cement company had come even close to doing what we had managed. The Modi Cement issue which came a month later, barely scraped through.

For me, the best part of the story was that out of the 27,000 or so shareholders who eventually got the minimum share allotment, more than 26,000 were small shareholders, the bulk of whom received 100 shares each. It was good news because I had done quite a bit of reading on the strategies of Mr Dhirubhai Ambani. He had been hailed for single-handedly creating the 'equity' cult across the country a decade earlier, by getting millions of small investors to put money in his public issues starting with his first IPO in 1977 (which coincidentally, was also oversubscribed seven times).

Attracting small investors who sought the minimum number of shares to invest in Reliance Textiles at that time was not an altruistic move on Mr Dhirubhai's part—it was a calculated strategy. In the unregulated pre-SEBI era, it ensured that no speculator could corner large chunks of shares on the stock market and conspire to beat down the share price or mount a takeover bid.

I had similar fears, because we as promoters controlled only 25 per cent of the company's shareholding. Having a few big investors owning large chunks of the company was not in my best interest. I felt more comfortable with the small investor. In any case, the big investors had shown they were less enthusiastic about what we were doing. It was the small investors who helped oversubscribe the issue. We were so happy that we sent each of them a thank you card with a beautiful rose printed on one side and a 1986 calendar on the other. The investors were thrilled with this kind of attention.

Now that the small investors had reposed their faith in Gujarat Ambuja's future, it was incumbent on me to work on the promises I had made during the roadshow. Besides publicly committing to honesty and ethics, I had declared my faith in the future of cement, promising to be as good or even better than the best in the business. Now I had the vital duty to deliver. The success of the public issue reignited my passion. It infused a greater sense of motivation in me about the company and its people.

The success of the IPO brought about a new sense of enthusiasm among our small staff. And we followed through with Nimeshbhai's suggestion of providing the best possible service to our shareholders in the quickest time. Since the plant had not yet started production, we were still functioning with skeletal infrastructure at the head office in Bombay. It was the pre-internet era and we moved heaven and earth to get all the share application forms and collection certificates from the banks to our office in the shortest possible time. Many of the bank branches were in remote areas and communication systems in those days were miserable. We mobilized our own people to go to many of these branches and pick up the certificates.

In the case of some banks, we sought help from their head office in Bombay. It was a round-the-clock job for many days. We even hired students from the local KC College to help us out part-time to sort out the thousands of forms. Eventually, we managed to make share allotments within weeks rather than months that most companies would take in those days. Also, unlike the prevailing practice at that time of delaying application money refunds, we returned the excess subscription money immediately. I believe it is unethical to make money in this manner. I was proud of what our company secretary, Mr Taparia and his team achieved in such a short time.

Another pleasant outcome of the IPO was that it allowed us to expand the ownership of the company to include our employees, loyal dealers, bankers and business associates who had believed in us when we were just starting. In those days, as part of the 'promoters' quota', company owners were allowed to make discretionary allotment of shares to employees, friends and associates up to the tune of 2 per cent of the company's equity, through the unique pink-coloured share forms.

I knew these forms would become a valuable tool in making our employees and business associates feel a sense of ownership in the company. In the early days of marketing the IPO, when we were not sure how well it would fare, my executives wanted to distribute these 2,000 or so pink forms freely to get our friends to invest. The idea was to get as many confirmed subscriptions as possible. I, however, did not think this would be necessary and was of the opinion that the pink form should serve the purpose it was meant for—rewarding employees and business associates for their steadfast loyalty and hard work.

In my mind, there was nothing better than employee ownership for strengthening the bond with the company. It would motivate them even better in the future. I asked for these forms to be passed around methodically, with proper record-keeping. Every form was valuable. I was particularly keen that each employee subscribed to at least the minimum number of shares. We even arranged funds for some who were short on money. The rest of the shares were given to our carefully chosen business associates. Towards the end, when the demand for these shares picked up, there was a rush of demand from various people and we ended up rationing them.

After the stock price picked up a few years later, I would have regular visits from employees to thank me for the wealth their Ambuja shares had created for them, which had come in handy for family occasions and emergencies. I derived great pleasure and satisfaction in seeing my colleagues benefiting from the wealth that we were creating for our shareholders. A few years later, when SEBI drafted the rules for Employee Stock Option, targeted mainly at IT start-ups, we were among the first in the manufacturing sector to embrace it unreservedly. Later, when the stock price rose significantly, there were even occasions when our marketing team rewarded high-performing dealers and stockists with company shares that we bought in the open market. It incentivized them to work harder.

The success of our IPO was a landmark event in the history of the company. It gave us the confidence in our belief that we were on the right path and the feeling that we were being acknowledged and appreciated for the good work we were doing. It was our first brush with the outside world of investors, the media and the public at large and we had done relatively well on all counts. For a company, whose plant was still under construction, the buzz and the goodwill it generated ensured that we never had a problem raising money from investors or banks thereafter. Six months later, when we floated a rights issue to raise ₹2 crore to help fund our plant capacity expansion to 7,00,000 tonnes, it sailed through without much of a hitch or publicity.

The IPO helped me understand and appreciate the power of marketing and advertising. The excellent work done by Clea Advertising had made a tremendous contribution to our success. The advertising strategy that we devised had two purposes—first, to build a public reputation for us as a start-up cement maker and second to make the Gujarat Ambuja issue stand out in a crowded IPO market dominated by well-established players. The advertising had worked remarkably well on both counts. It sparked a thought in my mind about using the same advertising strategy to make Gujarat Ambuja and its cement standout in public perception. More about this in subsequent chapters.

The year 1986 was supposed to have been our big year, when our plant would go on stream. Mr Kulkarni had the plant construction work under control and I was still enjoying the success of the IPO. However, the euphoria did not last long. I still remember the late-night phone call on Thursday, 13 February 1986. It was a trunk call from Kodinar and I knew there was trouble because no one called at that hour in those days unless there was an emergency. I was not prepared for what I was about to hear. The person on the other end told me that he had some bad news. Mr G.C. Kotwal, our joint president for manufacturing, had just died in a car accident on his way back from Kodinar to Ahmedabad.

I was alone in my study and it took a while for the magnitude of the tragedy to sink in. And when it did, I was shattered. I sat down and wept. Mr Kotwal was an indispensable member of our senior team and his main task was about to begin. He was our plant commissioning specialist. The kiln was to be fired in the coming months. And now he was no more. After a few days, we had a meeting and Mr Kulkarni said, 'You bring anyone as a replacement for Mr Kotwal and we will support him.'

I told him it was not possible to recruit someone at this late hour. 'We do not have that much time. You have to fire the kiln,' I said. 'Do whatever you know and whatever best you can do. You decide; I will support you. All we can do now is to learn on the job and get it right by trial and error.'

Keeping our fingers firmly crossed, we fired the kiln in May 1986. And expectedly, our lack of experience and expertise meant that things did not go well in the early days. The plant had to be shut down frequently on account of various problems, including overheating and the inconsistent quality of the clinker that we produced. Cement manufacturing is a simple process that has not changed in more than 100 years since the first rotary kiln was set up in the US. Limestone, the primary raw material obtained from the limestone mines, is crushed and ground into fine powder in crushers and grinding mills at the plant. It is then blended with small amounts of additives like alumina, silica and iron in the form of sand, clay, marl, shale, etc.

The raw-meal mix is then sent to the tall preheater tower for a process known as pre-calcination, where it is heated to a temperature of up to 1000 degrees Celsius using hot gas. The preheating removes most of the carbon dioxide and moisture. The hot mix then goes to the rotary kiln, the giant rotating cylindrical steel vessel, where the calcination process is completed by heating it to 1400 degrees Celsius using pulverized coal. The burning of the coal produces fly ash, which reacts with the melted limestone to produce nodules called clinkers. The clinkers are cooled down in a special cooler and then mixed with gypsum and fly ash before being sent to the grinder to be turned into the fine powder that we call cement.

We were still very new to the manufacturing process and Mr Kulkarni was finding it tough to stabilize the kiln. After trying for several weeks, he said that we should get help from an expert. I told him that I still had full trust and faith in his ability. He tried once again and as if by a miracle, a week later the plant stabilized. We got our confidence back. By trial and error, Mr Kulkarni had found that the varying quality of the limestone was the main culprit. We were mixing limestone from different mines which had created the problem. Once this was sorted, things became much more manageable.

As he experimented further, he realized that the quality of the cement was also dependent on the quality of the coal burning in the kiln. Burning is an art that takes a long time to master. The right temperature ensures the stability of the kiln, which, in turn, is essential for good-quality cement and improved output. He found that the coal had to burn within the first quarter portion of the kiln for best results. In our case, the burning was happening across the entire length of the kiln. It led to the production of something called coal flushing (unburnt or under-burnt coal) which was travelling back into the preheater and turning into clinkers that clogged the whole system. After this issue was understood and rectified, our cement quality improved tremendously. These lessons proved to be invaluable as we ramped up production.

I would be remiss here if I did not mention the role of Mr M.N. Rao, a manager on our account at IDBI. We had got to know him very well. He was a great believer in *vaastu shastra*. When he heard of the problem in stabilizing the kiln, he sent over a *vaastu* specialist to check out our plant. He asked us to make minor layout changes in the plant by shifting a gate and filling up a well in our premises. When we did that, lo and behold, most of our plant problems were settled almost immediately. I became a believer after that and we used a *vaastu* specialist every time we commissioned a plant.

The cement mill at Kodinar was commissioned by the end of August and the cement packing plant on 10 September. Our first bag of cement from the plant was packed the same day. The sale of our cement was inaugurated soon after by the then CM of Gujarat, Mr Amarsinh Chaudhary. He received the first consignment of 11 tonnes of Gujarat Ambuja cement, which we had donated to the scarcity relief work in the state.

It would be a few more weeks before we started commercial production, which finally happened in October. As against the original target of eighteen months, we were able to start production in twenty-two months, despite all our problems. No Indian cement company, as far as I knew, had built a plant and commissioned it in such a short duration. All our hard work had finally paid off.

Our technical problems, however, were far from over. In the weeks leading to the commissioning of the plant, we discovered that the process control computer system that L&T had supplied was not up to the mark. The response time was so slow that it would take three to four minutes to start each section of the plant. The engineers they had sent to implement the system had no experience or knowledge of the cement industry. I felt let down by this big-name Indian company that I had trusted over international giants like Asea Brown Boveri (ABB) and Honeywell. We had invested ₹80 lakh in this system and all we got were three PCs, some controllers and inadequate software. Their salespeople had sold us the system saying that they had been using it successfully in their own plants that were much bigger. However, their engineers could not fix our problem.

Unable to bear the delay, I told Mr Kulkarni to get someone else. In his opinion though, it was not prudent for us to approach the likes of ABB or Honeywell. They would have insisted on replacing the whole system, which would have further delayed the project. Instead, Mr Kulkarni decided that we could improve the existing system ourselves, with help from external software specialists. Luckily, Macmet Limited, the Neotia company, employed software engineers who had worked on similar systems. We called them in. Working with Ambuja engineers, it took them nearly three months to rectify the problems, by the end of which the communication response time of the control system had reduced to less than two seconds!

The Macmet engineers were not able to fix the stability issue of the kiln, however. After much searching, Mr Kulkarni was able to locate two experts based out of the United Kingdom (UK)—Hiron Chatterji and Alan Skull. We flew them to Kodinar and within a few weeks they helped us fix the problem. The whole experience left a bad taste in my mouth. It was a pity that in India you could not sue anyone for negligence.

We had a similar problem with Pune-based Thermax when it came to the supply of the baghouse as part of our emission control system. They were supposed to make it on behalf of their international partner Zurn & Co, whom we had contracted. After multiple delays, we discovered that Thermax had sub-contracted the work to UB Engineering, a Vijay Mallya company, also based out of Pune. They, in turn, had sub-contracted the job to a third company. When I contacted the owner of Thermax, the late Rohinton Aga, he was, to his credit, very apologetic. He offered me the design of the baghouse for free. He said that we could fabricate it ourselves under the supervision of the engineers from Thermax. We had it done as per the design and the equipment worked very well.

5

An Emotional Roller Coaster

Euphoria and nervousness • Quest for efficiency • Understanding the cement consumer

My joy at the successful start of production was tempered with the anxiety about the future. We had entered the market at a time when the Indian cement industry was going through its worst crisis in decades. Drought conditions in various parts of the county had led to excess supply combined with declining demand and had depressed prices to a level not seen in many years. At around ₹68 a bag, the price was almost the same as five years earlier.

The partial decontrol of cement in 1982 led to a flood of new companies rushing into the industry, even as existing manufacturers added large new capacities. As a result, the next five years would see the Indian cement industry transforming in more profound ways than it had in the previous five decades. Technologically, we went from a country dominated by wet process cement plants to a dry process-oriented industry almost overnight. The installed capacity for cement, which had grown at a snail's pace till the early 1980s, had now doubled to 60 million tonnes. Twenty million tonnes of this new capacity were added in the three years since we began work on our plant in 1984.

In the blink of an eye, we went from an economy built around shortage and imports to one of overproduction. Expectedly, with supply exceeding demand, there was carnage in the market, leaving the balance sheets of cement companies bleeding red. For the cement industry as a whole, the return on net worth (RONW)—a crucial measure of returns that a company generates on its invested money—turned negative in the period between 1986 and '88.

This meant that barring a few successful companies, the industry as a whole was making a loss. And unlike us, almost every new plant that was coming up in those days, including those of prominent companies like Modi Cement and JP Cement, were facing significant delays and cost overruns. We had no clue how the recession scenario would play out. Unlike the big players, we did not have the luxury of time and money or the ability to absorb losses till cement prices picked up. Our cost structure was such that we needed the plant to work at 100 per cent capacity right from the beginning to avoid making losses.

It was early days in my career as an industrialist and I worried that things could go south despite our best efforts. Rebuilding a ruined reputation at this stage was not going to be easy. The other reason for my anxiety was that I was a newcomer in Gujarat, a market dominated by three established players. The biggest of them, Saurashtra Cement, controlled 40 per cent of the market with its famous Hathi brand of cement. It was a company founded by the formidable Mahendra Mehta. His family had been among the state's leading businessmen since the 1930s and owned vast plantations in East Africa and a large textile mill in Porbandar.

Saurashtra Cement was set up in the mid-1950s. They were also in the process of commissioning the new plant for CCGL (later renamed Gujarat Sidhee Cement), their second company in Gujarat. Like ours, it was a joint-venture project with GIIC. The other big player was the Bangur-owned Shree Digvijay Cement, set up by the maharaja of Jamnagar in the 1940s. They had a 20 per cent market share. The rest of the market was distributed between Narmada Cement and smaller players.

Since they had been around for a long time, the depreciated value of their plants gave my competitors a distinct advantage. Obsolescence is not a big problem for cement plants, so our new plant did not provide us with any additional benefits. We were, in fact, at a disadvantage. Our plant had cost around ₹80 crore, while their much bigger plants probably had a nominal written-down value. It meant that our cost of production was much higher, while we were both trying to sell cement to the same consumer. Our pricing had to be competitive.

Gujarat Ambuja's challenge was twofold—to produce the best quality cement at the lowest possible price; and to establish our brand as a better alternative in the mind of the consumer. Were we up to this onerous task? I was not sure. Going by what we had done so far, I was confident that we would give it our best shot. The only thing that was clear to me was the enormity of the challenge we faced, without a clue about the way ahead. On the other hand, though, the advantage of being a newcomer in the business had its benefits. We were not burdened by history or tradition in our approach. The only thing that mattered was our mission to do the best for our shareholders and the consumer.

We examined and re-examined in minutest detail every aspect of running a cement company. From how we set up the plant to how we ran the plant to how cement was packed and transported, nothing escaped our scrutiny. Status quo was never acceptable. If there was a better way of doing any part of the operation that saved money and time while enhancing quality, we embraced it.

Besides the 40 per cent capital cost, the other big expenditure head in cement is energy. It constitutes another 40 per cent of the cost. If we had to succeed, the company would have to focus on these two issues. We had started well by building the lowest per-tonne-cost cement plant in the country and that too in record time. Now we had to build on this achievement. We had to run the plant consistently at more than 100 per cent capacity utilization, at the highest possible level of efficiency.

It was not as if the competition leaders—Saurashtra Cement or Narmada Cement—were not efficient. Their plants ran at around 90 per cent of capacity, which was a good performance by Indian standards. Our only way out was to make our plant even more productive and efficient. Any effort at raising productivity had to target reducing the cost of coal and power, the two components of the energy cost. Our efficiency levels had to be benchmarked not just against Indian cement companies but also the best in the world.

Within the first few months, Mr Kulkarni and his dedicated team proved that they were capable of taking us to the next level. With every passing month, the team grew more confident about getting the best out of the plant. Our capacity utilization went up from 21 per cent in October 1986, when we started production, to 57 per cent in December; and from 77 per cent in February 1987 to 121 per cent in March. It never dipped below 100 per cent after that.

The success on the production side was matched by the good work done by our nascent marketing and sales teams. They also hit the ground running. Our brilliant advertising and marketing blueprint was the brainchild of my friend Ravi Gupta and his advertising agency Trikaya. It was backed by some savvy work on the sales and dealer front by Rashmi Kampani, who had joined us as sales adviser a few months before the plant went on stream. I will talk about the strategy employed by these two gentlemen in the next chapter. Their effort made GACL a name to reckon with across Gujarat almost overnight. Simultaneously, a distribution network was created that made Ambuja cement available in every corner of the state within a short period.

The results of all these efforts became visible quite early. We achieved a rare feat for a cement company in those days, of making a profit in the first six months of operation. For the half-year ended March 1987, we turned in a small net profit of ₹32 lakh on sales of ₹20 crore. Less than a year earlier, we were struggling to stabilize our kiln. Now here we were in a position where we could humbly boast about some of our early achievements. An ad released at the time talked about a few of them:

- Today Ambuja Cement has overtaken several established brands in Gujarat. And is rising fast to the number one position. In just six months!
- Excellence in quality: We had nurtured a vision of making the best-quality cement. Today we are happy that Ambuja Cement is acclaimed by one and all as the best cement in the state.
- Excellence in distribution: We are fast expanding our network of dealers to reach even the remotest villages in Gujarat. The number of dealers increased from eighty-five to over 185 in March 1987.
- Excellence in technical service: We don't just sell cement. Our technical cell, comprising specialists in civil construction, provides complete guidance to customers for getting the best results.
- Excellence in sales promotion: The famous Ambuja Giant spells out a loud and clear message—the giant strength of Ambuja Cement.

The market was still tough. Cement prices continued to rule low through much of 1987 and '88, while input costs continued to rise. Prolonged drought conditions prevented demand from picking up. We were barely meeting the interest cost on our loan and any wrong move could prove to be fatal. We had to keep our heads down and concentrate on our singular purpose—raise production, improve productivity and cut costs. It was a mantra which over time would become second nature to everyone in the organization.

Around this time, we formulated a Corporate Objectives and Strategic Orientation document, which listed six clear goals and provided much clarity to our thinking for the future. These goals were: excellence in quality; a ceaseless quest for higher productivity; maximum customer satisfaction; an environment conducive to employee growth; providing fair returns to shareholders; and a vigilant search for opportunities for the growth and fulfilment of our social objectives. Achieving these six goals defined Gujarat Ambuja's mission for the next three decades.

The grim external conditions, in some sense, turned out to be a blessing. Mr Kulkarni and his team put together systems and protocols that helped create a culture of productivity, innovation and cost control all across the plant. Though computers were still new to India in the 1980s, we already had in place a fully computerized system for monitoring plant operations. It helped us consistently document and analyse every bit of data about the working of every equipment, every action and every input and output. As many as 3,000 parameters involved in the running of the plant were continuously monitored.

This helped in a variety of ways. The data provided the starting point for changing equipment parameters to improve their efficiency. Any fluctuation in data was an advance warning to the maintenance crew to be prepared for an equipment breakdown. When we started, quality control data was generated once a day. Within a few years, we were generating it as many as forty-eight times a day. If things were not going right, the engineer monitoring operations in the central control room was empowered to correct it. This accelerated the response mechanism and problems, if any, were fixed in double quick time.

Unscheduled plant stoppages were always the bane of the Indian cement industry. Our monitoring system made sure that we were able to anticipate breakdowns in advance, which helped reduce downtime to a minimum. Whereas in the first year we ran the plant for 270 days, we took that number up to 340 days two years later, a rare feat for a cement company anywhere in the world. Even the time taken for the mandatory annual maintenance of the plant was progressively reduced by better planning.

There was another reason why we had fewer plant breakdowns than most other cement companies—our very effective dust control system.

Dust is one of the biggest reasons for equipment malfunctioning and downtime in cement plants, leading to a loss in production. Any investment in dust control thus has a direct impact on the balance sheet. We invested in additional dust control equipment like the baghouse for the cement mill at a very high cost. The maintenance cost for the dust control equipment alone was more than ₹1 crore a year. But the benefits in terms of fewer breakdowns and prolonged working life of the plant and machinery made it worth the investment.

Despite the massive investment, dust continued to bother us for quite some time. Dust, like water, has a way of seeping through the narrowest of cracks and crannies that are otherwise not visible to the human eye. Then one day Mr Kulkarni launched an all-out war on what is known as 'fugitive dust'. The technical team perfected something called the 'whistle test'. When the plant was in operation, the machine operators were tasked with keeping an ear out for a whistling sound (created when air leaks from plant tubes and shells). This escaping air carried fugitive cement particles. Sealing such cracks became a top priority in the plant.

With continuous effort, we finally achieved the goal of a dust-free plant. To demonstrate our claim, we planted a rose garden right under the kiln. The flowers bloomed and became a showpiece of our commitment to a dust-free environment around the factory. I would tell all our visitors, including farmers from the nearby villages, that if roses could thrive so close to the kiln, they had nothing to worry. The rose patch became known across the cement industry as a symbol of our resolve to create a clean environment in and around Kodinar.

Despite consistently running our plants higher than a capacity of 130 to 140 per cent, our dust pollution levels of around 70 milligrams per cubic metre were well within the Swiss standard of 50 to 100 milligrams; Indian standards were much more lenient at around 150 to 250 milligrams. Not surprisingly, many of the cement plants were, in those days, blanketed with dust.

All these efforts also contributed to production increase, year after year. In the first two years, because of terrible market conditions, we deliberately restricted our capacity utilization to around 115 per cent. But the moment the market picked up in 1989, the figure rose to 130 per cent and a year later to 140 per cent. Every few weeks, Mr Kulkarni would tell me that he had modified some equipment, as a result of which the production had gone up by a few percentage points. It was a relentless effort to raise productivity.

Mr Kulkarni was not the only one firing on all cylinders in those tough days—every employee was. I had always believed that given the right platform, freedom and encouragement, everyone would perform regardless of their college degrees or even their past record of employment. We empowered people at every level. Failure, of any innovation that they had initiated, was not looked down upon. Everyone had free access to seniors to discuss grievances and new ideas and this engendered a feeling of ownership and a sense of responsibility. Every idea and suggestion that came from the employees was recognized and rewarded.

In the first two years alone, as many as ninety operation-related changes were implemented across the plant based on employee suggestions. No idea was too small to be discarded, every rupee saved mattered—I remember being told about an idea that led to savings of just one-tenth of a unit of power. In the first three years, the implementation of employee-suggested ideas led to savings of more than ₹70 crore in terms of today's currency value.

To implement their ideas faster, we introduced a three-year rule for our managers. We empowered them to make investment decisions up to ₹1 crore (₹10 crore in today's value) to modify machinery to conserve energy and increase productivity. The only condition was that the investment should have a payback in three years. These measures encouraged creative thinking across the company. A good example: when senior executives decided to follow the industry trend and replace mechanical conveyors with the seemingly more modern and efficient pneumatic version, one of our engineers came up with the idea of modifying the existing system to make it as efficient. Since pneumatic conveyors were energy guzzlers, the refashioned mechanical conveyors saved us not just new equipment cost but were also cheaper to run.

Similarly, a few years later, someone discovered that the discarded industrial waste from a nearby unit of Gujarat Mineral Development Corporation (GMDC) contained fluorspar. According to him, this industrial mineral could be used to lower the melting temperature in our kiln, thus reducing energy consumption. On implementation, we found we were able to cut down fuel consumption by 3 per cent. Cutting down electricity consumption by even a unit at the plant led to a saving of ₹20 lakh annually. And as our production grew, the savings multiplied.

The energy-saving measures that we implemented over the years led to a steady decline in power consumption, from 120 units per tonne of production in 1987 to 95 units in 1990. Indian companies at that time were averaging around 125 units per tonne and the international average was 110 units. A survey of the twenty-five most efficient cement plants in the world conducted at that time by the Swiss company Holderbank (renamed Holcim in 2001) showed that only two companies did better than Gujarat Ambuja.

Another major innovation that we introduced around this time was in the packaging. Surveys done by Trikaya as part of our cement marketing study had helped us understand the Gujarat cement consumer quite intimately. The most common grievance was that the 50-kilogram bags invariably weighed a few kilos less. There were two reasons for this—it is likely that some manufacturers were deliberately packing less than the stated weight of cement in their bags; it is more likely that a few kilos seeped out (cement is a microparticle), or even spilled out, thanks to the multiple handling of the bags at various stages, including transportation.

As a new player in the market, we saw this as an opportunity to set things right by introducing better packaging. We were keen to present Ambuja as a consumer-friendly brand. We worked closely with the vendors and improved the quality of our high-density polyethylene (HDPE) bags. These were tested repeatedly for spillage and only the best lots were approved and used for packing the cement. Each Ambuja cement bag came with a tag that guaranteed 50 kilograms of cement and the 'giant compressive strength' that our advertising promised. The bags were packed using zero error electronic rotary (ZEER), an electronic packing machine that ensured the exact weight. Every fifth bag was rechecked for the correct weight. This system guaranteed that every bag that left our plant had 50 kilograms of cement.

As mentioned above, cement is a microparticle. It can invariably seep out from the weaves of even the best of HDPE bags if not handled well during transportation. Since cement bags are handled manually in India, standardizing manual handling to the point of zero seepage or spillage was the impossible target we would have to achieve. I was keen to see if this manual-handling process could be switched to mechanization in any way. I was certain that there was a better way of handling cement elsewhere in the world. We sent our senior engineer Mr Hirpara to travel to countries like the US, Canada, Japan and many others to see how they handled the problem.

He came back with some ideas that could be implemented without much additional investment. We experimented with them and settled on a simple, low-cost solution—unitizing several cement bags into a single bundle using slings. Instead of handling one bag at a time, this allowed several bags to be packed into a sling and then loaded using a forklift. The process required minimum manual handling, leading to less leakage of cement particles.

As the slings were not produced in India, we imported some samples from Spain. And because of import restrictions in those days, our engineers replicated the design and got a local company to manufacture it. It was then sent to the Indian Institute of Packaging for testing, where it was approved without any modifications. We were now ready to create the infrastructure for slinging the bags, but we found that none of our dealers were prepared to handle it at their end. The idea died a natural death, though our sling supplier was able to find a lucrative market for the slings in Dubai.

We achieved similar results in our effort to cut down on coal consumption—among the biggest cost factors in the running of cement plants, responsible for nearly 20 per cent of all expenditure. We improved the efficiency of the coal burning in the kiln, which reduced consumption; more critically, we improved the quality of our coal and tried to cut down on the theft in our supply system. Every Indian cement maker has lived with all these problems for decades. However, the issue of theft needs special mention.

Coal mines are government-owned and the mafia that stole the coal, during transportation, was well-entrenched at this time. The racket involved cement procured from private companies on behalf of the Directorate General of Supplies and Disposal (DGS&D)—the Union commerce ministry arm responsible for all cement purchases for government projects. The cement would be picked up by the truck mafia from company plants, but on its way to government warehouses, large portions of the cement would be diverted via trucks and sold in the black market. Most companies had made peace with the fact that they could do very little to change the situation.

We decided to take the initiative and change it. We already paid the top price to transport coal to our plant located nearly 2,000 kilometres from the nearest collieries in eastern India. Since we were paying the top price, I was determined to get our monies worth.

The Neotias had old connections with people in the coal business and through them we were able to establish contacts in and around the mines that supplied our coal. Making use of these contacts, we were further able to establish contacts with people close to the coal mafia and make sure that the coal on our trucks was not pilfered. We were also able to station our people at the coal distribution centre to supervise the stockpile meant for us. This ensured that only the best-quality coal was loaded on to Ambuja trucks.

The whole exercise cost us money, but we were able to safely and regularly transport the best-quality coal with the best calorific value. The consistency in coal quality also helped reduce the strain on the kiln during burning and our coal consumption declined substantially as a result. It went from 870 kilocalories per kilogram in 1987 to 762 kilocalories in three years, as against the industry average of 900 kilocalories.

I found out that much of Gujarat's road transportation business was controlled by a truck mafia based out of cities like Porbandar, Jamnagar, Ahmedabad, Baroda and Surat. A large number of these truck owners made their money working for smugglers who landed gold and electronics on the Gujarat coast in those days; they also diverted trucks carrying cement to government warehouses and sold the cement in the black market, as discussed earlier; and overcharged all industries in the state.

Their rates were massively inflated and there was little that companies could do about this because of the cartelization by truck owners. In the case of cement companies, I was told that they were spending as much as 20 to 25 per cent of the sale price on transportation!

Our plant location (Kodinar) was not well serviced by the railways either. At the same time, our main markets were 500 and 600 kilometres away, which made us heavily dependent on trucks for our cement shipment. The only way I could solve my problems, I decided, was by setting up our own transportation network where we had complete control. As with other innovations, it happened because we were new to the business and unfamiliar with the traditional way of doing things.

I did not know anyone who was directly involved in the trucking business, so I decided to ask my good friend Dilip Swadi to step in. His family owned Swadi Automobiles, one of Bombay's best-known workshops for imported cars, which later branched into maintenance and restoration of vintage vehicles. They also ran a limousine service company that provided cars on hire to hotels, corporates and consulates. Dilip owned a few chemical tankers which he had deployed on the Gujarat–Bombay route to transport industrial chemicals. Though this didn't make for the perfect résumé for the job I had in mind, I was confident that he would be able to handle it.

I told Dilip to start a trucking service for Ambuja. Not being knowledgeable about the business, he was understandably wary. He spoke to his friends at Patel Roadways for help and they offered to send a director to meet me. When I got to know of this, I told him that I was not looking for any established players involved. I wanted to look at cement transportation through a fresh new lens and that I wanted him as our partner. Gujarat Ambuja would provide him with all the support that was needed, including financial help. Luckily for me, he took up the challenge.

Initially, Dilip was nervous and took some time to understand the business. When he began work, the plant was still in the trial production phase, which gave him enough time to learn the ropes before the start of commercial production. Besides his own trucks, he enticed a large number of small truck owners across Gujarat to work for his company. That way, he was able to work around the truck mafia in Gujarat.

What was important though was the way he and his team worked closely with our sales and marketing team across the state on the logistics. As required by us, his trucks delivered the cement bags directly to individual stockists rather than to some district warehouse. It cut down on multiple handling of bags and the resulting wastage. The cement was delivered factory-fresh to retailers, which helped our reputation.

The truck movements were monitored in real time by his team with the help of Ambuja's state-wide network of salespeople. This ensured the timely delivery of cement as well as quick turnaround of the trucks. The efficiency of the operation helped us keep our costs down, as compared to other cement companies. The truck drivers were provided with food and other facilities, including a place to rest at the Ambuja plant. It incentivized them to give their best and attracted more trucks to Kodinar.

We gave Dilip competitive rates for his logistics service. For the first few years, he made a loss. As promised though, Ambuja compensated him for the losses at the end of every year after auditing all the incurred costs, the details of which he would send us periodically. We also made sure that he made a small profit.

Dilip was transparent about the costs he incurred and it gave us a handle on the expenditure involved in running a cement transportation business. It also helped us benchmark freight rates for the future. All of this came handy in later years as our production increased and we added two more truck operators to complement Dilip's operations. The state was by then geographically divided between the three truck companies.

The same logistics model was replicated at all our plants over the years. And twenty-five years later, Dilip's company continues to be among the biggest logistics operators for Ambuja Cement. The trucking model that we set up in partnership with him benefited us not only from the efficiency perspective but also in keeping corruption out of Ambuja. From fudging challan documents to pilfering supplies and diverting trucks, the list of illegal activities that characterize large sections of India's logistics industry is very long. We were, in that sense, fortunate.

This innovative logistics model had a big impact on our bottom line. Not surprisingly, our trucking operations became a model for many other companies in the years that followed.

As our transportation system evolved, we initiated a different kind of trucking innovation by introducing bulk transportation of cement. In most developed countries, more than 90 per cent of cement is transported in bulk, something that was unheard of in India those days. Cement was sold in 50-kilogram bags, whether the consumer wanted one bag or 1,000. It was expensive because of the high packing cost, as well as the spillage due to the multiple stages at which it was manually handled.

We were convinced that bulk transportation would work in India. Once again we sent Mr Hirpara to study similar systems in other countries. He came back with the idea of designing special bulk tankers. We asked our engineers to develop and manufacture a prototype for the Indian market. A 10-tonner equipped with a self-unloading system was designed by Ambuja engineers and fabricated by a supplier in Bombay. But he did a poor job. We tried again with a fabricator from Delhi, who did a much better job. We ordered several of these tankers and used them successfully over the years. Seeing what we were able to achieve, many other companies shifted to bulk transportation as well. These tankers are a fairly common sight on Indian roads these days thanks to our pioneering effort.

The cumulative benefits of all that we did, big and small, added to our profits every year. The rising cement prices in 1989 helped push our sales beyond the ₹100-crore mark for the first time. Our gross profit margin of 19 per cent was the highest in the cement industry. We were honoured with the Best Corporate Performance Award by *The Economic Times*–Harvard Business School's Association of India, our first significant public recognition. Though the award was in the category of emerging companies, our performance was the best across the industry, beating prominent names like ACC, L&T, Dalmia Cement and Mangalam Cement. The same year we were also awarded the Certificate of Merit for Productivity in the cement industry by the National Productivity Council.

More than the profits and the awards, what put me at ease after a long time was the fact that now I had a cash reserve of more than ₹50 crore in the bank. It was a mental threshold, a target that I had set for myself, which I had finally achieved. Despite the best efforts of our competitors, we were now the dominant player in Gujarat with a commanding 25 per cent share of the 3.3-million-tonne state market.

Despite our lower capacity plant of just 7,00,000 tonnes, we were now selling more cement in Gujarat than our local rivals who were equipped with a million-tonne plant each. Our growing reputation also enabled us to sell Ambuja cement at a much higher price than our competitors. We were now in the driver's seat in the state.

Much as 1988 was the year when I felt that everything was finally coming together after years of hard work, the joy of the occasion was tinged with the pain of losing my father. He died that year of cancer at the age of seventy-two. The loss left a big hole in my heart. After my mother's death ten years earlier, also of cancer, he was my moral and spiritual anchor. He was the one I turned to whenever I needed answers to my troubles. And now that safe harbour was gone forever. The only consolation was that in the previous year he had been able to travel to Kodinar for the first and last time to do the *bhoomi pooja* (the ground-breaking ceremony) of our company temple.

Despite all the issues, we had managed to set up the plant in record time and start production. Our production had finally stabilized, we had started commercial dispatch and I felt God was exceedingly kind to me. We were not making money yet, but at least we were not in trouble, like many other cement companies at that time. I felt it was the right time to build a temple within our campus. The Birlas have a temple in each of their townships and I thought we should also build one. When I told my father about my idea, he could not have been happier.

In those days, he spent half his time with me in Bombay and the other half in Vrindavan on his spiritual quest. Even though he was weak and frail, he took it upon himself to buy the idols for the temple. He spent a week in Jaipur looking for the right kind of idol. He then came to Kodinar for the *bhoomi pooja* along with my sister's father-in-law from Calcutta. The two seniors jointly did the first *pooja*. It was a joyous occasion that I still remember. But he passed away a year later, before the temple was completed.

Set among a large grove of trees, the temple is one of the prettiest places in Ambujanagar and every time I go there, I still think of my father. It is a place that always inspires me. My only regret about his last years is that he was not happy with the way I was working. He felt I had taken on more than I could handle and was taking too many risks. It upset him that I was not spending enough time with him when he was in Bombay. Although we would all have our meals together whenever I was not travelling, he felt that I was not talking to him in the manner that I used to earlier. I was too busy setting up the plant to pay heed to his wishes. It is a guilt that I will always carry with me.

His death did not come as a shock because he was ailing for a long time. Once he was gone though, I started missing the mental and spiritual support that he provided. He was like my shock absorber; I could always rely on him to soak up bad news, tell me not to worry and assure me that everything would be fine. He gave me instant peace of mind. I have always had this feeling that he was constantly praying for me and that his prayers were immensely powerful, leading me on the right path. I believe his blessings had a big role to play in all our achievements. I still feel his invisible hand guiding me every step of the way.

His greatest legacy to me is the values he instilled in me and the love for spirituality that I picked up from him as a young man. Spirituality has helped me keep calm and centred even in the most turbulent of times. The values of ethics and compassion that he taught me steered me in everything that I did in my career. It was not just ethics for the sake of ethics. Beyond the moral obligation, he would tell me that high ethical standards are always good for business. I am glad that I took it to heart. It has paid off very well.

6

A Brand Is Born

Finding a marketing guru • Discovering the strength of cement • Birth of the Ambuja Giant • A new dealer paradigm

In this chapter I journey back a little, to the time in and around the period that we were commissioning the plant and the remarkable role that advertising and marketing played in our early success.

Honestly speaking, advertising and marketing were nowhere on my radar when we first made plans to set up Gujarat Ambuja in the early 1980s. I began thinking about both these aspects only in late 1985. Till then, all my energies were concentrated on getting the project off the ground and setting up the plant. The fact that every month of delay would cost us ₹1 crore in interest alone, bothered me no end. During many interactions with Mr Pai when he was the chairman of IDBI, I was privy to dozens of stories of project disasters because of delays in construction and commissioning.

The success of our IPO in late 1985 gave me time to think about the future. The plant was on track to become operational in a few months, but the cement market could not have been in a worse condition. The Indian cement industry, for the first time in nearly sixty years, was dealing with a wholly buyers' market. For far too long, the sellers had called the shots and now the market had turned. The buyers were in a commanding position with an unbelievable variety of choices in front of them. And it increasingly looked like a secular trend, in other words persisting for a long period. The situation was unlikely to revert to the good old days when demand invariably outstripped supply.

The challenge for us was to convince the buyer to choose a bag of cement with Gujarat Ambuja printed on it. Not many people in Gujarat had heard of the Ambuja name except during the public issue. The question was, why would anyone buy cement sold by an unknown company when so many known brands were finding it difficult to sell their cement?

With just a few months to go before the launch of our cement in the market, the immediate need was to set up a team to handle the advertising and marketing. I did not look for very long. I was blessed with chance meetings with two men who would go on to play crucial roles in the destiny of the company in these areas. Notably, both had their grounding in consumer marketing, which is as far from traditional cement marketing as chalk is from cheese.

The success of our public issue and the crucial role played in it by the advertising created by Clea Advertising was an eye-opener to me about the power of good advertising. Sometime around December 1985, not long after our IPO, I got talking to Mrs Gita Gopalakrishnan. She is married to Mr R. Gopalakrishnan, who in those days was a senior executive at Hindustan Lever. We had met while playing badminton, which I occasionally did in the winter months, at the Bombay Gymkhana. I knew she was an advertising professional, working at the Bombay-based Trikaya Advertising.

Gita was the only person I knew in mainstream advertising and I knew truly little about Trikaya. I remember sitting with her after one of our badminton sessions and telling her that I was looking for an advertising agency for my new company. She asked me if she could get her boss to come and meet me. His name was Mr Ravi Gupta. I told her I would be glad to meet him. The meeting was arranged for some time in January 1986.

I found Ravi to be gentle and mild-mannered, in the style of an old-world professional. I told him that I was looking for an advertising agency for my new cement brand. The assignment was challenging because we were an unknown company launching our product in a market that was flooded with cement. We had a long chat and I was impressed with his credentials as well as his knowledge about the Indian advertising and marketing scene. He had graduated from St. Xavier's College in Bombay and had trained in Cardiff to become a geologist but had drifted into advertising after he came back home.

After working with some of the biggest agencies in the country, he had set up Trikaya in 1978. The name came from the Sanskrit term for three bodies, in his case referring to the three areas his agency specialized in—marketing, communication and media. He told me about the successes he had had over the years, including his famous campaigns and the brands he helped launch such as Thums Up and the luggage brand Aristocrat.

I liked what I heard from him, his honesty and his seeming enthusiasm to work for us even though we were a commodity manufacturer. Later, after we became close friends, he would tell me that he was desperate for new business at that time and would have taken on anything that came his way. Ravi suggested we take a consumer-advertising approach to market Ambuja cement and I agreed. No other company had tried this before.

After a few more meetings, I told Ravi that I was willing to give him the Ambuja business without even talking to any other agency. But I had a vital precondition: he had to be personally involved in my work and not farm it out to some business head at his agency. He immediately committed to it. He said he saw this as an opportunity not only to learn about cement but also about how to market a commodity, something he had not done previously.

Thus began yet another vital chapter in Gujarat Ambuja's journey. Ravi was the man who built the Ambuja brand. He was also my marketing guru. Everything that I know about marketing, which I employed successfully in Ambuja, I learnt from him. Our ability at marketing was as much a vital pillar of our success as our ability at efficiently producing cement. Towards that end, I consider Ravi to be as much a creator of Ambuja as Mr Kulkarni and me.

With Ravi and his advertising agency in place, I began looking for someone to handle our sales and ground-level marketing in our main catchment area of Gujarat. This marketing was to be targeted towards the network of dealers, distributors and retailers who played a crucial role in the selling of cement. I needed a sales head who could understand the complex distribution network, market our brand to the distributors and establish a close relationship with each of the players. My partner Vinod Neotia recommended the name of his former classmate Rashmi Kampani. He had worked in the marketing departments of Hindustan Lever and Dunlop India and was now running his own cement-marketing company called Mitco. He impressed me straightaway with his knowledge of the Gujarat cement market and its dealer network.

Rashmi was a chartered accountant who started at Hindustan Lever in the production planning department. He then transferred to the marketing department, where he cut his teeth in consumer marketing. He then worked in a similar capacity at Dunlop before setting up his consultancy a few years later to help clients sell their cement in Gujarat. He came across as diligent and eager to come to work with us. He didn't want to join the company as an employee. So, we agreed that his designation would be Sales Adviser, with the full-time responsibility of managing Ambuja's sales in Gujarat. He joined in February 1986 and my brief to him was simple: I did not want him to market or sell cement in the conventional way that he had done so far. 'I want you to use your Hindustan Lever and Dunlop experience to market and sell cement as a consumer product and not as a commodity.' He took it upon himself as a challenge.

What did the consumer expect from the cement companies? The consummate advertising professional that he was, the first thing that Ravi Gupta asked me was if I had any knowledge of the Gujarat cement consumer.

I had absolutely no idea. He requested me to ask others in the company who might be better informed. I asked around and the most common answer was that people wanted the kind of cement that the government had imported from South Korea. They remembered it being green in colour and of a quality that was much better than any Indian cement. Since then, the colour green had become synonymous with quality cement in their minds.

I told Ravi this, but he felt it still did not provide him with the USP or unique selling proposition that he was looking for in our cement. He asked if I was open to the idea of doing a market survey by asking the actual consumers in Gujarat. I remember the study cost us ₹1.5 lakh.

He came back a few weeks later and told me that the Trikaya survey had revealed that the crucial thing people expected from the cement they bought was 'strength'. They wanted the house or anything else they built to be durable, for which they wanted 'strong' cement. I was a bit puzzled. Wasn't all cement strong? I asked Ravi if he believed in the findings of the survey. He did. Since I was still sceptical, he offered to do a second survey, this time using a different agency.

I didn't know anything about cement strength. I had no idea how it was measured. After reading some manuals, I found out that the technical term is 'compressive strength'. For its measurement, a block of cement concrete of a predetermined size is prepared by mixing cement, sand, crushed stone, gravel and water in pre-specified proportions and then cured by moistening it for a fixed number of days—three, seven, nine, or in most cases twenty-eight.

Curing allows the cement to gain its strength. The fully cured concrete block is inserted in a compression testing device where progressive force is applied from opposite sides. The pressure at which the block cracks is the compressive strength of the cement for the number of days it was cured. It is measured in megapascal pressure unit or MPa. A cement bag with OPC 43 grade written on it signifies Ordinary Portland Cement (OPC) that will attain a minimum compression strength of 43 MPa in twenty-eight days; OPC 53 grade cement will gain a compression strength of 53 MPa in the same period.

Ordinary Portland Cement is the most commonly used variety of cement in the world. The other variant is PPC or Portland Pozzolana Cement, which is made by grinding OPC clinker with fly ash. Fly ash is a by-product of burning coal in thermal power plants. Hence, most cement plants making PPC are located close to power plants. Though PPC is commonly used for dams and other marine structures, these days it is also used in regular construction. Our plant in Kodinar was set up to manufacture OPC.

Trikaya's second survey came back with a similar finding. Now there was no doubt that strength was indeed what most people looked for when buying cement. It meant that Ravi's advertising strategy would have to focus on using 'strength' as the selling point of Ambuja cement. He asked me if it would be possible for us to create the strongest cement available in the market. I told him I would have to think about it.

Our team at the time had no one who was a specialist in cement technology and would be able to develop this cement. We started looking for someone with the required qualification and experience. Luckily, it didn't take much time. We were directed to Mr J.P. Desai, a civil engineer with expertise in precast cement, who was just back in Ahmedabad after an assignment in the Middle East. He joined us in August 1986 and was given the responsibility of working on developing cement that was the best in the market in terms of strength and quality. He worked closely with Mr Kulkarni over the next few weeks to fine-tune the raw-meal mix, the grinding process and the burning in the kiln to deliver the quality that we were looking for.

The Bureau of Industrial Standards (BIS)-mandated minimum compressive strength for OPC in those days was 33 MPa over twenty-eight days, while the best of cement available in the market had a strength of 43 MPa. Mr Desai and Mr Kulkarni's work allowed us to manufacture 53 MPa grade cement. It was a significant achievement for us as the first bag of cement rolled out from our production line. We were among the earliest companies in the country to introduce it in the market. Within a few months, the Ambuja OPC 53 grade became the yardstick against which all cement was measured. A few years later, our cement won national recognition in the form of the Rajiv Gandhi Quality Award, the Government of India's highest quality award.

The fine-tuning of our production process to make the OPC 53 grade cement had the added benefit of raising our productivity. The readjusted grinding process ensured the production of uniform-sized limestone for the kiln and uniform burning of the limestone—not under or over-burnt—which was essential for producing good-quality clinkers.

A few weeks later, Ravi was ready with the advertising campaign to help us sell our OPC 53 grade cement. His presentation in the Ambuja boardroom was eagerly awaited. But it turned out to be nothing like what anyone had seen or expected. It was unconventional to the core. The campaign featured the hand-drawn visual of a man with notably exaggerated biceps and shoulders holding a dam comfortably in his giant-sized muscular arms. It would be no exaggeration to say that every Ambuja executive in the room, including me, was surprised by the visual. I could even hear some chuckling at the back. The image was a radical departure from what we were used to seeing in cement ads, which were usually a play on the visuals of cement bags. There were no cement bags in the Trikaya ad.

Ravi was a seasoned advertising professional and he was unfazed by the immediate reaction. He gave a very articulate and convincing explanation of the strategy behind the campaign. The idea, according to him, was to build the perception of the superior strength of Ambuja cement with an overpowering visual that grabbed the viewer's attention at first glance. The explanation made sense. The visual seemed to capture everything we wanted to convey.

The giant was not the only unusual bit about the campaign. The tagline was equally unexpected and atypical. 'Virat Compressive Strength'—a mix of English and Hindi. We felt the line was an odd combination of two languages and too technical for an ordinary cement consumer. Hinglish usage was not yet a big part of popular culture in those days. Advertising lines were either in English or in Hindi; the use of hybrid lines was still a few years away.

Ravi again was ahead of the times and had an explanation. The technical term 'compressive strength', he said, elevated the image of Ambuja cement in the public mind. It conveyed that ours was no ordinary cement, but a strong cement specially developed by the Ambuja laboratory. Similarly, the word *virat* (common to both Sanskrit and Hindi) worked at various levels. It evoked the image of giant strength, robustness, majesty, brilliance, durability, etc. The bilingual phrasing, he added, was to connect with the man on the street who comfortably peppered his everyday language with words in English and Hindi/or his mother tongue.

Ravi's suggestion to us was to make the giant the Ambuja mnemonic. Having never heard of the word, I asked him to elaborate. He said if successful with the consumers, we should make it our company symbol that would appear with every Ambuja communication. It would act like a memory aid that would help people remember what Ambuja cement stood for, every time they saw it.

I was new to the language and strategy of advertising. By then, though, I was convinced that I could trust Ravi with his expertise and experience to do the right thing. I asked him if our advertising could include a few of our findings of what people looked for in their cement, like the green colour and the use of HDPE bags. He ruled them out saying in advertising, even getting one idea across to people was a complicated process, conveying two or three was next to impossible.

Despite my reservations, once I am convinced of an idea, I believe in backing it wholeheartedly. That is what happened with our first 'Virat Compressive Strength' campaign. On Ravi's recommendation, we launched an advertising blitzkrieg across Gujarat with hoardings, banners and shop displays. Most importantly, we bought full-page ads in the Gujarati newspapers which no one had done before. He had earlier sent two of his team members all over Saurashtra to find out the nature of branding that retailers and wholesalers used in their establishments. They found that most of these places carried poor branding, so we had an excellent opportunity to make an impact, which we did.

Though I had no advertising budget figure in mind when we started, I was indeed taken aback when Ravi came up with a figure of ₹80 lakh. It works out to ₹8 crore in today's value, a figure unheard of in cement company advertising. I had thought of a figure between ₹10 and 20 lakh. Ravi was insistent that this was the only way to make an impact. I reluctantly agreed.

Having committed to spending the money that Ravi wanted, I was keen that his agency was fully focused on our work. I worried that being a small player compared to some of his other clients like Parle and Aristocrat, he would give me short shrift. I made it easy for Ravi and his team by extending our vendor payment policy to Trikaya as well. I told our accounts department to clear their bills as soon as they were presented rather than wait for the conventional thirty-day credit period. It was not something Ravi or his team expected in an industry where clients were notorious for not clearing payments for months. Expectedly, our work never suffered.

The 'Virat Compressive Strength' campaign proved to be a big success on multiple fronts. The consumer-style marketing of what was otherwise a dull commodity, helped build Ambuja as a brand name. In no time it propelled Ambuja's name into the top league of the Indian cement industry. Its impact stretched far beyond Gujarat. We were now well known across the country. Gujarat Ambuja was seen as synonymous with the strongest and most durable cement in the market.

In an industry where sales were driven almost entirely on competitive pricing, our brand-building exercise enabled us to command a premium on the prevailing market price, despite us being a new player. We were able to sell almost everything that we produced from the word go. We achieved better-than-expected price realization, which helped boost our bottom line. It was the primary reason we were profitable even in our first full year of operation.

The campaign helped cement our long and fruitful relationship with Trikaya that would last for nearly two decades and become one of the main pillars of the Ambuja success story. Ravi Gupta had fundamentally altered the way Indians looked at cement. The giant himself underwent a subtle transformation over the years. In the second stage of the campaign, he was shown holding a skyscraper in his hands, signalling our push into urban areas. In yet another campaign, the giant was turned into a mnemonic while the ads were in the form of educational stories targeting people building their own homes.

I have no hesitation in saying that Ravi was the father of brand Ambuja. He helped sustain and nourish it, with path-breaking ideas right till the days of his premature death in 1997. I had no marketing manager when we started, just a sales head in Rashmi Kampani. Ravi became our de facto head of marketing. I never bothered to recruit anyone in that position as he was the best in the business. In the ten years or so that I got to know him, he was my advertising and marketing guru. Everything that I know about both these disciplines—most of which I successfully implemented in the company—I learnt from him. We also became good friends.

The giant is still the Ambuja mnemonic three decades later. And the phrase 'Virat Compressive Strength' proved to be a precursor in Indian advertising's fundamental and successful shift towards the use of Hinglish taglines in the 1990s with phrases like 'Hungry Kya?' (Domino's Pizza), 'Yeh Dil Maange More' (Pepsi), 'Pal Banaye Magical' (Lay's), 'Taste Bhi, Health Bhi' (Maggi) and 'Kya Aap Closeup Karte Hain?' (Closeup).

A few years later, Ravi created yet another groundbreaking campaign for us with the tagline 'I Can' (which I will talk about later in the book). It not only pioneered the concept of corporate advertising campaign in India, but also had the double effect of image building for the company as well as boosting the morale of employees for what they had achieved.

Every Ambuja insider is grateful for yet another of Ravi's brilliant contributions to the company, the setting up of the Technical Services Division. After the success of the first Ambuja Giant campaign, he told me one day that I should set up a technical division in the company. It would disseminate knowledge about cement and its correct usage to dealers, retailers and end-customers. It should be, he said, something like an after-sales service for people dealing and buying Gujarat Ambuja cement. He even offered to lower the advertising budget to pay for this division. It was a great idea which I implemented immediately. Over time, it morphed into a capable marketing vehicle as well.

Setting up the division was not difficult since we already had a qualified cement expert in Mr Desai, our technical services manager based out of Ahmedabad. He and his team of civil engineers were the original mainstays of this cell. Besides their work in quality control at the plant, their mission was to educate people on the best ways of using cement. They would give lectures and physical demonstrations to dealers, retailers and home-buyers on best practices for cement.

The marketing team organized dealer meetings in small towns and cities across Gujarat, where the technical services engineers conducted workshops and training sessions. It proved to be a valuable addition to the cement we were selling. No other company had done this before. It helped enhance the image of the company, while spreading knowledge and awareness about the superior quality of our cement.

Not long after we had set up the technical cell, Mr B.T. Unwalla, a retired civil engineer, came to see me. He had spent a lifetime at ACC as an expert on concrete. He had come to tell me that the company was now selling its much-reputed Concrete Services Division and that I should buy it. I was certainly interested. But when I made a cold call to Mr Darbari Seth, who was the Tata director on the ACC board, he sensed that there was some value in the division and decided not to sell it.

Mr Unwalla was a vast reservoir of knowledge about cement and concrete. I retained him as an adviser and over the next few years, he became my teacher on all the technical aspects of cement. He would come and talk to me a lot. I remember him telling me that you could make a lousy house from good cement, but using good practices you could make a fabulous house even with bad cement!

He was also very well networked in the architects and structural engineering community. He was both an active participant and an organizer of seminars and conferences on issues related to construction and civil engineering. Once he told me that ACC had backed out of the sponsorship for a talk by the famous architect Charles Correa at a civil engineers' seminar in Bombay. He asked if I would like to step in. The money involved was only a few thousand and I was glad to provide the sponsorship. I also realized this was an excellent platform for us to create awareness about Ambuja among the architect and civil engineering community in the country.

Through Mr Unwalla, I began sponsoring many such events where the Ambuja name would be prominently displayed. I would encourage him to speak at many of these events and write for industry journals. All this contributed to building Ambuja's reputation among industry professionals across the country, even though we were still a small company restricted to Gujarat.

While Ravi Gupta built the Ambuja brand and provided us with the marketing direction, Rashmi Kampani led the charge on the ground. He was tasked with the thankless job of implementing our often-unconventional marketing ideas and experiments. Though he had some experience in cement marketing in Gujarat, even he was not well versed in the wily ways of our strongly entrenched competitors. When we first launched Ambuja cement in the big cities of Gujarat like Ahmedabad, Baroda and Rajkot, we were flummoxed as to why sales were not picking up despite heavy advertising and marketing. The bigger dealers told us that the pick-up was slow and stocks were piling up. A bit of sleuthing by our team revealed that the problem was not lack of demand. People were asking for Ambuja cement, but the dealers were not selling it despite stocking it.

We had walked into a trap laid down by our biggest competitor, who was then the market leader. This company had told the dealers to stock the cement, but ensure that it was not pushed or sold in large numbers. Once we became aware of the problem, we moved fast. We stopped dealing with many of the big dealers and instead started selling through the smaller ones. We got people who were not in the cement business to become our dealers. Baroda was a particularly challenging market in this regard. I sent my brother-in-law Arvind Nopany, who had never sold cement, to open a dealership there. He found it challenging initially, but once the buyers discovered the quality of our cement, he became remarkably successful.

The early problems we encountered with the dealers were a good indicator of how ignorant we were of the traditional ways of selling cement. But it worked to our advantage as well. Since none of us came from cement-selling backgrounds, we were able to devise innovative, out-of-the-box solutions. We started with no grand plan or strategy, just a hefty dose of common sense and an unfailing commitment to ethics and honesty.

The only thing that I was clear about from the beginning was that we would be honest and fair in all our dealings. Our first test came when we were to appoint dealers. The traditional way was to squeeze a massive cash deposit from them for the dealership. People were paying as much as ₹20 to 30 lakh (about ₹2 to 3 crore in today's value) to become dealers for products of big companies. I considered this immoral and unfair. I told my people we would take only a nominal deposit. If you do not trust your dealer, then there is no point in working with him. Our only condition was that the dealer should make his payment within the prescribed time.

I had always admired pharma marketing with its network of medical representatives who went from doctor to doctor explaining the details of each product. I thought it was an excellent system to emulate. The same kind of personal contact would help us build better relationships with dealers and retailers. When I first told Rashmi about my idea and that we should recruit twenty-five marketing representatives, he was quite taken aback. He asked me what he would do with so many of them.

I said we should spread them all across the state so that we could be in regular touch with each dealer and stockist. I insisted that they wear a tie as the pharma reps did. For reasons that are difficult to understand, a man wearing a tie or dressed in a suit is always better respected in India. I believed that wearing a tie would raise their stature among the dealers. The strategy worked. The dealers were happy that we were going the extra mile to stay in touch with them. We got valuable feedback on our product as well as those of our competitors. Most importantly, we were in a better position to anticipate trends and the supply-demand situation.

One of the earliest situations our marketing 'rep network' encountered was the OPC vs PPC debate. Which one was better? Two of our competitors, Digvijay Cement and Narmada Cement, made PPC. Most consumers and even dealers were not aware of the difference between the two types of cement. We used this as an opportunity to spread information and knowledge about cement varieties, particularly about OPC and its advantages.

The other significant change that we brought about was in dealer relationship. Within a few months of our launch, I realized that the whole system was rotten to the core. More than the manufacturers, it was the dealers who controlled the market. Each cement trader had dealerships of two or three companies. His expertise was in pitting one cement company against the other.

From my experience in cotton trading, I knew that pushing sales by cutting prices was always a bad idea. It would invariably backfire in the long run. We refused to join the discount battle between various companies, which was standard practice in the Gujarat market in those days. We declared that our price would always be ₹2 more than the next-best brand. Dealers and stockists would call our sales team often to say that our competitors had reduced their prices and we should do so as well, or else our cement won't sell. But we refused.

Daily price negotiations with dealers did not serve any purpose. I thought long and hard and decided that things could not go on like this forever. We could not work in an environment where we were always in an adversarial relationship with our dealers. With the profit margin being the only thing on their minds, my dealers would never work in my interest. They were concerned only about their bottom line, despite being provided with world-class cement, backed by great service and persuasive advertising. I was asking them for no special favours, yet they made no commitment to me. If there is no commitment, there cannot be a strong relationship between a company and its dealers, which is essential for the healthy growth of our business.

I told Rashmi that this had to stop. He said this was how the market had evolved and it would be impossible to stop it now. 'Why would a dealer want to give up his bargaining strength?' he added. I suggested that we organize a dealer conference in Bangkok to discuss the way forward in more relaxed surroundings.

Dealer conferences were common among pharma companies in those days. Once a year, they would fly their dealers to a fancy tourist location for a pep talk and some fun, which did wonders to their business. I decided to replicate this. Bangkok was cheaper than Kashmir and the fact that it was a foreign location added to the charm. Rashmi invited around eighty of our biggest dealers from across Gujarat, all of whom agreed to come. The Thai capital was a very charming place even then. Most of our dealers had never travelled outside India and did not possess a passport. We helped many of them get passports and visas, some of which arrived on the day of travel.

I had no prior discussion with Rashmi on what I was going to tell the dealers. After reflecting on it for a while, I decided that it was time to move towards developing a network of exclusive dealerships. That was the only way to eliminate the long-prevailing, multi-brand dealership problem which was causing so much stress and consuming valuable management time. Our sales were picking up month on month and I was confident that we would do even better with a network of dealers who sold only Ambuja cement.

After they had taken in the sights and sounds of Bangkok during the day, we ushered them into the ballroom of the hotel for a meeting addressed by me. I told them I was grateful for all they had done so far, but it was time for a change. Going forward, I said, we would be introducing a differential commission system for the dealers. Those who stocked only Ambuja cement would get the status of 'preferred stockist' and a special discount. They would be given priority cement allocation during times of shortage and could expect better service than regular stockists.

I assured them that they would sell more cement as exclusive Ambuja dealers than what they were currently selling as multi-brand dealers. Some of them asked me how I could guarantee that. I told them about the confidence I had in the quality and the popularity of Ambuja cement. 'Not only will you sell more, but your profits will also go up. Your prestige will be higher than what it is today.'

The dealers were not enthused; it meant radically altering the way they had been selling cement so far. I knew I was taking a big risk, more so by making a public commitment. It was not only the dealers who were surprised by my announcement, my people were a bit startled too. It was not something they were expecting. No one was more surprised than Rashmi. He was genuinely worried. He was the one who had to implement the plan. He felt no one would accept the proposal. I asked him to wait and watch.

As Rashmi had predicted, in the first couple of months only a few small dealers from small towns signed up. I could see that he was agitated at not being able to make the idea work. I told him to be patient. Rashmi then devised a new strategy. He and his team started going from dealer to dealer trying to convince them to sign up. In the areas where a few of them had signed up, his strategy began drastically reducing the number of multi-brand outlets we were servicing and helped push the sales of the newly joined preferred stockists. Others saw what was happening and more and more dealers jumped on our new bandwagon. Rashmi started cutting out even more multi-brand outlets from our network. And as demand for Ambuja cement picked up, the preferred stockists benefited even more.

News of their success made many others join until we had the threshold number of preferred stockists we wanted. In Ahmedabad, one of our biggest markets, we were able to shrink the number of dealers from around 400 to 100, but our sales doubled.

It was the biggest operational risk that I took after launching the company and we won. The reward was immense. Our state-wide sales network was now made up of only single-brand dealers. Nobody, including the great Aditya Birla, had done this in any market and he complimented me saying, 'We had always lived with the idea that the system cannot be changed. Only you had the courage of conviction to change that system. I admire your courage.'

'*Saab*,' I responded, 'I have a very limited quantity of cement to sell and that too in only one state, that's why I was able to take the risk.' Indeed, I am not sure I would have done this had I plants in several states at that time. I was able to take the risk because I was the owner of the company. No professional managers would have had the courage to take the risk.

The Bangkok dealer conference proved to be beneficial for another vital reason. It raised our standing in the Gujarat dealer community to a level that we had never anticipated. We began to be seen as a company that respected and valued its dealers. The dealers were thrilled by the fact that not only were they made to feel at home, but were also able to interact directly with the MD of the company. That was a time when they were barely recognized or appreciated for their service by cement companies. Many of them told us that a personal audience with even the sales manager of the company was next to impossible. Ambuja thereafter was viewed as a company that cared for its dealers and considered them part of its business family.

We also made another major decision around this time. Around 20 to 30 per cent of the sales of most cement companies in those days came from government agencies. The government would open a tender and companies would bid to supply the cement, often at lower prices than in the market. Invariably, the tender documents would ask for more cement than was required. This was done deliberately by corrupt government officials, who would then steal that cement and sell it in the black market. It would lead to a situation where a brand seeking a higher price in the open market had to compete with its own cement pilfered from government godowns and sold by unscrupulous dealers for a lower price!

We were by then commanding the highest price in the market and there was a growing demand for our cement. I made a principled decision that it was not in the company's interest to bid for government contracts. Even at the risk of losing a large chunk of assured business, I did not want to diminish our growing brand image.

Government officials were surprised by our decision. I told them that there were enough cement companies prepared to supply cement to the government, so my absence would not be felt. My cement was fetching a higher price in the open market, so it did not make sense from a business perspective either. After all, I was answerable to my shareholders which included the Gujarat government itself. I promised them we would be more than willing to supply to the government if there was a shortfall in the market.

I did make one small concession for the government officials. The Gujarat government was our partner, so we decided to give state employees a ₹5-discount on every bag of cement. The only condition was that the cement should be used for building their own house. This scheme became a hit and the best part was that these government officials became our goodwill ambassadors, talking up the brand all over the state.

Another significant achievement of ours in the early days was compressing our dealer payment cycle. Cement manufacturing is not a working-capital intensive business. However, it was essential to me that the capital was used efficiently. For this to happen, a meaningful payment cycle was vital. I believed that it would benefit everyone in the long run. The standard credit period for dealers in the early days when we started was thirty days and most dealers would delay on that as well. It made no logical sense to me. Why should it be thirty days, why couldn't it be much less? Soon after we reached our threshold level of preferred stockists, I decided that we should issue instructions to dealers to reduce the credit period to seven days. So that everyone was prepared, we gave the dealers a few months to adjust to the new reality.

Expectedly, as with the other changes I had initiated, I had to first convince my own people about the feasibility of implementing this plan. They thought I was crazy because no other company had done this. They said that the dealers would never agree, but I knew the dealers would be more amenable now since they were our exclusive stockists working only for us. I told my salespeople we would make it happen and everyone would benefit from this, including the dealers themselves.

The dealers were all unhappy at the beginning. Eventually, they all fell in line. After a few months, I heard from our people that some of them wanted to thank me for bringing about this change. Earlier, they used to have a thirty-day credit period with us and their customers would demand and get a thirty-day credit period from them. Now that we had reduced our credit period to seven days, they were able to force their customers to pay up in seven days since we needed to be paid. It helped bring down their debt in the market.

Besides benefiting everyone's cash flow, the new system helped further bolster the company. A company that is paid immediately after making a sale is always looked upon with envy in the market. The implication is that the dealers find us indispensable because of the quality of our product and services. Once we established this practice, other companies were quick to follow. Despite their best efforts, though, to our knowledge, no company was able to match our seven-day payment cycle at that time.

To run an efficient business, you need to have the courage to make the right decision, even if it is unconventional or radical. And then you have to sustain it by the quality of your actions and persistence. Despite being a small company, we had, in less than two years of operation, managed to do many things that others could not do even after decades. We transformed the way cement dealership worked in India—by creating consumer-style branding for our product; by changing the way cement was packed; by turning away government business because it didn't adhere to our principles; and finally, by compressing the payment cycle, which made businesses more efficient.

The most satisfying part of initiating these changes was that our bottom line continued to prosper. In June 1989, just a year after our memorable Bangkok dealer conference, we had the best results since the start of the company, both in terms of sales and profits.

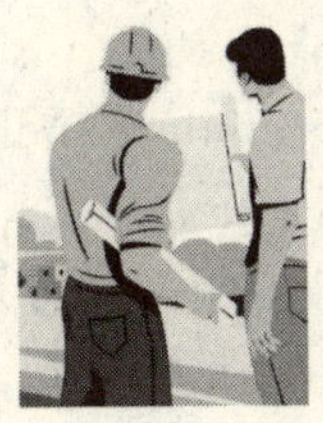

7

A New Sense of Confidence

Cutting the GIIC umbilical cord • Looking beyond Gujarat • Media and the stock market discover Gujarat Ambuja

The late 1980s saw great political and economic turmoil in India. The Bofors scandal had blighted the tenure of Prime Minister Rajiv Gandhi. His former finance and defence minister V.P. Singh, who had been expelled from the Congress Party after he exposed alleged government corruption, was now leading the charge against him in the Lok Sabha election. Singh eventually became the PM, but with support from an odd mix of parties from the left and the right. Everyone knew it was just a matter of time before his coalition collapsed (it lasted eleven months).

The economy was in a similar situation. The effects of uncontrolled imports that followed the 'light' reform by Rajiv Gandhi's government over the previous five years, had now come home to roost. Fiscal and trade deficits were heading into dangerous territory, which eventually led to the infamous balance of payment crisis and the mortgaging of RBI's gold. Amid this all-round uncertainty though, I felt strangely calm and relaxed. For the first time, since we started work on Gujarat Ambuja seven years ago, we had enough cash in the bank for us to feel comfortable, our market share in Gujarat was on an upward trajectory and I felt confident of our ability to withstand competition and do better.

Looking back, I feel that there were two phases in the Ambuja story. The first, from 1982 to '89, was the learning stage, along with the struggle and hard work to establish our name in the market. By 1989, I felt we had successfully entrenched the Ambuja culture across the organization. It was a culture of low-cost, high-productivity, innovation, ethics and inclusive growth where everyone benefits—the consumer, the employees, our vendors and shareholders and the community around us. We were now moving into the second phase, the post-1989 period. I felt that my core team of executives, including Mr Kulkarni, Mr Bhandari, Mr Taparia and Mr Kampani, were doing such a good job that I could step back and let them run the day-to-day operations. At the same time, I could involve myself with the larger picture of growth and expansion.

In March 1989, the government had at long last fully decontrolled cement. It was the first time an entire infrastructure-related industry had been deregulated in India. The deregulation had come at the urging of the World Bank, which at that time was helping India deal with its financial crisis. The partial decontrol earlier in the decade had resulted in significant new investments in the industry and the thinking was that full decontrol would accelerate the process.

Luckily, complete deregulation came at a time when cement prices were climbing and most companies were reporting improved bottom lines. As a result, the cement decontrol was deemed a success by many people. Massive new investments followed. In less than ten years leading up to the late 1990s, the total installed cement capacity in the country more than doubled to 100 million tonnes. Even with our team now managing the affairs at Kodinar, there was plenty of action that year to keep me fully occupied. It started with Suresh Mulani, a London-based NRI friend of mine, who had invested ₹1.25 crore in the original equity of Gujarat Ambuja to take a 6 per cent stake. In 1987, he increased his stake by picking up the unsubscribed part of GIIC's rights issue. He was on the board of the company and had a cabin for use at our Bombay head office whenever he was in the city.

Around mid-1989 he came to me, unexpectedly saying that his investment in the company was not fetching him adequate returns and that he wanted out. Our share price in those days was quoting at around ₹14. I told him that these were early days and despite our decent performance the share price had not moved due to the problems in the cement industry. Also, we had declared generous dividends starting from the first year itself. He said he was not happy and was also in need of cash for which he wanted to sell his stake.

I tried to persuade him to stay, as did Suresh Neotia who was in town at that time. Mulani, however, was determined to get out. After a point I decided enough was enough and offered to buy back his stake. He wanted an 18 per cent return in dollar terms on his investment, which worked out to around ₹22 a share. It would cost me a few crores. I arranged for the funds and bought him out. He resigned from the board soon after. He was so happy to get his money back that he threw a party in London for his friends. Unfortunately for him and fortunately for me, the Ambuja share price more than tripled in little over a year and sometime later it crossed ₹100. He missed his chance to make a killing.

Mulani's resignation also made me rethink Dr Jain's role in the company. He had been on the company board since 1983 and had helped recruit many of our earliest team members. I valued his contribution at board meetings over the years. Gujarat Ambuja was now performing much better than his own company, Andhra Cements, which by then was almost sick. It was an increasingly uncomfortable scenario, both for him and me. I decided it was the best time for us to part ways. A few months after Mulani's departure, I spoke to Dr Jain about my decision and we parted amicably.

The third and most crucial exit at this time was that of our biggest shareholder and joint-venture partner—GIIC. The company was the main reason behind our very existence. The advice and help from the GIIC team in the early days and during the IPO had been invaluable. Being a state industrial-development organization with limited monetary resources, the company had not participated in our rights issue in 1987. As a result, it had ceased to be the dominant shareholder, leading to its nominee being replaced as chairman by Suresh Neotia.

One day in April 1990, out of the blue, I got a call from Mr Madhusudhan Dayal, MD, GIIC. He said he was in Bombay at his guest house at Churchgate and wanted me to come over and meet him. I had known him for a long time and thought of it as a routine meeting, since things were going very well in the company. He came straight to the point as soon as I arrived. 'We have a situation,' he said. 'We are in the business of promoting joint-sector projects. Our philosophy is that we will invest for five to seven years and then allow the promoters to buy us out.'

He revealed that the Gujarat government had told GIIC it would not be getting any more funds, all fresh investments would have to come from internal accruals and disinvestment. This had led GIIC to think of selling its stake in those joint-sector companies that had started production. It would be the first time in its nearly two-decade-long history that GIIC had embarked on a disinvestment programme. And Gujarat Ambuja was to be the first company where it would be implemented. I asked Mr Dayal if they had spoken to any other joint-venture partner. 'No, you are the first,' he told me. I asked him why we were being made the guinea pig.

'Of all our partners you appear to be the most rational and committed promoter,' he said. 'The board felt it would be good to start with you. You can set the standard on how this disinvestment programme will work. We want to exit, but we cannot exit unless the partner buys us out.'

The GIIC board had worked out a formula on valuing its stake, said Mr Dayal—the company should either get a minimum 15 per cent return on investment, or be paid the valuation based on the average share price over the previous three months, whichever was higher. Gujarat Ambuja's share price in those days hovered between ₹12 and 14 and as per GIIC's calculation we had to buy them out at around ₹15 a share.

Mr Dayal recommended that we grab this opportunity as it was in our best interest to give GIIC an early exit. 'You will have greater flexibility in your operation, we will not question every move you make,' he said and added, 'You can expand beyond Gujarat. You might not get this opportunity later if the government changes its policy.'

I agreed with him. We had built a great relationship with GIIC over the years and this was a chance for us to part ways amicably. I had been looking for opportunities to invest outside Gujarat and GIIC would not have been enthusiastic about this since its mission was to bring investments into Gujarat. I calculated that I would need ₹6 to 7 crore to buy back the shares, which I could manage. I told Mr Dayal that I was glad to take up the offer. I was confident that the Neotias would have no objection either. As we shook hands, Mr Dayal said the deal had to be completed in three months. If we went beyond that, we would have to pay GIIC penal interest at the rate of 15 per cent per annum on the buy-back amount.

I went back to the office and spoke to Mr Bhandari, whose financial wisdom I trusted. He sounded happy and said it was a good deal. Then I talked to Suresh Neotia. He also said it was a good deal but added that at this point he and Vinod were in no position to participate in the buy-back because they were short on finances. 'You buy the shares and increase your holding in the company,' he said.

I was taken aback by the response. This was not what I had expected. If I bought the entire GIIC stake myself, as Suresh had suggested, it would lead to the Neotias' stake getting diluted. That could be potentially calamitous. I feared they would lose interest in the affairs of the company once they were reduced to minority shareholders. And they would eventually ask me to buy them out as well. The prospect of this alarmed me. My children were still in college and the Neotias were the only family members that I could fall back on in case of any problems. I had a lot of personal affection for the Neotias and the way they treated me as a younger brother. We had a tremendous amount of regard and respect for each other. They were not involved in the day-to-day operations of the company, but their advice, wisdom and moral support were invaluable. Suresh was a picture of grace, dignity and serenity when he conducted the board meetings as chairman. Vinod would frequently travel to Bombay and spend time at the office, talking to almost everyone. Because of his calm demeanour, genial temperament and a remarkable ability to listen, many of our senior executives were more comfortable talking to him than to me. They would use him to convey their unhappiness at some decision I had taken, instead of telling me directly. And he would pass it on to me in the mildest and most diplomatic language possible.

The Neotias were immensely helpful to me in other areas as well. Running a company in those 'licence raj' days meant much more than producing cement at the lowest possible cost and selling it at the highest possible price. It meant dealing with a number of government departments and agencies, spending time with bureaucrats and massaging their egos. I did not have much of an appetite for this. While I was okay with doing it at the state level, Suresh managed it at the Centre. And with our plans to expand outside of Gujarat in the near future, I knew that I would need help in Delhi more than ever before. Suresh was particularly good at it and loved this aspect of his responsibility. Over the years, he had built an extensive network of friends and acquaintances among the Delhi bureaucrats, particularly in ministries like coal, industry, environment, power and the railways. Whenever I was in Delhi, he would spend the entire day with me, introducing me to all the relevant government secretaries.

Taking all this into consideration, I decided to go all out to persuade the Neotias to buy their portion of the GIIC shares. I phoned Vinod who was closer to me in age and more like a friend. I told him that they had to buy the shares because I was confident about the future of the company and the upward trajectory of its share price. And I offered to help them get finance to buy the shares since they did not want to spend their own money. Vinod asked what would happen if the share price fell and they were unable to sell the shares. I promised to buy back their shares. Persuaded by this, Vinod spoke to Suresh and got back saying they would agree to the deal on the condition that I would buy back their shares if they ever felt like selling. Since I had already made this promise, the issue was settled.

With the Neotias on board, we informed GIIC that we would buy back its shares in two tranches within the period mandated. Gujarat Ambuja's share price began inching upwards after we bought the first tranche. As a result, GIIC wanted more money for the second tranche. We objected since we had already agreed on a price. Mr Bhandari and I flew to Ahmedabad to talk to their top people in person. Despite a heated exchange, they refused to budge and we ended up paying the higher price. Notwithstanding the last-minute haggling over price, we ended our partnership on a happy note.

I told them how beholden I was for their unstinted support and assistance over the years. This kind of project, I told them, would not have been possible in any other state. I genuinely meant it. I am glad that they still mention the Ambuja name proudly on their website as one of their biggest success stories since inception. Unfortunately, GIIC did not have much success in its effort to duplicate the same buy-back exercise with other joint-venture partners. On our way back from Ahmedabad, we met a senior bureaucrat who told me that I should consider myself lucky that the state government had allowed us to buy back the shares, because state governments were not normally good at letting go. The GIIC withdrew its nominee directors from our board in July 1990. However, I requested one of them, Mr Mohan Patel, to continue in his personal capacity as I valued his wisdom and advice.

The end of our seven-year partnership with GIIC was a significant turning point in Gujarat Ambuja's journey. We will always be grateful to

GIIC for nurturing us through our fledgling days, but the time had now come to spread our wings. It was as if destiny had chosen this to be the moment. We were now free to pursue expansion and growth in other parts of the country. Coincidentally, the same month that GIIC withdrew its nominees, our board approved the setting up of a new 1-million-tonne plant at Suli in Himachal Pradesh. It was a project I had been pursuing for some time, about which I will talk in detail later.

Potential new investors, especially institutional investors, had become increasingly aware of the Gujarat Ambuja story with all the positive press we were getting. The company stock, which had been comatose since the days of the IPO, was now showing signs of life. A combination of factors, including our impressive profit figures, had changed things. Cement prices were climbing and the stock market was finally turning bullish after a long time. It was a surprise for me. I had been prepared to wait for the long haul and even experts like Dr S.A. Dave, who was then the executive director of IDBI, had told me that it would take time for the price to pick up.

The first sign that big investors were indeed looking at us came in late 1989 and early '90, when Mr Harshad Mehta visited me. He was known as the big bull of the Indian stock market in the days before the infamous securities scandal brought him down. He said that he had done a thorough study of ACC and was now looking at Gujarat Ambuja. He was known for aggressively speculating in ACC shares, having pushed the share price up to ₹10,000 once.

Around this time, a young man by the name of Vinod Sethi also called to ask if he could come and see me. He said he was in charge of investing in emerging markets for the American investment bank Morgan Stanley. Foreign institutional investors (FIIs) were still not allowed to invest in the Indian stock market (it was permitted only in 1992). But Mr Sethi, who had an engineering degree from IIT, Bombay and an MBA from the Stern School of Business, New York, had worked out a special dispensation through SBI to start operations here.

He said his research team had been following our company carefully and had already bought 7 to 8 per cent of Gujarat Ambuja shares at around ₹17 per share. It was the pre-SEBI days, when the so-called 'creeping acquisition'—buying a large stake in a company quietly, without the knowledge of the company and without informing the stock market—was legal. I was happy that he had such confidence in Ambuja. I asked him what his target for the Ambuja share price was. He said ₹50. I told him not to be stupid. He said that was the assessment of the Morgan Stanley equity analysts.

Mr Sethi wanted more information about the company and its operations. I told him we were always transparent with our investors and gave him all the details he needed. Two weeks later, he came back and informed me that they had raised their holding in Gujarat Ambuja to over 10 per cent. 'After my conversation with you, I am even more confident about the company,' he said.

For the first time since the IPO, I could see a slow but distinctly upward momentum in our stock price. I now felt confident about the future. With the likes of Morgan Stanley and (pre-scam) Harshad Mehta, then widely respected for his keen ability to pick up undervalued stocks, reposing their faith in Ambuja, I felt it would be a missed opportunity if I didn't invest in my own stock, something that promoters were allowed to do in those days. I asked Mr Taparia and our treasury manager Mr Anil Singhvi to engage our broker at the BSE to buy the stock on my behalf. They must have purchased about 3 to 4 per cent of outstanding shares by which time the price of the stock touched ₹25.

My original intention was to acquire these shares in the name of my personal investment company, Radha Madhav. The idea to invest in my own stock was not to make a killing or to increase my stake in the company. It was about seizing the opportunity to buy an undervalued stock. I knew that sometime soon the stock would find its real value. There could be complications however, if I as promoter and MD increased my personal holding in the company without informing the other directors. Also, I did not want to do anything unethical. Then it struck me—why not get Gujarat Ambuja employees, dealers and well-wishers to buy these shares?

Four years earlier, I had persuaded many of my colleagues to invest in our IPO, but this time I knew it was not going to be easy. Persuading the same people to invest once again would be difficult, that too when the share price had hardly moved for a long time. Nevertheless, I would take my chances. I decided to start with our sales adviser Rashmi Kampani. He was a chartered accountant, who I knew was wealthy and invested in the stock market. I spoke to him about my interactions with Mr Harshad Mehta and Mr Vinod Sethi. I guaranteed him an 18 per cent return if he bought the Gujarat Ambuja shares. He said, '*Saab, nahi hua toh* I will take that money from you.' I told him that was my promise. If I remember right, he invested more than ₹10 lakh in the company stock.

Unlike Rashmi though, others in the company, including the senior executives, came from middle-class backgrounds where stock market investment was not looked upon kindly. I figured the best way to get them to buy stock was to offer it at my cost price. The quoted price at that time was around ₹25 and my average price was ₹18. The near-40 per cent immediate profit would be a powerful motivator for them to find the money to buy the stock. I made a list of shares we would give to each executive and employee. Many of the senior executives were given close to 1,00,000 shares each, the next rung of executives 10,000 shares each and so on.

Every employee of the company, including entrants, got some shares, even if it was just fifty. I don't think there were many who did not take up the offer. We arranged personal loans for some from Citibank, to buy the shares. It was the first time, in my reckoning, that any Indian company had done something like this. SEBI itself had still not been set up and its employee stock ownership plan (ESOP) rules were many years away. Ours was a rudimentary version of the ESOP.

The stock price continued its secular upward climb through much of that year, inching closer to ₹100 by December 1990. Suddenly, we were the darling of the stock market. I was getting periodic visits from many of Bombay's biggest brokers—including Mr Nimesh Shah of Enam and Mr Manu Manek, one of the biggest speculators in those days—to understand our story. I also had several big-name Wall Street investors coming to see me about Gujarat Ambuja and the economy in general, including the likes of Mr Barton Biggs the (then) chairman of Morgan Stanley Asset Management and legendary hedge-fund investor Julian Robertson of Tiger Management.

In July 1991, Finance Minister Manmohan Singh's big bang economic reforms ignited an even bigger bull run on the market. The Gujarat Ambuja stock peaked at around ₹275 that year. The next year (1992) provided fresh highs with the stock touching a record ₹675 in April and then settling at around ₹300 after our rights issue in July. Later that year, the government allowed FIIs to invest directly in the stock market for the first time. Their exponentially growing investments kept the market buoyant over the next decade. Along with the likes of Housing Development Finance Corporation (HDFC), Hero Honda and Infosys, Gujarat Ambuja was part of the core blue-chip holdings of most of these FIIs.

The stock kept buzzing over the next few years, providing handsome returns to the investors. I certainly did not anticipate this. Even the most astute of investment bankers like Mr Sethi had predicted that the price would climb to only around ₹50. The gains brought smiles to the faces of everyone—from the Neotias whom I had had to persuade to buy the GIIC shares, to Rashmi Kampani who had trusted me with his big investment in Ambuja, to all my other colleagues who had invested in the company.

This had the immediate effect of raising the motivational level of company employees. Everyone felt they were being rewarded for the hard work put in over the previous five to six years. Their new enthusiasm was a clear indicator that they were getting ready for our future growth. I am sure this elevated spirit played a major role in our fast-paced growth in the decade starting 1991, when we went from a 7,00,000-tonne cement producer to a 10-million-tonne company.

The other big takeaway from the rising stock price was that I was able to reduce my dependence on IDBI and other institutional banks for our new projects. I had figured how Mr Dhirubhai Ambani's financing strategy worked. He would raise money from the capital market and not depend on term loans from financial institutions. The problem with term loans was that they came with numerous restrictions and conditions that became onerous over time, restricting your freedom to do things your way. Instead, if you raised money from the stock market directly, you had much more freedom and flexibility in the use of the capital, particularly in the early stages. Once the project was up and running, loans from the likes of IDBI came with limited, rather than numerous, conditions. We decided that in the future we would raise money directly from investors for our new projects. Our impressive stock market performance had, at long last, provided us with that freedom.

8

Against the Odds

Setting up a plant in the Himachal hills • A promise to Punjab • The spirit of 'I Can' • Pioneering corporate advertising

As our bottom line started picking up, I became increasingly conscious of the risk we faced on account of what we called the 'Gujarat trap'. We already had 25 per cent of the market share in the state and growing beyond that would have been difficult because of intense competition. At the same time, our small size and the fact that we were selling 90 per cent of our cement in the state, made us vulnerable to any new competition. Any new plant in Gujarat, especially from a business house with a national presence and money power, could easily depress prices and end our competitive advantage; L&T was already in the process of putting up a 1.5-million-tonne plant in Gujarat.

I knew the way forward was to expand by putting up a new plant in another state. The question was, which state? I was sure that I did not want to be in any market where big companies were already fighting for market share. I did not have the resources or the stomach to join such a fight. I wanted to be as far as possible from the traditional markets. I had first thought of putting up a plant in Assam. At that time, only a small 2,00,000-tonne grinding unit serviced the entire 1-million-tonne cement market of India's north-east region. The rest of the demand was met by cement coming from outside. However, sporadic insurgency still plagued Assam and its neighbouring states, the region had abysmal infrastructure and accessibility was not easy. Also, despite my best intentions, I was not very familiar with the state. On the balance, there were too many negatives to go ahead there.

The second option was Himachal Pradesh. The state was first brought to my notice by Mr K.R. Lakhanpal, an IAS officer who was then the country's cement controller (yes, a post in those days) based out of Delhi. I got to know him well and used to meet him often in Delhi. He was from the Punjab cadre and would ask me to invest there. Mr Lakhanpal knew there was no limestone in Punjab, so he suggested that I put up the plant in Himachal Pradesh and a grinding unit in Punjab. He was the first one to tell me that Himachal Pradesh had some of the best limestone deposits in the country. That got me thinking.

Himachal Pradesh on its own was a small consumer of cement, with an annual demand of only 3,00,000 tonnes. What made it attractive were two factors—first, along with the then state of Jammu and Kashmir, Himachal Pradesh was the only north Indian state with significant deposits of good quality limestone. Second, the proximity of its western and southern fringes to the booming markets of Punjab, Delhi, Haryana, north-western Uttar Pradesh and northern Rajasthan would give us access to a region that in those days consumed more than 8 million tonnes of cement but had only one large cement plant servicing it—ACC's million-tonne plant at Gagal in Himachal Pradesh's Kangra district.

The Gagal plant had been set up by ACC in 1982 and, not surprisingly, it was the company's most successful plant and the one responsible for most of ACC's profits for many years. The public sector Cement Corporation of India Ltd (CCIL) operated a much smaller plant at Paonta

Sahib located on the southern tip of the state. Other than ACC Gagal, the region's cement requirement was met by units in Rajasthan and in the Satna cluster in eastern Madhya Pradesh, located 500 to 1,000 kilometres away. The galloping demand in this market gave me the confidence that the region could support much more than one large plant.

Besides limestone, Himachal Pradesh had another major advantage. It had surplus power because of all its hydroelectric sources. At around a rupee a unit, power in Himachal Pradesh was probably the cheapest in the country. Entrepreneurs, though, were still wary of setting up capital-intensive industries in Himachal Pradesh. The state's infrastructure was underdeveloped, a problem compounded by the hilly terrain which made accessibility difficult in those days. The rugged terrain also meant that finding large tracts of flat land for a cement plant was difficult. The state was in an eco-sensitive area with strict environmental regulations. Considering all this, setting up an industrial unit in Himachal Pradesh was not everyone's cup of tea. No wonder most investors kept away.

For us though, Himachal Pradesh ticked all the boxes. Our Ambujanagar plant was not only the cleanest in India but also on par or even better than many of the cement plants in Europe and America. I was not intimidated by Himachal Pradesh's stringent environmental regulations. As for infrastructure, my thinking was that if ACC could put up a million-tonne plant in 1982, then things could only be better now. We drew up a plan to put up a million-tonne plant in one of Himachal Pradesh's western districts bordering Punjab and set up grinding units in Himachal Pradesh, Uttar Pradesh and Punjab. This would enable us to service an entire swathe of north Indian states—Jammu and Kashmir, Himachal Pradesh, Punjab, Delhi, Uttar Pradesh and Haryana.

Fortuitously, the office of the cement controller was abolished around this time and my friend Mr Lakhanpal, who had held this post, was transferred as industries commissioner to his home cadre, Punjab. I remember this happened a few months after Operation Black Thunder in May 1988, Prime Minister Rajiv Gandhi's final police operation to flush out Sikh militants from the Golden Temple. Punjab was still in the throes of militancy and no industrialist wanted to invest there. Mr Lakhanpal invited me to Chandigarh to meet him and his bosses in the hope that we would invest in the state, which had lost nearly a decade to militancy.

I always had a soft corner for Punjab. Our family had bought from Punjab farmers for generations and our offices in places like Bathinda and Abohar had been in existence since the early part of the last century. Our cotton operations still employed more than a 100 people. We had never faced any militancy-related problems, so I was not as worried as many others were. I also knew the state was desperate for industrial investment, but I realized just how much by the red-carpet reception I received on my arrival in Chandigarh. Besides Mr Lakhanpal, I was welcomed by Mr I.S. Bindra, who was then the industry secretary and would later become nationally famous as the president of the Board of Control for Cricket in India (BCCI). He was the one who built the very modern cricket stadium in Mohali, which was named the IS Bindra Stadium. Mr Bindra told me how keen he was for Gujarat Ambuja to invest in Punjab. I told him about my Himachal Pradesh plan and that I was exploring the possibility of setting up a grinding unit in Punjab.

'We would welcome any investment you make in Punjab,' he said. 'We are here to provide you with all the help and assistance you need. Whatever you want, will be yours. Tell us what you want.'

I knew that Punjab had a problem with the disposal of fly ash—the non-biodegradable waste produced by thermal power plants—particularly the 1,200-megawatt Guru Gobind Singh Super Thermal Power Plant at Rupnagar (then known as Ropar). When mixed and ground with clinkers, fly ash is a valuable ingredient for making Portland Pozzolana Cement or PPC, which is 65 per cent cement and 35 per cent fly ash. Fly ash thus makes the cement stronger and more durable and increases its volume and weight. Sixty-five tonnes of clinker gives you 100 tonnes of PPC. Nevertheless, fly ash—though available free from the thermal plants—is exceedingly challenging to transport because of its powdery nature. There were no thermal power plants close to Kodinar and this was one of the reasons we made Ordinary Portland Cement (and not PPC) in our Gujarat plant. Now that Punjab had provided me with the opportunity to make PPC, I wanted to set up the grinding unit next to the Rupnagar power plant. Just 50 kilometres north of Chandigarh, Rupnagar was close to the Himachal Pradesh border.

I told Mr Bindra about my plan. He was more than happy to oblige and said that land and electricity would be made available whenever I was ready. It was agreed that we would be provided tax relief for fifteen years, including sales tax, octroi and electricity duty exemption. I also asked him for permission to build a special silo for the fly ash within the premises of the Rupnagar power plant. We planned to lay a pipeline through which the fly ash would be transferred pneumatically from the silo to our grinding unit. It would provide us with a steady flow of fly ash. To the best of my knowledge, no other cement company has been permitted to build such a facility at a government-owned power plant. I also demanded that no one else be allowed to put up a cement plant in Punjab for some time.

Everything was agreed to on the spot, except for the non-compete clause about other cement plants. 'We can put that into your contract, but the courts will strike it down,' Mr Bindra said. 'We had a similar case related to a sugar factory and the courts overruled it, saying it was bad in law.'

I then settled for a clause that prevented the building of new cement plants within a 100-kilometre radius of our unit and also gave us the first right of refusal over the Rupnagar plant's fly ash. This was accepted.

'Please let us know if you need any more concessions,' a colleague of Mr Bindra said to me at our celebratory lunch later. I had no further concessions to ask for. They had agreed to give us more than any other government had promised. I assured them I would be back as soon as our Himachal Pradesh plans were finalized. In appreciation of the generosity of the Punjab government, we put up another grinding facility further south in Bathinda, next to the Guru Nanak Dev Thermal Power Plant, a few years after the Rupnagar unit came up, to service the Haryana and Rajasthan markets.

Back in Bombay, when I told my colleagues about the concessions, their first reaction was that of disbelief. 'Why would anyone want to go to Punjab in this kind of political climate?' was the common refrain. I told them things were not as bad as they were made out to be. Our family's cotton operation had continued unimpeded all through the insurgency without any mishap. And the situation was improving. 'When you go there, which you will someday, you will see that it is a safe place. Nothing will happen. I can assure you all,' I told them. They still did not believe me.

It would be another five years before the Himachal Pradesh plant was built and made operational. In August 1995, a month before the Rupnagar plant started commercial production, the terrorists made their last stand in Punjab. They sent a suicide bomber to kill Chief Minister Beant Singh and blow up the secretariat in Chandigarh. Seventeen people died, including the CM, but we never wavered from our commitment to the state. Everything went ahead as planned and, as stated above, we even made fresh new investments in Bathinda a few years later.

The grinding units we built in Punjab were the main reason our Himachal Pradesh plants turned out to be massively profitable. I always viewed them as complementary entities. One without the other would not have been possible. They also led to us becoming one of the main sponsors of the Mohali cricket stadium and one side of the ground being called 'The Ambuja End'.

My first impression of the small mountain-state of Himachal Pradesh was based on our frequent family holidays in Shimla when I was young. I thought of it as a beautiful place with lots of tree cover and friendly people. Though it did not have the kind of problems that Punjab was facing, it was mostly underdeveloped. I was confident that the state government would still be very keen on seeking new investment. There was never any doubt in my mind that our project in Himachal Pradesh would pay off in the long run. We had the success of ACC Gagal for reference. It was that company's most profitable plant at that time. This fact stayed at the back of my mind when we started working on our plans. Our Himachal Pradesh plant became a mission for me—it was our best insurance against anything our competitors would try in Gujarat.

By April 1989, we already had the CEO in place—Mr R.N. Jain, a former senior executive with Modi Cement, who had experience on the commercial and engineering side. He started work out of Ambuja's office in Delhi because we had nothing in Himachal Pradesh as yet and it would be nearly a year before the company board formally approved of the project. Though we eventually did get all the permissions and concessions we asked for, the help stopped at that. It was becoming clear that Himachal Pradesh was going to prove much more challenging than I had anticipated. In fact, the experience was not very pleasant, especially during the project phase.

Getting work done in Himachal Pradesh proved to be more punishing than expected. Because it was a small state, everyone seemed to have a direct line to the CM and his ministers. We were forever addressing complaints from people in the neighbourhood who had gone all the way to the CM's office. If someone living nearby was not provided with a job, we were sure of some complaint being filed against the plant within the next few days. At one point, the truck owners in the state formed a cartel against us demanding exorbitant freight charges for transporting our cement and clinker. Though we went to court and won a stay against them, it was not heeded. We ended up bringing trucks from our Kodinar vendors to move the materials.

Our first big challenge was to find the right location for the plant. It was more difficult in Himachal Pradesh than anywhere else in the country, because of the topography. The land had to be along the state's south-western border to feed the grinding unit we were setting up at Rupnagar in neighbouring Punjab; and it had to be in the proximity of viable limestone mines. There were too many variables and getting the combination right was going to be a challenge. The Himachal Pradesh government's geology department was of very little assistance. Unlike geology departments in more advanced states such as Gujarat, it did not have detailed geological maps of the terrain. Instead, we had to conduct the geological survey ourselves.

Our team was led by our mining department head Mr Y.R. Rao and set up camp in several villages over a period of many months to drill and explore the soil. It was a back-breaking job. The weather was often mercilessly cold and the limestone deposits were located in valleys and near riverbeds. The downhill route through treacherous ledges and narrow walking paths was invariably tricky. I remember walking down to a site outside a village called Alsindi near Shimla, along the banks of the Sutlej; we eventually abandoned the area because of the challenging logistics in getting there. Therefore, though we started work in 1990, it took us nearly a year to find the right location.

We finally zeroed in on a mine at the bottom of a valley in a place called Kashlog in Solan district and began hunting for flat terrain nearby, for the plant. We were able to find land near a village called Darlaghat. We also shifted a smaller neighbouring village further uphill for some extra land. The terrain was not exactly flat, but manageable. It was also close to a state highway and an electrical substation.

The best thing was that Darlaghat sat on the top of the valley where the Khaslog mine was located. While the driving distance was 15 kilometres along a winding unpaved road, the straight-line, downhill drop to the mine was less than 4 kilometres. This shorter distance would prove crucial as we explored options for transporting the limestone. After the team gave me the good news about the location, I flew down to have a look at it. Access from the main road, as stated above, was not easy. We climbed a small hill for about half a kilometre and then walked another 500 metres to reach the plant site. But once there, I was thrilled by what I saw. It was a moderately large piece of land hemmed in by two hills, glistening against the bright morning sun. For a moment, I was overcome by the same ethereal feeling I had experienced when I had first seen the Kedarnath Temple set against the Garhwal Himalayas. I felt the same vibration. It was as though a divine force was sending me an internal message that this was the perfect location for the plant. It instilled in me the confidence that we would overcome every impediment in the way of building the plant here. And indeed, we had to overcome several obstacles to get the plant on stream.

From the plant site, the team took me to the mine. It was a long drive and an equally long walk downhill. What I saw made my heart sink. Everything seemed impossibly tricky here. The road leading to the site looked extraordinarily fragile and treacherous. It looked incapable of supporting the weight of the dozens of trucks that would have to travel with the limestone to the plant every day. Access to the mine from the top of the valley along narrow ledges and walking paths was equally bad.

As I looked up from the floor of the valley towards the high hills on all sides, I realized the kind of challenges that lay ahead. It would be a logistical nightmare to have the limestone sent by truck from the bottom of the valley to the main road and then to the plant. The options were either ropeway or a conveyor belt to the top of the valley where our plant would be located. It was an ascent of around 3.5 kilometres over two hills to the higher mountain on the rear where the plant was to be located. The cost implications of this were going to be massive, maybe in hundreds of crores. It was not a happy sight or a pleasant thought. I remember we were mostly silent as the team walked back to the car. I could see the look on the faces of my senior colleagues as if asking whether I was still serious about going ahead after what I had seen.

I was indeed despondent at the thought of the additional costs and the engineering challenges that lay ahead. But there was never any doubt in my mind about going forward with the project. I was confident that whatever the final cost, we were going to make it work. Mr Kulkarni and my senior team members were well aware of my thinking on this, so there was no question of backing out. All my life, I had taken risks. I think they worked every time because I had the habit of making difficult decisions without thinking of the consequences. If I worried about the potential ramifications and the costs involved, I would likely have not made those decisions. I cannot say if this was good or bad. Luckily, it worked every time. Maybe, subconsciously, I had more confidence in the abilities of my senior colleagues to execute seemingly impossible projects than they had in themselves.

Of the two people who were to lead the project, Mr Kulkarni was risk-averse himself. Still, he would never say no to a challenge I threw at him and executed even the most difficult of assignments to perfection. The other colleague was Mr A.V. Rao, our construction adviser. A no-nonsense technocrat, he was much older than all of us, a highly regarded civil engineer. He had joined us from Lakshmi Cements where he had headed construction-related activities. Mr Kulkarni, who was his colleague at the JK group, had lured him to join us to tackle the construction challenges we faced at Kodinar.

Mr Rao, like Mr Kulkarni, was not a risk-taker. But he was always determined to prove his ability to get work done. Nothing deterred him, not even the mountainous terrain of Himachal Pradesh. With these two fantastically able men by my side, the question was never about whether we would be able to execute the project. It was about how we would do it in the least possible cost and time.

Finally, it was not as if plants had not been built in these kinds of terrains before. I had seen cement plants constructed in the similarly hilly and wooded countryside of Japan and Switzerland. I was well aware that the civil engineering expertise in India in those days was not up to the level in those countries. At the same time, this project was essential for our long-term survival, considering we were not yet a million-tonne company.

The civil engineering challenges were immense. The roads leading to our plant site from the highway had to be first reinforced. Then the highway itself had to be widened in several sections to enable it to bear the load of trailer trucks carrying heavy construction equipment and large dismantled parts of the plant. In several places, we had to shift roadside shops and dhabas that hampered the free movement of vehicles. Similarly, we had to strengthen several road bridges so that they did not collapse under the massive load.

At the plant site, we had to flatten the highly uneven land and then strengthen it as well, because of the weak load-bearing capacity of the Himachal Pradesh soil. We also had to cut parts of the hill to make extra space to squeeze the plant in. Finally, we had to buttress the hills around so that there were no mudslides during the rains. This was nothing like our experience in Kodinar.

It stands to reason that every large industrial company operating in Himachal Pradesh, including ACC Gagal, would have gone through similar infrastructure problems at the time of erecting their plants. The ACC plant, though, was built on relatively flatter terrain and hence construction would have been more straightforward. Their limestone came from a nearby hill and was brought down on conveyor belts. We had the opposite problem. Our limestone mine was on the floor of the valley, while the plant was at the top, hundreds of feet above. Unlike the Gagal plant, it was not a straight climb to the top of the valley from the mine. There were two hills in between that had to be traversed. It was a civil engineering nightmare.

We had to choose the most economical and efficient option between a ropeway and a conveyor belt to get the limestone up. We sought the help of the well-known Japanese company Onoda Cement (now Taiheiyo Cement), Japan's oldest and largest cement-manufacturing company, with several such plants in similar topographies. We hired them as consultants for mining operations and the basic engineering of the plant. We also requested Usha Breco—an Usha Martin company and the only Indian manufacturer of ropeways for industrial use at that time—to make a presentation.

After much discussion, it was finally decided that the ropeway was not feasible in terms of speed, cost and maintenance. Going by our original plant size of a million tonnes (which would later go up to 1.5 million), we would have had to move 7,500 tonnes of limestone every day. For a ropeway to carry that kind of load daily would have meant designing a gigantic system, which was unviable.

The conveyor belt of the kind ACC was using at Gagal was the only other option. When we began looking for someone to build it, our first option was L&T. Their construction and engineering division had already been contracted for the civil and plant erection work. The L&T engineers surveyed the mine and the location and said that they would be able to take up the project only if we first reinforced road access to the valley. Considering the costs involved, this was out of the question. We asked a few other construction companies and all of them laid down similar conditions.

Finally, we decided to do it ourselves through our own Project Planning and Development (PPD) department. This department had been set up two years earlier on Mr Kulkarni's recommendation, to handle small in-house projects related to improving efficiencies and productivity at the Kodinar plant. Its role was later expanded to the planning and execution of all our projects in the most cost-effective manner. The department was peopled by some of the smartest technical brains in the company and headed by Mr C.N.J. Setty, a very experienced engineer hand-picked by Mr Kulkarni. A transfer to PPD was considered a matter of honour among company executives. The department played a crucial role in all the nineteen or so large projects Ambuja executed in its first twenty-five years.

~

Led by Mr Hirpara, the PPD engineers spent several months physically mapping the valley in the harsh Himachal Pradesh weather. The idea was first to create a precise engineering model of the terrain on which the conveyor belt would run. It was gruelling work. They had to set off for the mine site every day at 6 a.m. in the biting cold. Since the valley was accessible only by foot, the survey equipment had to be carried on mules, the only beast of burden in the region. Quite often, a fog would descend on the valley reducing visibility to nearly zero. The team had to wait till it cleared, sometimes for hours, before starting work again.

From the floor of the valley, the team would climb up and down two hills, before ascending the third to the top, where our plant was to be located. Each of these hills had to be scaled several times during the mapping process, sometimes using rappelling techniques while carrying surveying equipment such as theodolites and optical levels. Precision measurement was the key, because even a degree of mismatch in the modelling of the conveyor-pathway would render it inoperable.

The entire path from the mine to the top of the valley and into the plant was on a gradient. The work was so complicated that a German expert we hired for advice gave up after the first day. We were still in the pre-computer era, so all the recording and marking was done on paper. The nature of the terrain was such that we had no option but to plan for a 4-kilometre-long conveyor belt held together with trusses and no breaks in between. The belt would be laid over the first hill and would pass through the other two hills via specially drilled tunnels.

The topographic map drawn by Mr Hirpara and the team was turned into a scale model in Bombay and the best local experts were hired to design the system based on our specifications. The conveyor belt was manufactured by Krupp of Germany, a world leader in the field. Since it was to carry close to 7,500 tonnes of limestone daily, we wanted the best.

Installing the system was another big challenge. Every part was specially made as separate components and each piece carried on mules down the valley and then bolted on (since welding was out of the question in these conditions) and assembled on-site. The tunnels were planned, designed and executed by our team with the help of local contractors. The custom manufacturing and putting it all up took nearly a year. However, once it was up and running, we had no problems; a tribute to the meticulous work done by the team under Mr Rao. However, while the civil engineering work was in full flow in and around 1993, I was forced to deal with the big problem of cost overrun. The company continued to do well and we were the darling of the stock market. Still, the ballooning cost of the Himachal Pradesh project was giving me sleepless nights. Two years earlier, IDBI had assessed the cost of our million-tonne plant at around ₹267 crore. Though budgeted at 30 per cent higher than usual, to account for the additional civil work that was anticipated in Himachal Pradesh, the amount turned out to be a gross underestimation.

Civil work was now expected to cost more than the plant itself. Our estimates of the total cost were beyond ₹500 crore and this did not include the price of the grinding units. I was worried that the Himachal Pradesh project would sink the company much as the 2-million-tonne Wadi plant in Karnataka had emasculated ACC. Unfortunately, this was the time I was first diagnosed with mouth cancer (which I will talk about in detail in the next chapter). It was as if everything was going wrong now.

Our only option was to increase the capacity of the plant to spread out the cost. We called the local representative of our plant supplier Fuller, a Danish–American company, for a discussion. Our meeting took place at The Belvedere, the business club at The Oberoi in Bombay. Mr Kulkarni was with me. We briefed him about the problem we were facing and our desperate situation. I told him that at the existing capacity, we would not be able to break even.

He was unfazed. 'Even with the size of the current kiln, you can raise the production by 30 per cent,' he said. 'But if you want, at a small extra cost, we can increase its size to raise production by 50 per cent. We will have to do some slight modifications to the other parts of the plant like the raw mill, coal mill and the preheater.'

This was music to my ears. I asked him how much extra it would cost and he said ₹10 crore. I was relieved to hear that. With a marginal 2 per cent additional investment, we would be able to take our capacity to 1.5 million tonnes. That meeting saved us from a potential disaster. Nevertheless, the massive amount of civil work involved delayed completion by three years. Thereafter, working at a tremendous pace, Mr Kulkarni made sure that the plant was installed within twenty-four months.

After five years of hard work, we fired the kiln at long last in August 1995 and began commercial production a month later. It was the longest we had ever taken to build a plant. And it was the most expensive as well. But once we started production, as though by some divine intervention, our problems suddenly disappeared. Mr Kulkarni and his team were able to stabilize the plant within three months, which probably was a record for an Indian cement unit. This enabled us to achieve 100 per cent utilization in the first year itself, from where we never looked back.

The key to the success of our Himachal Pradesh project, of course, was our grinding unit in Punjab. Rupnagar was our focal point. It was built on schedule in eighteen months and went on stream as soon as the first shipment of clinkers arrived from Darlaghat. The decision to make PPC though, got us into an uncomfortable situation. North India at that time was an entirely OPC-dominated market and PPC was considered an inferior product. Ambuja, until then, had been associated with the OPC we made at Kodinar.

Our advertising and marketing communications had always hailed OPC as the most durable cement in the market. Our image, the mnemonic giant and the long-running 'giant strength' campaign, were all centred around the superior strength of OPC. The messaging had also indirectly implied that PPC, which some of our Gujarat competitors made, was inferior to OPC. The question was how to reconcile our own OPC image with the decision to manufacture PPC in north India.

The problem surfaced quite early during our first dealers' conference in Chandigarh. Since it was our first interaction with north Indian dealers, I had decided to attend the conference myself. When I reached Chandigarh airport, I was surprised to see a glum-looking Suresh Neotia waiting to receive me. He was accompanied by a few other company executives, including Mr P.C. Jain, the CEO of the Himachal Pradesh unit. For a moment, I was worried about what had happened. Suresh had never come to an airport to greet me. He immediately got to the point. 'We are in a state of confusion here. The dealers are saying that Ambuja cement has always been associated with the "Virat Strength" of OPC.

But we are making PPC here. How do we sell this cement? Why would people believe us?'

I was quite good at handling these kinds of situations. I calmed everyone down and asked them not to worry. 'You are right. We have in the past said OPC is a stronger cement than PPC. We can tell the dealers that in Punjab and north India our PPC will be superior to any OPC in the northern market.' I could see each member of our team react incredulously to my suggestion.

'How can we say that?' Mr Jain asked me, looking worried. 'Everyone knows that OPC is always stronger than PPC.'

'I will make sure that the PPC we produce in Punjab is a much stronger cement than any other OPC or PPC currently in the market,' I replied. 'You can tell the dealers that.'

No one, including me, had any idea about how I would make it happen. Just as so many times in the past, I had again spoken before thinking. Nevertheless, I told the dealers the same thing in my address so that there was no ambiguity about the message. I said, 'You can check the strength of our PPC. If you find that it is not the strongest cement in the market, you can send it back.' They seemed convinced by my confident assertion, but my team was not.

After the meeting, I told our executives that it was now entirely up to them to translate my promise into action. There was a stunned silence. I said I had already made the commitment and there was no going back. I was confident that my people would find the answer if they tried hard enough. 'Are you ready to do this?' I asked and the answer was a resounding yes. They did not have much choice. The team worked with Mr J.P. Desai, our concrete specialist and his R&D lab at Kodinar to devise a method to make the 'high-strength' PPC I wanted.

They discovered that the secret to making PPC stronger lay in grinding the clinker–fly ash mixture into extremely fine particles—the smaller the particle, the stronger the cement. There was a scientific reason for this. Fly ash is a fine powder, tinier than even cement particles. At the molecular level, the role of fly ash in construction is to fill the microscopic voids that are formed when the wet concrete mix (consisting of cement and aggregates like gravel, crushed stones and sand) combines and matures. As more and more voids get filled, they become impermeable over time, making the concrete stronger.

Fly ash is a powdery by-product of the burning of coal in a power plant. It usually consists of a mix of coarse and fine grains and is found in the exit flue gases from the plant. The flue gas is passed through a bank of electrostatic precipitators (ESPs) that capture most of the fly ash. The cleaned gas is vented to the atmosphere through the massive chimney of the power plant.

Our arrangement with the Rupnagar power plant ensured that we were able to take only the finest of the fly ash collected from the ESPs. It was pumped into the fly ash silo which we had built at our cost. It was then transferred pneumatically to our grinding unit through the specially made pipeline. This arrangement assured us the finest quality fly ash for our PPC. Fly ash is a waste product from a thermal power plant which not many people would bother to analyse. We did, with surprisingly good results and returns.

Having manufactured the high-strength PPC, the question now was how to market it. How do we get the message across to the buying public without being at cross-purposes with our earlier OPC advertising? I fell back on our marketing guru Ravi Gupta to come up with a solution. He and his team came up with an interesting answer. They decided to call our cement neither OPC nor PPC. Fly ash contains substantial amounts of silicon dioxide, which reacts with the various calcium compounds in the limestone to form calcium silicate. Their research indicated that people responded very well to the name 'Silicate'. Despite being a technical term, it created a perception of superior quality. The cement was named Cement Ambuja Silicate. The cement bags were specially designed using yellow and blue colours for a premium feel.

Our marketing message about Silicate was that Ambuja technology enabled the cement to gain strength over time. Your house built with it, which was strong to start with, would get even more durable as it aged.

To our original Ambuja brand positioning of a strong cement, we had added an additional message—a product that became more durable with time.

Cement Ambuja Silicate was unveiled at a function in Mussoorie in the presence of all the newly appointed dealers from across Punjab, Uttar Pradesh, Delhi and Haryana. Bhangra star Gurdas Maan was the star performer. We followed this up with a loud press and TV campaign in the region. The tagline in the Punjabi newspapers was 'Cement *ke* Sardar Punjab *Mein*', which worked wonders for the sales.

With the addition of 35 per cent fly ash, we were able to turn the 1.5-million-tonne clinker that Darlaghat produced, into 2 million tonnes of cement at the Rupnagar grinding plant. Because of the high demand in the Punjab region, we were able to sell our cement within a 30 to 50-kilometre radius of the plant, saving a considerable amount in transport cost. In the first year itself, we captured 20 per cent of the state market. And with no sales tax and excise duty, we ended up with a handsome profit.

In the early days, we were making over ₹100 crore in profit annually after interest and depreciation from this plant alone and were able to recoup our substantial investment within a few years. Three years later, we were able to further enhance the capacity of the Darlaghat plant to 2 million tonnes of clinker and 2.7 million tonnes of cement, by changing the preheater top with an additional investment of only ₹25 crore and that too in twenty-six days.

The best part of Darlaghat's success was that we were making high profits while running a zero-pollution plant. Part of the initial funding for the project, around ₹110 crore, had come from the World Bank. It entailed adhering to strict emission control norms, since the plant was in an ecologically sensitive zone. We did one better. We promised them that the plant would produce less pollution than even an equivalent

Swiss plant. It was a promise that we more than fulfilled. A few years later, we also got ourselves rated for environment management by the prestigious Tata Energy Research Institute (TERI; now known as The Energy and Resources Institute). They awarded us the Gold Eco-Star, their highest rating.

The Punjab government also appreciated our work in recycling more than 0.5 million tonnes of fly ash into cement annually. It was non-biodegradable waste from their thermal power plants and was, until then, dumped entirely in fly ash ponds near the power plant, rendering hundreds of hectares of farmland in the vicinity, fallow. Both in Rupnagar and in Bathinda (where we set up our second grinding unit in 1999)—and where the state's two largest thermal power units were located—we did our bit for the environment.

Darlaghat was a bittersweet experience for me. It was our longest and most challenging project. We never faced as many problems in putting up a cement plant elsewhere as we did here. Personally for me, the situation was compounded when I was diagnosed with cancer, midway through the project. On balance though, there were more positives than negatives. We created, as anyone who has been there would attest, a civil engineering marvel. And despite all the impediments, it turned out to be massively profitable. It drove the next stage of Gujarat Ambuja's growth. Secondly, the difficult challenges we were put through turned out to be a real test of character for all of us. I was glad that our grit and determination won the day. Darlaghat proved to be a tremendous confidence booster within the company. It gave us the feeling of being able to achieve anything we set out to do.

We built a reputation of being made of sterner stuff, a company that was unfazed by the biggest of challenges. We were now in the big league, having broken India's then dominant player ACC's monopoly in the northern market. Our plant was bigger, more efficient and several times more profitable. Himachal Pradesh also gave me another two lifelong lessons—first, never put up a plant in a smaller state; and second, people are not what they seem to be.

The phrase 'I Can' sums up the spirit behind the long years of struggle, hard work and leap of imagination in bringing Darlaghat to fruition. It was first coined as a corporate advertising slogan by Trikaya. But soon it evolved to become the company motto because it helped capture the passion, single-mindedness and selflessness that everyone brought to their jobs at Ambuja.

The origin of 'I Can' was intimately linked to the success of our 'Virat Compressive Strength' advertising campaign which helped establish Ambuja as India's most reliable cement. Sometime in 1991, a thought struck me: if an advertising campaign could successfully infuse a commodity like cement with character and positivity, why not harness its power to do much more? Why not use a similar advertising campaign to build a public image for all the things that we were doing at Gujarat Ambuja to make it India's best-run cement company?

I broached this idea with Ravi Gupta during one of our routine meetings. I told him, 'I have a big worry. For all practical purposes, our bad days are over and good days are starting.'

He started laughing and said, 'You are the first person who worries about good times.'

'I know I am going to be successful,' I replied, 'but I worry that people might say we are doing well only because the cement industry is currently doing very well. They won't know about all the extraordinary work we are doing to make Gujarat Ambuja a successful company. They will say the prices are going up and that's why Gujarat Ambuja is making good profits. Any cement company can make money in a good market. I do not want that kind of image for Ambuja. I would like people to know about my philosophy of how to run our company, which has produced great results.'

He asked me what my philosophy was and I summed it up: 'Unlike large companies, I don't believe in setting targets for my executives.

With Maa and Babuji on my adoption day, circa 1956.

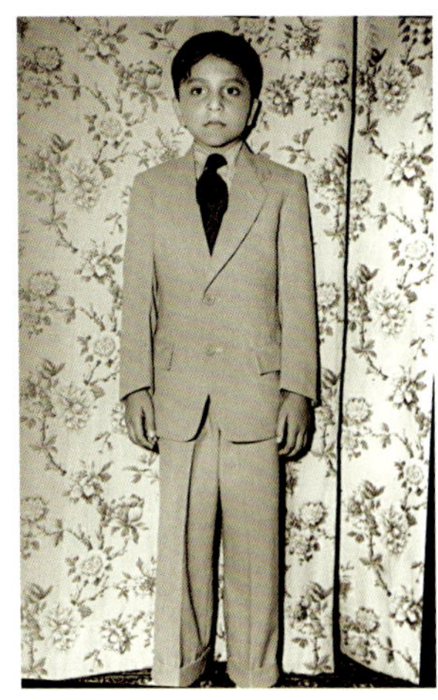

I liked to dress up even when I was very young. Posing here at at the age of 8.

This perhaps wasn't the most appropriate attire for a young cotton trader in those days, but I knew I was building myself up for the future.

Marrying Nilu in January 1971 was one of the most wonderful times of my life.

With the Class of 1970 and the faculty of chemical engineering. Much of what I am today is because of the four years I spent at the University Department of Chemical Technology, Bombay.

Early success in cotton trading allowed me the luxury of long holidays with my family. Here I am with the kids in Kashmir, circa 1976.

Bai was not just my elder sister, she was a mother and my best friend growing up.

Maa was in tears to see me travel overseas for the first time during my cotton trading days.

Nilu and I at Somnath during the temple *pran pratishtha* ceremony of the Kodinar plant, 1989.

Three generations in one frame: Maa and Babuji with Nilu and our kids, Pulkit and Padmini.

The Ambuja Cement logo and slogan were a runaway hit, making the brand a household name in the country.

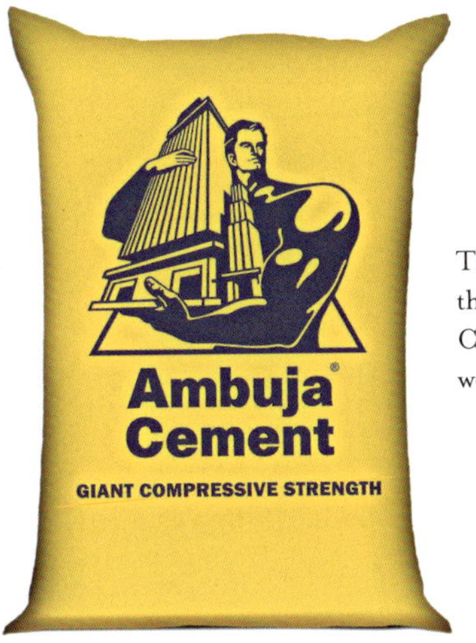

The Ambuja Cement bag with the giant and the tagline 'Giant Compressive Strength' worked wonders for us.

Our first ship *Ambuja Shikhar*, which kick-started Ambuja's shipping operations, being loaded at the port of Muldwarka, Gujarat.

The Birlas have a temple in each of their townships and I thought we should also build one. When I told my father about my idea, he could not have been happier. With Nilu at the *pran pratishtha* function of the temple at the Kodinar factory's campus.

A critical piece of our equipment, the limestone conveyor belt at the Gajambuja plant.

His smile is priceless. Physically challenged students are provided skill training as part of an Ambuja Cement Foundation project.

With my business partner Mr Vinod Neotia and team members Messrs Kulkarni, Bhosale and Kotwal during the construction phase of the Kodinar plant. L-R: Mr Vinod Neotia (wearing a safari suit with his hand in his pocket), Mr Kulkarni (he has his right hand stretched out), late Mr Kotwal (wearing a helmet, arms folded), and Mr Bhosale (in between Mr Kotwal and me).

Community development forms the core of everything we do. Here's the check dam on the Singoda river in Chhachar village, built with help from Ambuja Cement Foundation.

Atmanirbhar and proudly—the thermal power plant which made the Kodinar facility energy self-sufficent.

Aerial view of the temple inside the Kodinar factory's campus. Even though my father was frail, he took it upon himself to buy the idols for the temple.

One of the key people responsible for making it happen, our first chairman Mr H. K. Khan with his wife Hamidaji at the Kodinar project site.

Firing all cylinders, finally. The kiln at Kodinar took some time to stablize,but thanks to the efforts of Mr P.B. Kulkarni it went off smoothly.

Work finally commences at the Darlaghat plant in Himachal Pradesh, our longest and most challenging project till date.

Always acutely conscious of our role as a responsible corporate entity, we invested heavily to create one of India's greenest factory complexes in Kodinar, Gujarat. Seen here is the block crusher at Kodinar, surrounded by greenery and used mine pits filled with water.

By 2003, we were responsible for as much as 53 per cent of the country's cement exports. The Muldwarka port that year handled a record 4 million tonnes of cargo. Seen here is a vessel waiting to be loaded at Muldwarka.

Work continues full steam at the Darlaghat plant through heavy snowfall.

Early renderings of the 'I can' logo, which became a symbol of the company.

The Ambuja IPO was oversubscribed seven times. It was a success beyond our wildest expectations. Here, I am addressing one of our earliest annual general meetings after the company went public.

Feels like it was just yesterday, but it was twenty-five years ago that we laid the foundations of success. At the silver jubilee celebrations of Gujarat Ambuja in 2008.

Engineering marvel, the preheater at the Kodinar plant.

Darlaghat was challenging but it pushed us to do our best. Building these long conveyors at Darlaghat was a civil engineering feat for my team.

One of the high points of Gujarat Ambuja in its first ten years was when Aditya Birla came to the Kodinar plant. 'It seems very well run and very clean,' he told me. It is a compliment that I still treasure.

The cement mill hopper at the Gajambuja plant. We invested in additional dust control equipment like the baghouse for the cement mill at a very high cost. The maintenance cost for the dust control equipment has a direct impact on the balance sheet. But the benefits, in terms of fewer breakdowns and prolonged working life of the plant and machinery, made it worth the investment.

The Muldwaraka jetty construction goes on in full swing. The payback of our sea-transportation project went way beyond our own initial calculations.

Ambuja Cement Foundation has created a cadre of women called 'Sakhis' for health-related interventions in poor villages around our Chandrapur plant in Maharashtra. These well-trained women go from village to village providing basic healthcare-related advice, especially for women and children. Here's a Sakhi volunteer providing educational information to new mothers.

The need to achieve targets, in my opinion, invariably leads to people stressing about underperforming. It results in them lowering their goals because they are worried about not being able to meet a high target every time.' I pointed out that in such organizations, people were afraid of overachieving because they could be held to a higher target next year, which might not be achievable.

'In my view,' I said, 'this system of working, where people are always worried about failure, kills initiative and enterprise. At Gujarat Ambuja, we follow a different route. We encourage people to do their best without setting any target. We empower them and provide them with the necessary resources. Then we ask them to aim for the moon. We trust them to do their best for the company and failure is not held against them. Failure is seen as an investment in the future. Our employees own their successes while we own their failures. No targets, no budgets. Encourage everyone to do their best. It is a corporate philosophy that has achieved excellent results.'

I told Ravi that I wanted a campaign to project the Ambuja way of running a business, without boasting about our achievements. Within a week, Ravi and his young protégé Alok Nanda came back with an idea. It was called 'I Can'. The title had a ring to it; it captured the essence of what I wanted. The copy was an almost perfect elaboration of Ambuja's corporate philosophy: 'Give a man orders and he'll do his task reasonably well. But let him set his own targets, give him freedom and authority and the task becomes a personal mission'.

The ad went on to tell a granular-level story of how this corporate philosophy worked in practice at the level of the people working in the plants. The title of the story encapsulated how the project team had set up the plant in record time—'You can't build a cement plant in less than three years. We naturally did it in two'. In less than 100 words, the ad had captured it perfectly; the play was around the theme of 'I can do it faster'.

I found the campaign brilliant at various levels. Instead of shouting from the rooftops about how good we were, it told the story of our success in a style that was sensitive, subtle and engaging. The slogan 'I Can', though a simple phrase, was loaded with meaning. It superbly captured the culture that we had engendered at Ambuja, where each employee was inspired to go out of the way to do extraordinary things. They did it in the spirit of 'I Can'.

A second ad in the series ran under the heading—'We have one of the most sophisticated pollution-control systems in the world: a rose garden'. It told the story of our success in cutting down emission levels to Swiss standards. It connected our achievement to the worried farmers who came to meet us and the rose patch that we planted next to the kiln.

The 'I Can' ads ran in major newspapers across the country and were a great success. They helped boost the image of Gujarat Ambuja by successfully positioning us as a professionally managed company that used modern management techniques, ethical practices and social commitment to stay ahead in the game. The 'I Can' ads were hailed as a pioneering example of corporate advertising to boost the image of a company, as against only selling its products.

We continued with the series for many years. Each ad spoke about various aspects of our growth story, including rising efficiency levels and capacity utilization, the pioneering sea-transportation project, our success at getting the ISO 9002 quality certification for our plants that was a first in the Indian cement industry and much more.

With the success of these ads, corporate advertising became a key area of business for ad agencies in the country. Dozens of companies, big and small, used it to build public profiles. Many failed because you have to be truthful about what you mention in these ads. I remember Ravi telling me a story a few years later about a well-known industrialist calling him with a request for a similar campaign. When Ravi asked him about the message that he wanted to convey, the industrialist told him to make something up. Ravi had to tell him that such an ad campaign would not serve any purpose. He could not build him a lasting image based on nothing, which was what lies amounted to.

While the 'I Can' ads helped reposition Gujarat Ambuja in the eyes of investors and the public, it had an equally powerful impact inside the company. For our employees, it was a validation and recognition of the excellent work they had done over the years. It instilled a sense of pride in them for what they had done and what the company had achieved. Over the years, 'I Can' itself became a rallying cry and an anthem within Gujarat Ambuja. The simple expression could be understood and interpreted by anyone. Its power of exhortation and persuasion carried the force to motivate and inspire people to do their best for the company, to push boundaries, to innovate and achieve the best results.

Like the mnemonic of the giant, it has evolved to become a trademark statement of intent of the company. Its most recent interpretation goes like this:

- The 'I CAN' spirit encapsulates the management philosophy at Ambuja Cement Ltd.
- It signifies that every individual contributes to the best of his potential to achieve the collective goal of many. This process of tapping individual initiative for team synergy is at the heart of the culture nurtured over the years.
- It emboldens employees to have an equal voice in the functioning of any system that they are a part of, enabling them to achieve goals more efficiently as a team.
- Ambuja Cement entered the cement business with the driving conviction that challenges are there to be met and opportunities are meant to be seized. As a David among the established Goliaths, Ambuja Cement saw a way to put the competition at a disadvantage by achieving maximum efficiency and productivity at the lowest cost.
- The 'I CAN' rationale promotes the virtues of accountability and empowerment at each level. It keeps the employees motivated by letting them share equal responsibility.

I could not have said it better myself.

9

Stepping into the Unknown

Failed acquisitions • Making history with sea transportation • Travails of Darlaghat • Gajambuja is born

We began exploring other expansion opportunities in the early 1990s, when it became clear that the Darlaghat project would take more time than expected. One route I seriously pursued, though not very successfully, was acquisitions. My first attempt was sometime in 1990, when the cement division of Coromandel Fertilizer was put on sale by the Madras-based Murugappa Group. It was a relatively new million-tonne plant located in Chilamkur, in southern Andhra Pradesh's Cuddapah district. Set up in 1980, it had fallen on bad times on account of poor management, electricity problems and poor-quality coal. There were two bidders besides us—L&T and the Madras-based India Cements Ltd.

I was quite keen to get a foothold in the fast-growing southern market and this seemed like a good opportunity. At around ₹92 crore, ours was the highest bid and we should have got the plant under normal circumstances. I was at that time, not aware of the resolute ways of my friend Mr N. Srinivasan. He had recently regained management control of India Cements after a ten-year battle with his extended family. He would later become famous for his role as BCCI president. But in those days, he was keen to prove himself on the Madras business scene after spending nearly a decade in the wilderness. He offered the Murugappas ₹10 crore more than our winning bid.

The Murugappa people called to tell me about Mr Srinivasan's new offer. They wanted to know if I was willing to top it. I was furious. It was unethical to the core, as they had committed that the highest bidder would get the plant and that there would be no negotiations once the bid was opened. 'What is the point of open competitive bidding if you are going to use it only for price discovery and then get the loser to outbid the winning bid?' I asked them. 'What is the guarantee you won't ask Mr Srinivasan to outbid me again if I offer you more money? I am not interested in this way of doing business.'

The plant went to Mr Srinivasan. Later, when I heard about how he operates, I was relieved that I did not buy Coromandel Cement. Mr Srinivasan guarded his southern territory zealously and he would not have let me settle down. I also learnt that Cuddapah district in Andhra Pradesh, with its infrastructure and employee-related issues, was not the easiest of places to operate a cement company. As for Mr Srinivasan, this was to be the first of my many run-ins with him.

My second tryst with a failed acquisition came roughly around the same time. This time it involved CCGL, the second cement company (besides Saurashtra Cement) of the Mahendra Mehta group, our big Gujarat rival. Its recently built million-tonne plant in Junagadh district had been delayed on account of which the company was in bad shape. Moreover, the company had recently been declared sick by the Board for Industrial and Financial Reconstruction (BIFR).

Every time we met IDBI executives, they would tell us about the problems they were having with CCGL's loan dues. Once, for a lark, I told them that if they allowed Ambuja to take over the company, we would clear the loans and invest in the company's revival. The executives got excited and put up our suggestion for discussion at their next board meeting. They were so convinced of getting the board's approval that they told us to be prepared to take over the company. In my exuberance, I shared the news with a few colleagues in office. My secretary got to know of this and shared the story with my brother-in-law Arvind Nopany. He was also a business associate of Gujarat Ambuja and was based out of Baroda. He told some industry people in Baroda that Ambuja would be taking over CCGL in the next few days. The news somehow reached the owners of the company. They were very well connected in Delhi and called their friends in the government who rushed to their aid.

Lo and behold, the deal was settled. The message was: 'No Indian company should be allowed to take over another company. We do not want a Swaraj Paul–Escorts kind of takeover scenario.' The CCGL board met as expected but did not take up the matter. I had only myself to blame for mishandling this chance at an acquisition.

The drama was repeated two years later, this time when the CCGL case came up before BIFR, the statutory government body tasked with reviving sick companies. At the final hearing in the BIFR court, IDBI once again argued vehemently that the only way out was to sell CCGL to a stronger player like Gujarat Ambuja, which had the ability and the inclination to invest and revive the company. As the arguments continued, we got a feeling that even the BIFR chairman was inclined towards inviting us to take over. But in its final verdict, BIFR mysteriously went against its own rule of not allowing existing promoters any role in the revival and handed the company back to the Mehtas.

The three failed attempts and the unsavoury incidents around them soured my attitude towards acquisitions. It convinced me that for some reason, I was not good at it. As a result, I steered clear of this route of expansion for many years, before successfully taking over DLF Cements and Modi Cement towards the late 1990s. But even those were not the best of experiences. I was happiest when setting up our own plants.

Getting more cement out of our existing facility was now impossible. We had pushed the Ambujanagar plant to its limit. The capacity utilization had peaked at 149 per cent in 1992. Anything beyond this would damage the plant. The question was, how and where were we to grow? Staying still was the worst thing for a young company like ours. We, no doubt, had the option of putting up a new plant at Ambujanagar. But where would we sell the cement? Gujarat was by then a saturated market.

The only options were the smaller market of Rajasthan or the large Bombay region. But from our location in south-eastern Saurashtra, Rajasthan was over 700 kilometres away and Bombay nearly 1,000 kilometres by rail and much more by road. At the prevailing freight cost, sending large quantities of cement to Rajasthan or Bombay by train was unfeasible. We would have never been able to compete with established players in the market because of our high cost. We knew this because we had been sending a few thousand tonnes of cement to Bombay every month by train. My idea was to seed the market, in the hope that someday we would have a larger presence there.

As has often happened with me in the past, destiny has a way of intervening when things are looking grim. A young Danish student came to see me around this time. He was in India writing a research paper for his university project on sea transportation of cement in India. Since we were closest to the coast, he wanted to use us as a case study about the feasibility of transporting cement by ship from the Gujarat coast to Bombay. Though the study would cost around ₹50 lakh, it was to be paid for by the Danish International Development Agency (DANIDA) that funds development work in emerging markets. As it was no cost to us, I asked him to go ahead.

A few years earlier, in 1988, not long after we started commercial production, we had explored sea transport as a way of cutting down our cost of getting cement to Bombay. I had got my senior executives Mr

Hirpara and Mr Prabhu Rajaram, to work out the logistics of sending a small shipment of 700 tonnes to Bombay by sea. We sent it by truck to Veraval, the nearest port, around 45 kilometres from Kodinar. There it was loaded on to a barge to be taken to the cargo port at Hay Bunder in Sewri, on south Bombay's eastern edge. Unfortunately, it was the monsoon and the barge ran aground, destroying our entire shipment.

Following this disaster, I got Mr Rajaram to spend time at Essar Shipping to study the basics of coastal shipping. We sent another shipment after he came back. This time we chartered an entire cargo ship to transport 2,300 tonnes of cement. The shipment did reach the market, but we were not too happy with the way the cement was handled and the resultant wastage. The cement bags had been manually transferred from the trucks to the ship in Gujarat. The same action was repeated at the port in Bombay. From there the cement was transported by truck to the retailer's warehouse.

Multiple manual handling resulted in substantial leakage of cement, dust emission, long waiting time and high labour cost, which made the operation unviable. Add to these, the cumbersome and time-consuming bureaucratic procedures at the government-run ports. That is when we decided that sea transportation to Bombay in this form was not worth the effort or the money. However, the decision of the Western Railway General Manager to raise our freight charge made me revisit the idea.

Like many international cement companies, I wanted to explore the possibility of setting up our own ports in Kodinar and Bombay and to use our own ships to transport the cement. It was not a radically new idea. One of our rivals, Narmada Cement, was already transporting cement clinkers made at its plant in Jafarabad about 100 kilometres north of Kodinar, by barges to the company's grinding unit in Surat, across the Gulf of Khambhat.

Clinkers are tiny cement nodules and transporting them is relatively easier than transporting cement. Both are different from the handling perspective, particularly in the case of sea transportation. Cement reacts instantly with moisture and degrades into clumps, which makes it virtually useless. Clinker, on the other hand, is relatively more stable. It deteriorates if subjected to moisture over a prolonged period. What we were planning was to ship bulk cement, which no other company in the country had done before.

Everything depended on getting permission from the local government, as well as the land for our private port. If we did manage to pull it off, we would be at a tremendous advantage in the Bombay market. We would decrease our transportation cost by nearly 70 per cent, while reducing the time taken to under a day. In contrast, the two dominant players in the Bombay market at that time, ACC and L&T, were sending cement from plants located 580 kilometres and 850 kilometres away, respectively. I was eagerly looking forward to what the DANIDA-funded research had to say.

It was an excellent report, comprehensive and authoritative. It convincingly made the case that sea transportation would be hugely beneficial to us in terms of cost and time. In great detail, the report delved into the infrastructural feasibility of the project. It talked about a scenario of us building a port near Kodinar. The report was supported by valuable research material from two premier government establishments, Pune-based Central Water and Power Research Station (CWPRS) and Delhi-based Water and Power Consultancy Services (WAPCOS) which specialized in coastal mapping, port construction and ship hydrodynamics.

This report convinced me of the enormous benefits of using the sea route to transport cement from Kodinar to Bombay. But when I first mooted the idea in the office, everyone was aghast. Those were the days when in most people's minds, it was unthinkable for a private company to set up ports, build ports and run ships. The common belief was that only the government could do it. My finance people thought I had gone mad. The cost of building a port and the breakwater alone would be half the cost of the plant and they reminded me that we had only one plant with a capacity of 7,00,000 tonnes, at that time. We should not be overconfident others said, pointing to the construction problems we were having in Darlaghat. My thinking, though, was very different. What we needed was a leap of imagination.

Though Gujarat today has more than thirty captive company ports, there were hardly any at that time. I was confident about selling my idea to the Gujarat government. For the project to succeed, we also needed to build a suitable port in Bombay. That, I knew, was not going to be easy.

~

Once again fate played a hand and this piece of the puzzle too fell into place by happenstance.

A few years earlier, I had helped my old friend Mr R.C. Sinha in selling CIDCO's first luxury housing project. Mr Sinha was an IAS officer of the Maharashtra cadre and at that time the MD of the City and Industrial Development Corporation (CIDCO; the Maharashtra government agency charged with developing the 'New Bombay' project, now Navi). I had got to know Mr Sinha well in the early 1980s, when I had helped him and the Maharashtra government recover cotton export dues from the Romanian government (discussed earlier in the book).

In the intervening period, Mr Sinha had built a reputation as a no-nonsense civil servant with the ability to get big projects done. It was because of this image that then Maharashtra CM, Sharad Pawar, had put him in charge of reviving the New Bombay project. Though conceived in the 1970s as a sister city of Bombay, it had turned moribund with time and was seen as a suburb of Bombay known for its cheaper housing colonies, built for industrial workers escaping Bombay's high real estate prices.

The New Bombay that we see today is largely Mr Sinha's creation. When he took over, CIDCO's finances were so bad that he had to borrow money from the market to pay the employees. But in less than five years he transformed New Bombay into a vibrant, well-planned metropolis—with fancy housing projects, malls, modern office complexes and some of India's best-looking railway stations, designed by the country's leading architects, for use by a suburban train network linked to Bombay.

The project that really helped Mr Sinha transform New Bombay's image was an upmarket gated NRI housing complex of 1,200 flats. Called Seawoods, it is still a landmark in the city three decades later. Mr Sinha had conceived of it as a project whose success would draw others to come and invest in the city. His plan was ambitious. He would pre-sell the flats and use the money for the construction. He had no experience in housing but managed to convince the well-known Bombay-based architect Hafeez Contractor to design the complex and promised potential residents world-class amenities.

No one in the Maharashtra government, including fellow bureaucrats, state ministers or the CM himself believed that the project would work. The image of the Maharashtra government as a provider of housing was poor and so was the image of CIDCO. Even leading builders in Bombay were calling Mr Sinha to say that such a large-size upmarket project would never work in New Bombay.

Mr Sinha had negotiated full autonomy for his decision-making process from Chief Minister Pawar, when he took over CIDCO. He had the courage of his convictions, but was still nervous that the plan would flop, in which case his name would be mud in government circles. It was in this state of mind that he had come to see me. I saw his presentation and was convinced it would work. Out of 1,200 flats, he told me that he had to sell a minimum of 780 units to break even; the rest would be CIDCO's profit.

I told him that if the NRI plan failed for any reason, I would buy 350 flats and get my friends to buy another 350. That gave him some peace of mind because then he would have to sell only eighty more flats to break even. I got the Ambuja advertising agency to work on the project, create a slick brochure and a classy advertising campaign.

Mr Sinha did a great job conducting IPO-style roadshows in various cities around the world, including London, New York, Los Angeles and Dubai. When the day of the sale arrived, he was shocked by the response.

A large number of the apartments were sold before noon on the first day itself! He called me in the evening to say that I wouldn't have to buy my promised 700 apartments since his sales had already exceeded that number. In Bombay, the queue outside the CIDCO office was so long that he had to call the cops for security. Within a few days, all 1,200 units were sold.

The project proved to be a massive success and a big image booster for Mr Sinha and New Bombay. Overnight, the twin city became a desirable location for Bombay's middle-class. Builders flooded CIDCO with applications to construct new apartment complexes and shopping centres. Several large companies expressed their desire to shift some of their offices to the upcoming central business district. So did many Central and state government agencies. The building of an entirely new city suddenly picked up pace after being in limbo for more than a decade. Not surprisingly, within a few years, construction activities were to be seen everywhere in New Bombay.

It was around this time that I had mentioned my sea-transportation idea to Mr Sinha. I wanted a piece of coastal land to build a port and onshore facilities to receive my cement shipment. I planned to approach the newly built Jawaharlal Nehru Port Trust (JNPT), at Nhava Sheva, 40 kilometres outside Bombay. But Mr Sinha dissuaded me saying that the bureaucracy at JNPT would thwart me. Instead, he offered to give me a piece of sea-facing land at the southern end of New Bombay to build a port. 'It is our land and so the decision process will be faster,' he told me. In Mr Sinha's opinion, the port we proposed would be a business activity which was in sync with his objective of attracting large corporates to the city. From CIDCO's point of view, this would be a business partner facility. They saw us as a supplier for high-quality bulk cement at a cheaper rate, without the wastage involved in transporting vast quantities of cement in bags by trucks and trains.

Around January 1991, CIDCO allotted us the land for the port. I was not aware that CIDCO land could be used to build a private port. It was a godsend for us because the port we were looking to develop would be closer to Bombay than JNPT. I gladly took up Mr Sinha's offer and bought the land without having seen it. But when I went there with my team for an inspection, we were not very happy. The 10-acre property was part of a marshland abutting a hill by the Ulwe creek near Panvel town. Besides the issue of reclaiming the land from the marsh, the bigger problem was that the creek was shallow and the water level was subject to the action of the prevailing tide.

While it was okay for small fishing boats, we planned to use ocean-going cargo ships. The water level was only about a metre at low tide and around 4 metres at high tide. I asked Mr Sinha, who had accompanied us, how we could build a port under these circumstances. His answer was simple: high tide comes in twice a day and you can bring the ship in at high tide and take it out at the next high tide.

After the initial disappointment, we realized that we did not have much choice. The positives far outweighed the negatives. We could use the time between the tides for unloading and maintenance. On the plus side, if we got permission from the state government, which Mr Sinha told me should not be a problem, we would have a private port close to Bombay over which we would have full control.

Two years later, we began building the port and the cement silos. We did run into some problems with nearby villagers, but were able to earn their trust by investing in their village infrastructure through funds we had allocated for corporate social responsibility (CSR) activities. As Mr Sinha had promised, we didn't have any problems getting the necessary approvals from the state government. Our project fell under the purview of minor ports, for which no permissions were needed from the Central government.

In keeping with our principle as a responsible corporate citizen, we built a showcase port, one that looked more like a garden. We used the best dust-control equipment to ensure that no cement particles escaped into the air around the creek. We did not want in any way to breach the trust that Mr Sinha and the state government had placed in us when allocating the land. (I have discussed the building of the port below, as it ran in tandem with the building of the port in Gujarat.)

I had always been confident that the project of building our own ports in Maharashtra and Gujarat would be a reality once we had all the permissions in hand. Between the two states, Maharashtra was unpredictable and complicated in my view and now that was sorted. We were extremely fortunate because it turned out that we were the first and last private company to be permitted by CIDCO to set up a port near Bombay. I knew Gujarat would be relatively more straightforward.

As expected, the Gujarat government was more than encouraging. Their first suggestion when I approached them was to recruit the highly regarded and recently retired chairman of the Gujarat Maritime Board, Mr M.V. Vora, as an adviser. He would be the best man for the job, I was told. It turned out to be true. I am not sure if we would have been able to do everything that we did, that too in record time, without his overall supervision. A civil engineer who was still only sixty, he was at that time arguably the most knowledgeable person about port construction in Gujarat. Despite his tremendous knowledge and experience about the port scene in the state, he was a simple man, incredibly unassuming, soft-spoken and humble. He readily agreed to join the company as the adviser for the Gujarat operation.

After he had a look at the DANIDA-funded report, Mr Vora said that there was no reason we could not set up our port somewhere near Kodinar. I asked him about the horror stories one heard of other minor ports—of small ports in Porbandar and Veraval being washed away after a few years. They had been washed away, he replied, because they were poorly designed and badly constructed. 'Because of the corruption involved, poor-quality cement and steel was used, which you cannot do for building a port. If built properly, I don't see why any port would be washed away,' he said. Most people had discouraged me, saying that only large commercial ports survived in India. Mr Vora convinced me otherwise.

I asked him to prepare a project report on building a port near Kodinar. It would take a minimum of nine months, he told me. Besides on-site research and analysis, the most crucial part of the study was the modelling tests at CWPRS and WAPCOS. They would create scale models of the port and the precise seabed topography of the intended location, undertake laboratory simulation of the tide and wave action seen in the region and then evaluate the results. It was a long-drawn process and the design and durability of the ports were entirely dependent on their study.

We constituted a team led by Mr Hirpara to find a suitable location for our port in and around Kodinar. They explored the entire coastline from Veraval (45 kilometres to the northwest of Kodinar) to Una (45 kilometres to the east) to find the right location. There were not many sheltered seafront areas in the region, so we eventually settled for a small fishing village named Muldwarka, about 11 kilometres from our Kodinar plant. The water depth here was adequate for mid-sized ocean-going vessels and a small hillock on one side provided some protection from the wind.

With the location finalized, the next task was to build the ports and the accompanying facilities at both locations. In Bombay, we needed to set up a packing plant as well, because the cement was to be transported in bulk and then distributed from our port. An equally big task was to procure the right kind of bulk-carrying ships that would suit our port requirement. We were new to this task and no private sector company in India had the expertise in this area. We decided to send our go-to person in these matters, Mr Hirpara, to countries around the world to study sea transportation and ports of the kind we wanted to set up. He did some research and suggested that we appoint Lassing Dibben Pacific, a Canadian bulk-handling engineering specialist as a consultant to help us plan the project.

Coincidentally, the consulate general of Canada in Bombay was then talking to business houses to enhance Indo-Canadian trade. Mr Hirpara got to know about this and persuaded the Canadians to fund Lassing Dibben for a detailed study and analysis of the project. Their team visited India to study the Muldwarka–Bombay coastline and Mr Hirpara visited Canada to see their facility and the work they had done. We benefited considerably from their advice. They also opened doors for us around the world to ship designers, equipment suppliers, manufacturers of bulk handling and other port equipment.

Subsequently, our engineers travelled around the world visiting bulk terminals, shipbuilders, equipment makers and cement companies that use sea transportation. It gave us an excellent perspective on what companies were doing around the world. We decided to take the best of what everyone had to offer and get the ships built to our requirements and specifications.

Next we approached the local construction companies in Muldwarka and Bombay to build the ports. But we were put off by the kind of prices they were quoting. After much discussion, we decided to design and build the ports ourselves under the watchful eyes of our very own Mr Rao and Mr Vora. I had full trust in both these gentlemen, so I knew the ports were in good hands. The work itself was contracted to specialist port-construction companies.

Like the ports, the bulk cement-carrying ships also needed to be custom-made, because of the port conditions in New Bombay. The cargo hold and the handling equipment were designed to our specifications, because we were planning to transport bulk cement and not clinkers. Our engineers found a cement company in the Malaysian region of Langkawi that was using sea transport in shallow-water port conditions like ours. Our engineers visited the port and came back with valuable feedback. Their ships had flat bottoms and featured a self-unloading system, which we thought would be useful for us. Our engineers met the ship's designer and got many ideas from him.

Our research took us to Shiptech Pte, a Singapore-based firm founded by an expat Britisher, which specialized in bulk carriers. The specifications itself were based on a mix of references our engineers had seen around the world. The Malaysians gave us the idea of the flat bottom. The cement-handling system inside the ship was based on what the team saw in Denmark. The aeration system in the hold was based on a ship under construction in Singapore. The system handling the cement at the port was based on a bulk cement terminal in Stockholm.

For building the ships, our first instinct was to approach the best shipyards in Canada, Singapore and several European countries to do the job. But when they quoted exorbitant prices, we thought it was best we got it made in India, under the supervision of international consultants. We hired FT Everard & Co, one of the oldest and most reputed shipbuilders in the UK, as our adviser. We hired a few Indian advisers as well.

After exploring all options, we contracted the work to ABG Shipyard, a Surat-based company that had recently started operations. They specialized in barges and other kinds of bulk carriers at their yard in Surat. Their founder Rishi Agarwal was a nephew of the Ruias of Essar for whom they had built bulk carriers. I knew the Ruias and Rishi well. When I first spoke to Rishi, he was excited but also nervous about taking on the project.

We were looking to build three ships to start with, each with a capacity of 2,500 tonnes. In terms of capacity, they were much bigger than what ABG had built till then. Then there were the complexities of the design of the kind of cement carrier we wanted. I assured him that we would fully support him, including having our experts stationed at the Surat shipyard. We negotiated a reasonable price, which was almost a third of what was quoted by international companies.

We spared no expense in getting our ships built to the highest international shipping standards in terms of robustness, safety and functionalities. We sourced the best equipment from around the world. The main engines came from Yanmar, Japan, a world leader in our class of vessels. The cement-handling equipment came from BMH Marine, Sweden and the onshore cargo-handling system was designed and supplied by another Swedish company, Consilium.

Looking at the scale of the task, Rishi wanted three years to deliver the first ship, but I convinced him to do it in one. Three years would have been unthinkable. The timing had to match the completion schedule of our new million-tonne plant coming up adjacent to our existing facility at Ambujanagar. We named it Gajambuja and work on it had started as soon as our sea-transportation plans had been finalized. The entire production from this plant was targeted at the Bombay market. The ships and the port facilities were expected to cost us in the region of ₹75 crore, while the new plant was priced at around ₹270 crore. It was an expensive project and there was no time to waste.

When work on the ships started, we began our search for an experienced industry professional to head our shipping operations. The first to respond to our recruitment ad was Sudhansh Gupta, a young man still in his early thirties who was already a fleet manager with eight ships under him at Century Shipping. I met him with William Everard, the MD of FT Everard, our consultant from the UK for the project, who had come from London. We were impressed by what we heard and Sudhansh's credentials. He came across as simple, straightforward, honest and methodical in his approach to work and responsibility. He seemed right for the 'I Can' culture we were fostering in the company.

At the next meeting, I made him an offer, which he accepted. I was relieved that he had agreed to join. He was on a fast career path and we were still a small company venturing into an area that was alien to all of us. We sent him to London to spend time at the ships and facilities of FT Everard and see the operations of cement companies around Europe who were using sea transportation.

Our ports were under construction and the ships still being built when Sudhansh joined. He immediately took charge and built a strong team. The Gajambuja plant went on stream in June 1993 and our first ship was delivered two months later. The ports in Muldwarka and Panvel became operational in December that year and ABG delivered the other two ships by March the following year.

The shipping operations proved their worth almost immediately. The journey from Kodinar to Bombay was cut down by nearly 850 kilometres to just 315 kilometres, the travelling time to less than a day and our transportation cost dropped by more than 70 per cent to ₹189 a tonne. That was nearly 60 per cent less than what the established players like ACC and L&T were paying to ferry their cement by train to Bombay.

Much was now dependent on Sudhansh and his team delivering on the efficiency parameters. Coastal shipping in India, except for a few cases, had failed because of poor management. Sudhansh proved to be an asset, a valuable member of our core team. He hit the ground running, imbibing the Ambuja culture of efficiency and productivity remarkably early. Our ships made the Muldwarka–Panvel journey in less than twenty hours. And despite the tide constraints, they were turned around in fifteen hours.

~

In the first year of operation, the ships carried 7.5 lakh tonnes of cement. And with minor modifications, we were able to import coal through Muldwarka as well. It ensured cheaper and much better quality coal for both our cement plants and the captive power plant. In the first year alone, we imported a million tonnes of coal. And in the same year, we exported nearly 2 lakh tonnes of cement from Muldwarka. This figure would rise to a million tonnes over the next few years. The pay back of our sea-transportation project thus went way beyond our own initial calculations.

Unlike other shipping companies which started with a bang and then withered away, Sudhansh managed to improve our turnaround time with every passing year. Each ship was making more than 150 trips a year, with virtually no downtime, like our cement plants. It was mainly on account of the excellent maintenance facility that we had built in Panvel. Except for some major repairs, we did everything ourselves. It is one of the reasons that more than twenty-five years later, our fleet of ten ships is as efficient today as the day they were launched.

Around the world, the average life of a cement carrier is around ten to fifteen years. However, our first three ships from the 1993 to '94 period are still as good as they were when they first arrived. Sudhansh tells me that they are good for another twenty-five years. It is a remarkable testimony to the great work done by our maintenance people and ABG Shipyard's rugged design.

I remember, at the time of our negotiations with ABG, some of my senior colleagues wondered whether I was taking an unnecessary risk. They felt Rishi Agarwal was too young (he was still in his late twenties) and lacked experience for fabricating the kind of ships we wanted to be built. But I was confident that his company would deliver. And they did, consistently. We would get them to build four more ships over the next decade.

The early success of Panvel and Muldwarka immediately spurred us to build a port in Surat. The highly industrialized area in and around Gujarat's second-largest city was our most significant market in the state. It was located nearly 600 kilometres by road from our plant and this made our cement much more expensive to sell there, than that of most of our competitors. Sea transportation would cut down that distance to less than 150 kilometres, giving us the price advantage.

We got Mr Vora, who knew the area intimately, to explore a suitable location. On his advice, we built the port at Magdalla, near the mouth of River Tapti. WAPCOS suggested a T-port, like that in Panvel. The challenge here was the soft soil and erosion. The tide problem was like that of Panvel, which we had mastered by then. This port was built and made operational in considerably less time. Over the years, we extended our shipping operations to south India by building ports in Mangalore and Kochi (earlier Cochin, the city was renamed Kochi in 1996).

When we started work on our interstate coastal sea-transportation project, it was seen as a revolutionary idea that was beyond the imagination of any private company in India. We were, in that sense, pioneers. Soon after our success, dozens of other companies began replicating the strategy. Our success was a testimony of our ability to think outside the box, coupled with our skill in handling complex projects. They were beyond our area of expertise, but we were able to execute them to perfection. We had once again taken a big risk and come out on top.

The start of production and the arrival of our first ship, *Ambuja Shikhar*, happened when I was in New York for my first cancer surgery. It was a source of immense joy and satisfaction for me during a tough time in my life. Like our other seemingly impossible venture, the Darlaghat plant, the success of our sea-transportation strategy was a triumph of will for my colleagues. They believed in my vision and worked to make it possible. Successful organizations are built by the spirit of the people who work in them. It is never the technology, but how you use it that matters. It is never the idea, but how you implement it and break new ground that leads to excellence. I was lucky I was leading such an organization at Ambuja.

In our quest for expansion, before we embarked on the sea-transportation project, I had bought a company called Indo-Nippon Special Cements from the Bombay-based KEC International, which had a licence for limestone mining in the Marwar–Mundwa area of central Rajasthan. My thinking was that if all else failed, I would use the licence to put up a plant in Rajasthan to service the northern market. We were then a darling of the stock market and a bit of arrogance had crept into me. I knew I would be able to raise money to fund any new project I floated. Shortly after that though, it became clear that our idea of sea-transportation to and from Muldwarka to Bombay would become a reality. So we put the Rajasthan plant on hold and turned our attention towards the new Gajambuja plant in Kodinar.

~

Our original plan was for a 7,00,000-tonne plant next to the existing Ambujanagar plant. Then we found out that we would be eligible for tax concessions if the new plant was set up as a separate legal entity. So, we decided to raise the capacity to a million tonnes and put it up next door, with a common boundary wall separating the two plants. That way the plants were physically separated but shared a common infrastructure leading to significant savings in erection and running costs.

As per our ambitious schedule, shipping operations were to start mid-1993. Mr Kulkarni drew up an equally aggressive plan to erect the Gajambuja plant in twelve months from the time we ordered the equipment. He wanted the cement to be dispatched by the end of twelve months. If we succeeded, it would undoubtedly be a world record. The project cost, estimated at ₹270 crore, was raised through a rights issue and debentures and Mr Kulkarni's team began work simultaneously. The share price in April 1992 had peaked at ₹675 and settled at around ₹350 towards the time of the issue in October. Not surprisingly, the response from shareholders was tremendous. The key to Mr Kulkarni's accelerated timetable was to order the same equipment that we used next door at Ambujanagar from the same suppliers, Krupp Polysius of Germany. Familiarity with the equipment would help reduce installation and engineering time. As for the manufacturer, he was already in possession of the drawings and the specs for the customized equipment from our earlier order and thus things would move faster. Also, the plant supplier gave us an extremely competitive price as it was a repeat order and he would save on design and fabrication costs.

The compressed schedule was announced to our employees, contractors, suppliers and our corporate office. The response was electric. Every agency tried their best to deliver before time. No one wanted to be seen as the laggard that was responsible for the delay if it were to happen. The only suitable land near our plant was an adjoining excavated limestone mine quarry. The decision was made to ask our mining department to reclaim the gigantic pit. They did an excellent job of transporting and filling it with close to 5,00,000 tonnes of marl from our newer limestone mine in a matter of weeks. The civil work started within four months and the equipment started arriving soon after.

Mr Kulkarni called me one day to inform me about our high-tension motor supplier's inability to keep to our schedule. I asked him to cancel the order and get a new supplier even if it meant spending more money. I did not want to curb the enthusiasm of the team. I was sure that early commissioning of the plant would more than make up for the extra expense.

A similar situation arose with the international supplier of the kiln tyres. Though the manufacturer promised to have it ready earlier than usual, transportation by ship from Germany was expected to take more than a month. Mr Kulkarni asked me for approval to have it transported by air, which I gave immediately. His team then started hunting for a charter aircraft that could carry the three sets of tyres, each weighing more than 25 tonnes. They could locate only one transport aircraft in the world at that time that could take such a heavy load. But it was in Russia, a country that was in chaos in the aftermath of the break-up of the Soviet Union. As a result, procuring the necessary permissions proved to be too complicated and time-consuming. Our team abandoned the idea of expedited delivery and instead worked on compressing the installation time.

Everything went almost as planned and Mr Kulkarni and his team were able to finish the installation by early 1993. It took only a few weeks to stabilize the plant and we started commercial production in March that year, within thirteen months of ordering the first set of equipment. We missed our twelve-month target by a month on account of supplier constraint, but I think it was still a world record for setting up a cement plant that size.

Mr Kulkarni had followed up his success—putting up the original Kodinar plant in record time—with this equally groundbreaking performance with Gajambuja (and Gajambuja II a few years later). He is the man responsible for making Ambujanagar what it is today. The company recognized this feat by dedicating the Ambujanagar staff colony and the clubhouse to Mr Kulkarni and to Mr Jain, our commercial head at that time, who made a significant contribution as well. I recall our director Mr Bhakta complimenting us at the board meeting soon after, saying that not many company promoters would recognize the accomplishments of their own people in the manner we did.

We also learnt a few lessons from the Gajambuja project experience. First, the project leader needs to announce the schedule, however ambitious, well in advance and to convince all partners, including colleagues and suppliers, to try their best to stick to it. Second, the top management needs to make quick decisions to overcome unexpected hurdles that are inevitable despite the best of planning. Finally, the project team itself should be empowered as much as possible to take decisions at their level. These key learnings stood us in good stead when we implemented other projects in the subsequent years.

With Gajambuja, the ports at Muldwarka and Panvel and our first ship *Ambuja Shikhar* all fully functional by late 1993, Bombay—India's biggest cement market—was now closer to Kodinar than most prominent cities of Gujarat. Our seeding activity over the years had already created a small market for us in India's biggest cement market. We used to sell about 5,000 tonnes every month, which was sent by train. Once our silo became functional at Panvel, the figure rose to 10,000 and then to 20,000 tonnes.

The city, with its annual cement consumption of 2 million tonnes, was an intensely competitive market. It was at that time dominated by established giants ACC, L&T and Aditya Birla group's Indian Rayon subsidiary Rajashree Cement. No existing player likes competition and our Bombay friends were no different. Their approach was even more aggressive than what we had faced in Gujarat from the likes of Saurashtra Cement and Digvijay Cement. They ganged up and tried to bludgeon us with the biggest arsenal in their armoury: price. They depressed the cement price to ₹90 a bag, whereas in Gujarat it was ₹100.

Our competitors thought we would not be able to match their low prices, since we had already incurred considerable cost in setting up the new marine infrastructure. But they were bringing their cement to Bombay from considerable distances—Indian Rayon (550 kilometres), ACC (580 kilometres) and L&T (850 kilometres)—thus incurring substantial transportation costs. In contrast, my variable cost was a third of L&T's and half that of Rajashree Cement and ACC. They did not have the full picture. I played along with the price battle. It was a war of attrition. They thought they would be able to wear me down. Instead, with every passing month, their costs went up as inflation picked up in the aftermath of the economic liberalization by the Narasimha Rao government. The inflation effect on us was restricted to the rising fuel price (which was less than one-third of the cost), while our competitors had to deal with many other expenses. They offered massive discounts to big builders like the Hiranandanis and Rahejas and got them to boycott us. We managed to entice some of them, including big consumers like CIDCO, with our facility of bulk transportation with reduced wastage. However, we realized that 80 per cent of the Bombay market was made up of small builders who were constructing one or two buildings.

We decided to focus on them, instead of the big builders. We offered them the comfort of a fixed price that was the same for all dealers, big or small. Unlike the others, we did not discriminate. They liked our honesty and transparency. But we strictly enforced our seven-day credit rule and this ensured that we were not stuck with the payment delays that many of our competitors were facing. We also began looking at the retail segment, which was a large part of the Greater Bombay region. The retailers sold to people looking to build their own houses or to repair existing ones. There were as many as 1,000 retailers for this segment in the city. Our sales department worked closely with them.

Through our interaction with retailers, we found that because of lack of storage, cement dust was a huge problem for the stockists and the buyers. A decision was then made to shift to paper bags. We imported a packing plant for this. It eliminated the cement-dust problem at the Panvel port. The joke was that you could have lunch next to the packing machine there and not see dust. The trade liked the paper bags. Our marketing team then launched a festival targeted at small retailers called Ambuja Parivar Mahotsav. It was an eighteen-month-long multifaceted programme that included a grand launch function for the family, followed by a series of smaller events. Within three months, more than 500 retailers had signed up with us to become exclusive Ambuja retailers.

We backed it up with a strong advertising campaign. Ravi Gupta and his team at Trikaya transformed the 'Virat Compressive Strength' slogan into a more creative and innovative idea of an unbreakable wall built with Ambuja cement. It first appeared as a plain white poster with a broken sledgehammer. It was a subtle statement on the superior strength of Ambuja cement. The idea was later turned into a series showing how the Ambuja wall was unbreakable. The only way the hero could get to the other side to save his heroine was by pole-vaulting over it.

It was a big hit. Within a few years, we had a firm grip on the Mumbai market, with a 60 per cent share of the retail segment. We had now become the largest player in two of the wealthiest markets in India, Mumbai and Gujarat. We had taken on and beaten the combined strength of India's three biggest cement makers—ACC, L&T and the Aditya Birla group—through original thinking and innovation. It gave us the confidence that we could achieve anything we wanted if we put our mind to it.

Interestingly, this was the time when L&T was going through problems of its own. It was viewed as an excellent takeover target by one of the country's most prominent companies, controlled by a big-name business family. Out of the blue one day, the scion of that family came to see me. His family wanted me to partner with them in an L&T takeover attempt. I said I was honoured they thought of me, but I was still too small a player to get mixed up in this kind of battle. I politely declined, but the incident was a clear indication that Ambuja was a force to reckon with in the corporate arena.

Sometime around 1992, a young man named Prakash Bhopatkar, an ex-McKinsey consultant, came to see me with an idea for all-round improvement in the quality of our work. He was a quality specialist and offered to conduct workshops in the company. Bhopatkar had recently finished writing a book called *Quality Is Free*, the essence of which was that it doesn't cost anything to improve quality. He wanted to implement the ideas in Gujarat Ambuja. All that was needed was a motivated workforce prepared to work towards self-improvement. Impressed by his sincerity and passion, I told him that the seminars should be conducted for everyone, not only the seniors.

The seminars were conducted both at our offices and plants. Bhopatkar started by saying that there was no extra cost involved in producing good-quality work as compared to the usual style of working. All that was needed was for everyone to be more attentive, vigilant and concerned about quality. And by everyone, he meant everyone who worked in the office and plants, down to the level of office assistants, canteen servers, cleaning staff and security guards. The idea was that only if each one of us was conscious of improving the quality of our work would productivity improve and the company benefit.

To achieve this, one has to start with the assumption that there is always room for improvement in every area of the company. Finally, quality is a never-ending mission. The journey is one of continuous, small measurable improvements. Once you have achieved your quality goal, you start all over again by setting a higher goal. It is a constant process. Here was a thought that jelled perfectly with our concept of 'I Can'.

Bhopatkar made everyone, including the office boys, write one page on what improvements they would like to see in their area of responsibility. Everyone came up with constructive suggestions on what they could do. He then used a formula he had developed to express the suggested improvements, in terms of monetary value. He trained us to use the method. We were now able to assess the quality improvements in monetary terms.

The sessions that he conducted made a deep impression on everyone. We distributed copies of *Quality Is Free* to everyone who wanted to delve deeper into the subject. I have no hesitation in saying that Bhopatkar sparked-off a quality revolution in the company. Quality became a buzzword in every department. It produced a lifetime of benefits for the company.

No one absorbed the mantra of continuous upgrading of quality better than Mr Kulkarni himself. When we started producing 2,500 tonnes of clinkers a day in the Ambujanagar plant, we were thrilled about achieving what seemed to be India's highest level of production from a kiln that size. Mr Kulkarni, though, was not content. He began looking at the production figures of comparative international cement manufacturers.

The Japanese, he found, were achieving far superior results with their plants. He got in touch with the research department of the Japanese company Onoda Cement through an Indian acquaintance who worked there. They were more than happy to show him around. He made a few trips there and we learnt quite a few things that helped us raise production and productivity. Onoda Cement eventually became a consultant for our Darlaghat project.

Mr Kulkarni, during his visits to Onoda Cement's research centre, found that there was a direct correlation between the quality of the cement and the microscopic structure of the clinker in the kiln. To get the best-quality clinker, the raw limestone mix that is fed into the kiln must be as per a predetermined specification in terms of quality and the size to which it is crushed. Even the burning process inside the kiln has to be manipulated in such a manner that no limestone residue is left behind. Optimum burning improves the energy efficiency of the kiln, leading to significant savings in the energy cost. These learnings helped improve our productivity tremendously while cutting down our electricity consumption.

We also found that the production level in our plants, which were among the highest in the country, fell way short of what the Japanese were able to achieve from a similar-sized kiln. While we were producing

2,500 tonnes of cement per day, they were able to produce 3,500 tonnes per day. The Japanese scientists told us the trick lay in increasing the size of the preheater. It is the tower-like structure adjacent to the kiln in which the raw limestone mix is preheated to get rid of carbon dioxide and water before it is fed into a kiln.

After learning about this, Mr Kulkarni made the preheater at Kodinar two sizes bigger with a small investment. Along with some other minor changes in auxiliary equipment, we were able to raise the daily production at both Ambujanagar (to 3,300 tonnes) and Gajambuja (to 3,500 tonnes). Similarly, we later raised the capacity at the Himachal Pradesh plant, from 5,400 tonnes per day to 6,300 tonnes. We were able to get nearly a million tonnes of extra cement every year through these changes! It was the equivalent of setting up a million-tonne plant for free! By doing this, we set a new gold standard for the Indian cement industry.

10

Cancer Is Just Another Distraction

Diagnosis, surgery and relapse • Getting back to work • Joining the UTI board • The GDR issue

The early 1990s were among the most exciting and hectic years in Ambuja's history. Darlaghat was progressing full steam, the sea-transportation project was in an advanced stage, ports were being built, bulk carriers had been ordered, work had been initiated on our new plant at Kodinar and we were simultaneously raising capital in the stock market to fund everything. Our senior team was still the same size as when we first started, so each one of us was flitting from one site to another across the country, scarcely taking a breather.

I enjoyed the unrelenting pressure and the stress of the frenzied pace of working. It felt like a permanent adrenaline rush. The high it gave me made me push even harder and take on more things to do. And then, as it happens very often, it all came crashing down. In August 1993, I was diagnosed with cancer of the mouth. Though it did unsettle me for a short period, I was lucky that my spirituality helped me bounce back.

Did the frenetic work schedule contribute to the cancer? We will never know. But it did have a role to play in its two subsequent recurrences, in 1995 and 2000, as we pushed towards becoming a 10-million-tonne company.

The primary cause of my cancer, of course, was my two-decade-long habit of chewing tobacco in the form of paan masala and zarda. I had been an occasional smoker and drinker since my college days. I rarely bought cigarettes by the pack and was more of a social smoker. It was the same with alcohol. I loved whisky and with time took a liking to single malts. I was more in the class of people who savour and enjoy a drink but are not big drinkers. However, paan masala with zarda, in many ways, consumed me. I was addicted to the tobacco in it. It was my constant companion. I loved the high. I thought it helped me through the stress of hectic activity that was part of my life at Gujarat Ambuja.

For years I had been warned by Nilu, my parents, my friends and my doctors that chewing tobacco caused cancer. I was prone to ulcers in my mouth since childhood. The condition aggravated with time because of the paan masala habit. I remember consulting the renowned Bombay ENT specialist Dr Joe De Sa in the 1970s, when I was still in my twenties. 'Narotam,' he would say, 'please give up chewing tobacco. It will give you cancer one day.' So would many others. Paan masala, they would say to me, was even worse than smoking. When you ate paan masala, the tobacco was directly and continuously in touch with the fragile skin inside your cheeks.

I had a fatalist view of tobacco. I knew it caused cancer, but at the same time I knew a vast majority of consumers who had never had a problem. Both Suresh and Vinod Neotia were compulsive users of tobacco and paan masala, as were many of my Marwari friends. I hoped that I would also be among the multitude that remained healthy. It was a probability game and I turned out to be the unlucky one. When one is addicted to something, the mind always finds ways and reasons to continue doing it. I justified the use of tobacco, telling myself that I was trying to cope with my heightened levels of stress. On occasions, I was so busy that I would miss my meals, but paan masala would sustain me for hours.

I had a feeling that my mind was hyperactive, more active than that of most people and I was always trying to cope. All my life, I had been trying to keep up with people who were smarter and older than me. At the elite Hill Grange High School, where I was transferred mid-term, I was a Hindi-speaking boy trying to keep pace with kids to whom English came naturally. In college, I was always in a class higher than I should have been for my age. In the cotton trade, I dealt with people who were much older and more experienced. In cement, I butted heads with companies that had been in the business for decades. I was a fast learner, but there was always the anxiety and the stress of catching up. Tobacco calmed me down.

Stress for me was of both kinds, positive and negative. Negative stress had disappeared by the time Ambuja had enough cash in 1990, only to be replaced by the positive version brought about by anxiety, impatience, overworking, etc., as we embarked on a path of furious growth and expansion. I was anxious about wanting to protect our market share, our expansion efforts, the acquisition of new companies and living up to our reputation as a star performer in the stock market. My lifestyle had hardly changed from the time when we were struggling. I was still working non-stop and suffered from hyperacidity, which was aggravated by stress and tobacco. I gave the impression of being calm and serene on the outside, but my mind was forever overstrung.

I had a packed schedule every day, working from morning to late evening and travelling around the country and abroad. Besides, there was a new point of pressure. Suresh Neotia, who had taken over as chairman in 1988, was a low-key presence in the company in the early days, preferring not to get actively involved. However, once we started doing well, he suddenly became more active in his communications. He was not happy that I was not regularly keeping him in the loop about the many things that we were doing. I was too busy running around and had neglected him, which I later realized was a mistake. I told him about my pace of work, but he was unmoved. He kept writing letters to me, criticizing my attitude and style of working. He was an avid letter writer and this was yet another point of stress.

The first sign that something was wrong with my health came in May 1993 when I was in London. There was an ulcer in my mouth which refused to go away. I tried to ignore it for a while, thinking it was a recurrence of my old oral problem. This time though, it wasn't healing. In August, when I was back in Bombay, I went to see my ENT specialist Dr Dara Anklesaria. He examined me and said it did not look good. He was sure it was not my usual, harmless ulcer. He wanted me to have it tested immediately for cancer. I was shattered. What if cancer had finally got me? I could not bear to think about the consequences.

Dr Anklesaria suggested that I go and see Dr Sultan Pradhan, the cancer specialist at Tata Memorial Hospital. I was worried and jittery. I told Dr Anklesaria that I was not ready to see any cancer specialist in Bombay. He said that if I did not go, he would physically drag me there. I was worried both about getting the cancer diagnosis and of the Bombay doctors messing up my mouth. I was also concerned about the news getting out. In light of all this, I made an appointment with doctors at the Sloan Kettering Cancer Centre in New York, the world's most prestigious cancer hospital.

Within a week, I was in New York with my wife, Vinod Neotia and his wife. Vinod came with me for moral support. He and I shared a special bond formed over many years. It was a relationship built on trust and affection. In New York, I still hoped that by some miracle Dr Anklesaria's alarm would be proved false. Then I got the diagnosis. It was indeed cancer of the mouth. I was devastated. I was only forty-three. Until that point, I felt I had dodged the bullet, but now cancer had finally got me.

The only silver lining was that it was caught before it had spread to other parts of my body. It was restricted to my mouth. I felt that this was God's signal to me that I was not on the right path. He had given me a tight slap to put me in my place. It took me a few days to gather the courage to accept the new reality of my life. Once I reconciled myself to the diagnosis, I felt much better. I was no longer given to brooding or moaning. I slowly came to terms with my new condition and started thinking about the way forward. Though the cancer was not caught in the early stages, it was not at an advanced stage either. It was detected within the crucial first year.

Cancer of the mouth, they told me, was not very life-threatening if caught in the first year and surgically removed before it spread to the glands. Unlike cancers of the liver and rectum, cancers of the breast, bone and mouth do not spread as fast. My surgery hardly took any time. It was more like a tooth extraction where they removed a piece of my inner cheek. No chemotherapy or radiation was needed and I was back at work in Mumbai in less than a month. No one outside my family and the Neotias knew or was told about the diagnosis. Work continued as usual.

I gave up chewing tobacco immediately after my diagnosis, but not my whisky. The surgical wound inside my mouth showed signs of getting better in the first few months, but then the recovery stalled. It wasn't healing fully. The doctors said it would take time to settle down, but it never really did. It kept bothering me for the next two years. I felt unwell all the time. But I worked through it.

The second half of 1993 was packed with action. Our first ship, the *Ambuja Shikhar,* made its maiden voyage from Muldwarka to Bombay in September; Gajambuja started commercial production in October; we successfully recalibrated the Darlaghat capacity to 1.5 million tonnes; the ports at Panvel and Muldwarka were completed by December; and work was underway to build a port at Magdalla in Surat.

I was forced back into the thick of things quite early. Because of my cancer, I had asked Suresh Neotia to oversee Darlaghat, while Mr Kulkarni was handling the day-to-day affairs. I thought he might offer a helping hand. After attending a few plant meetings in Himachal Pradesh and Punjab, he said he did not want to be involved in daily operational details. Suresh was one of those people who found it tough to make decisions despite being the chairman of the company. It would always fall on me to make the decisions.

This was something that I found common in quite a few business people and professionals. They were exceptionally good at execution if given proper direction. However, they would be numbed into inaction when asked to make a major decision. They would dither, procrastinate and kick the can down the road. I was the opposite. My philosophy was that in business you needed to be decisive even if the decision eventually ended up being wrong.

That was an early learning for me and the man who told me about it was our head of civil engineering, Mr Rao. He narrated the story of the scion of a leading Delhi-based business house who looked after the cement operations of a leading north India-based cement company where he had been previously employed. He would fly down every month to the remote location where the plant was situated and spend a few days conducting meetings from morning to night. However, he would take no decisions and this left everyone confused.

The meetings concluded, he would fly back leaving behind a close lieutenant of his. This man was much more decisive and would step in and make all the decisions, doing in an hour what his boss could not do in three days. Similarly, Suresh would leave all significant decisions to me. A few weeks after my surgery, he called to say that the Darlaghat responsibility was getting to be too much for him and he wanted to give it up. Once again, I was drawn back into supervising the Himachal Pradesh operations.

On the positive side, being back at work kept my mind off the unhealed wound in my mouth. It was a source of constant discomfort and I could hardly stop thinking about it. I never wanted anyone to feel that my work was suffering because of this. I was worried it would have a direct impact on the morale in the company. I had to maintain a facade of confidence, of being entirely in control of the situation.

Internally though, I was racked with anxiety, wondering if the cancer was indeed in remission or was still lurking inside me. I did not know what lay ahead.

I had also added to my responsibilities while I was in New York, still recovering from my surgery. It began with a call from Dr S.A. Dave, the chairman of UTI. He said he wanted me to become a trustee of UTI as the IDBI nominee. I could hardly say no. To be a UTI trustee was a prestigious appointment in those days. I felt it was an honour for me to accept the offer on behalf of myself and my company. I had known Dr Dave since his days as executive director (ED) of IDBI, which was the promoter of UTI, India's monopoly mutual fund company at that time. It had raised thousands of crores each year from investors across the country.

Traditionally, IDBI had two nominees on the UTI board, the chairman and a second nominee to provide the industry perspective. This was a position usually reserved for a prominent industrialist or business professional of high repute. Besides a high level of knowledge about the intricacies of project and corporate finance, the job demanded ethical standards of the highest order. Every large business house was a borrower from UTI and UTI also invested in many companies through the stock market. It was important that there be no conflict of interest. 'I know that you will not do anything that would help one industrialist over the other,' Mr Dave had told me on the phone.

For me, this was not just a public recognition of my ability and stature as a self-made industrialist, but also an acknowledgement of the high ethical standards at Gujarat Ambuja. We had never borrowed from UTI and our dealings with IDBI itself had come down considerably in the previous few years. Dr Dave went one step ahead and made me a member of UTI's all-powerful executive committee which sanctioned the big loans. While the other three members—Dr Dave, Mr P.J. Nayak (who would go on to become the chairman and CEO of UTI Bank, which later became Axis Bank) and Mr S.H. Khan (managing director of IDBI)—were powerful bankers, I was the only outsider.

For the five years that I was a member of the committee, I was involved in the sanctioning of loans worth thousands of crores to the biggest of Indian companies and dozens of smaller ones. It was a job that involved extensive research and analysis of companies and industries, followed by prolonged debates in the UTI boardroom. After my earlier stint with IDBI's Western Committee, this was another great learning experience that I had the privilege of enjoying. The only thing was that it came at a time when maybe I should have slowed down. I could not; UTI would not have waited for me.

~

This was also the time when we launched our first Global Depository Receipts (GDR) issue. Cheaper foreign funds were for the first time made available to top-rated Indian companies and we did not want to miss the moment. The $80 million-GDR issue that we floated on the Luxembourg stock market in November 1993 was a big success. We were only the third Indian company to tap the international markets after Grasim (Aditya Birla) and Reliance. To be in that league and to pull off an international capital-raising exercise spoke not only of our standing in the financial market but also of our desire to be in the big league and our ability to push the envelope in innovative financing.

Our issue was co-led and managed by the International Finance Corporation (IFC), Washington, though they had been reluctant to invest in many other Indian manufacturing companies because of the poor environmental regulation in the country. A year earlier, the World Bank, which owns IFC, had provided us with a loan for the Himachal Pradesh project. They were convinced that our pollution-control standards were on par with the cement companies in Europe and America.

At the GDR roadshow in London, I beamed with pride when IFC bosses Jamil Kassum and Farida Khambata stood in front of some of the world's most prominent investors and said, 'We have invested in cement companies in sixty-seven countries and we have no hesitation in saying that Ambuja is the best.' We received subscription offers sixteen times the issue size, exceeding $1 billion. We used the funds to retire old and expensive debts and to finance the plethora of our ongoing projects, including Darlaghat, the cost of which had more than doubled by then.

On the health front, even in early 1994 and more than six months after my surgery, I continued to suffer. The wound in my mouth would get inflamed periodically and then settle down. The cycle continued. The doctors kept telling me to give it more time. My frequent visits to the doctor were now being noticed by some of my colleagues, particularly the secretaries and the assistants who were fixing the appointments. I got a feeling that some of them suspected cancer, but I was not ready to tell anyone yet.

It did not slow down my pace. With the arrival of the *Ambuja Vaibhav* and the *Ambuja Gaurav* in early 1994, our first fleet of three ships was ready. By July the sea-transportation project was in full flow, with the commissioning of the Surat port. Besides providing an impetus to domestic sales, it provided us the opportunity to step up exports. In the past, we had exported bagged cement from the nearby Porbandar port. Handling and transportation of bagged cement, as I have said earlier, comes with associated problems of waste and pilferage. Muldwarka now afforded us the infrastructure to export bulk cement. With a bit of redesign, we could ship clinkers as well.

We moved fast on this, built a new silo and worked out arrangements for exports with big dealers in Sri Lanka, the Middle East and Africa. Muldwarka, however, was not yet designed for berthing of big ocean-going bulk carriers. For exports to be viable, we needed to move large quantities of cement. We did what large ports do in these kinds of situations. We worked out a system of transporting the cement on our smaller vessels to the larger carrier anchored on the high sea. Our engineers reworked the pneumatic pumps so that we could pump the cement into the bigger ship. The operation was challenging because none of our team members had experience in this area. But they pulled it off. That year we exported close to 0.5 million tonnes of cement.

Gujarat Ambuja's export department was now not intimidated by the idea of procuring large export orders. They were confident that our engineers would find a way to move the cement from our port. The spirit of the 'I Can' culture that we fostered was on full display here. The export department figured out something equally innovative while shipping cement to the Dangote Group in Nigeria off the coast of West Africa. On the way back, the ships could pick up high-quality coal from South Africa and bring it to Muldwarka for our consumption. South African coal was cheaper and superior to Indian coal.

Importing coal was proving to be an unviable proposition for most Indian cement companies because of the high handling charges at the country's public ports and the rising transport cost. With Muldwarka, we discovered that coal import had suddenly become much cheaper. Our engineers creatively tweaked the handling facilities. In the first year alone, we imported more than 1,00,000 tonnes of coal, a figure that would rise steadily over the years as we expanded our cement and captive power capacities.

While the news on the work front continued to be better than expected, my cancer wound was going from bad to worse. After I came back from New York, I was under the care of Dr Sultan Pradhan, the eminent cancer specialist whom Dr Dara Anklesaria had recommended. His name was also recommended to me by the two doctors who were treating me in New York, who were coincidentally both Indians—Dr Ashok Shaha and his senior Dr Jatin Shah, the chief of head and neck surgery at Sloan Kettering and both originally from Baroda Medical College.

By late 1994 and early '95, my condition had deteriorated enough for Dr Pradhan to feel that I might need a second surgery. This time though, I did not want to leave my colleagues in the dark. Once it was clear that I would have to go back to New York for another surgery, I broke the news to my senior executives. The entire company now knew of my cancer. Their reaction, surprisingly, was normal.

By then, I think, we had reached a stage where I was not required for the day-to-day operations and it did not look like they would miss me.

I was still worried about the morale and to make things look normal, I decided to ask Mr Kulkarni to start work on a few new projects. The hope was that this would make people less concerned about my absence. Why would I sign-off on projects worth hundreds of crores if I was not confident about the future of the company despite my cancer?

I asked Mr Kulkarni to go ahead with the second million-tonne plant at Gajambuja. It was an idea we had discussed after the early success of our sea-transportation project. Our ports in Panvel and Surat were working to capacity and we had drawn up plans to build new ones in Kerala and Karnataka to tap the south Indian market. Muldwarka also helped us open new markets abroad. Our exports were picking up. I asked Mr Kulkarni to place orders with ABG Shipyard for three more ships to meet our growing need.

The Gajambuja II plant would eventually cost us ₹400 crore. It was to be a duplication of our first plant in terms of design, size, supplier, infrastructure, engineering, etc. And the plan again was to finish it in thirteen months, as we had the first one. When commissioned in December 1996, it would raise our cement capacity at Kodinar to 4.5 million tonnes.

I went back to New York for my second surgery in early April 1995. Besides my wife, Vinod and his wife, Dr Pradhan also accompanied me for support. I was placed under the care of Dr Ashok Shaha, who had performed my first surgery and had worked closely with Dr Pradhan in Mumbai for my follow-up treatment. Dr Shaha decided to reopen the area of the first surgery and discovered that the cancer had spread to my jaws.

This time, the surgery lasted nearly twelve hours. They removed my entire jaw on one side, including my teeth. An artificial implant was inserted to hold the face together and prevent disfiguration. The veins and arteries were then reconnected using microsurgery. My face was swollen like a balloon and took several days to settle down. Once the wound healed, I had to go through thirty-five sittings of radiation treatment.

While the early sessions were mostly uneventful, the final week was the most painful experience of my life.

The surgery, the radiation and the recovery process took more than six months, all of which I spent in New York. It was September by the time I came back to Mumbai. I was physically a completely changed man and the next few weeks were spent trying to adjust to the new realities of my life. My teeth had been removed, so I could not chew. It meant I was forever on a diet of soft, non-spicy food. I was free of cancer, but the radiation treatment had lowered my immunity, so I had to be careful when I was out with people. I had to be extremely vigilant when travelling on flights and invariably ended up with an infection.

The most visible change was on my face. The microplastic surgery on my face did not work very well. Things seemed fine for about six months. But after that, the good side of my face began to slowly pull away because of the dynamic tension caused by muscle loss on the other side. This resulted in a distortion of my looks. It happened slowly and subtly, so not many people noticed it. However, it was visible to the doctors and me. Luckily, that too settled down after some time.

The two cancer surgeries in the space of two years transformed my life. I was still only forty-five and in the prime of my life. Looking back, I realize that I could have easily fallen into the self-pitying trap of 'God, why me?' But I did not. I refused to be downbeat or crestfallen. That was not my character. I was never given to excessive brooding or bitterness when things went wrong. I was not afraid of death, possibly because I had seen many illnesses in my family and both my parents had died of cancer. I believed that like all the good things that had happened to me, this was also part of my destiny. I should take it on the chin and move on.

Unlike the first surgery, the doctors managed to remove the cancer tissues in the second surgery. As a result, the wound healed well, which was a significant relief. Luckily, the operation had no impact on my speech. In September 1996, I took over as the president of the Cement

Manufacturers Association (CMA) and gave some of my best lectures at their meetings and seminars.

The good news was that the company had done even better in my absence. We commissioned our Himachal Pradesh plant in June and it was stabilized in a record three months. Our all-important grinding unit in Rupnagar was brought on stream during my absence. There was also a potentially damaging fire in the main electrical substation of the Kodinar plant in June. The alert staff first contained the fire from spreading into the operational area and then worked round the clock for the next two weeks to get the plant running. We were lucky that it was not a big fire and that we were quick to respond.

Expert opinion was that the fire could have set us back by three months and cost us hundreds of crores in lost business. It brought to the fore the sense of commitment and the selflessness of the employees. In spite of the two-week shutdown of production, the team more than made up for lost time. Our production touched a record high of 3 million tonnes that year. I told my colleagues that since they were doing such a good job, I should probably be on sabbatical much more.

At a personal level, 1995 turned out to be a lousy year besides my own cancer recurrence. In October, when I was still convalescing in New York, a few hundred miles away in Baltimore, Aditya Birla—one of India's greatest industrialists and a man I greatly admired as a corporate role model and for the way he ran his cement companies—died of prostate cancer aged just fifty-two. He was an inspiring leader who had achieved a great deal at a young age; the cement businesses of Grasim and Indian Rayon were among the best performing in the country. He was among the first cement company owners to have recognized and complimented us for what we had done. Whenever we ran into each other, he praised me for what I had achieved and would always have a word or two of advice.

One of the high points of Gujarat Ambuja's first ten years was when Aditya babu came to our Kodinar plant. Sometime in the early 1990s, one afternoon I got a call in Bombay from the plant general manager. He said that Mr Aditya Birla's people had called to ask whether he could come for a visit on his way to the airport. He was at the Birla group's Indian Rayon plant located half an hour away. I told my people that since it was short notice, all we could do was to welcome him graciously without any ceremony. He spent time going around the plant and on his way out called to congratulate me on the great work we were doing. 'It seems very well run and very clean,' he told me. It is a compliment that I still treasure.

Aditya babu once told me that he was flummoxed by Grasim and Indian Rayon cement not being able to get the same price as L&T in the market. I had replied that within two years, I would make sure Ambuja commanded an even higher price. He had laughed it off then, but we achieved that distinction much earlier. He was not entirely convinced about the power of brand building in cement. Years later, though, his son Kumaramangalam took an altogether different approach after he took over UltraTech. He set aside a considerable budget for marketing and advertising. It was not surprising that UltraTech went on to become India's largest cement manufacturer a decade later.

By some strange coincidence, Aditya babu was diagnosed with cancer around the same time as me in 1993. I remember that we were in the US roughly around the same time for our respective treatments. And in 1995, we were once again in the US at the same time; I was at Sloan Kettering and he was at Johns Hopkins. When I was first told that he had been detected with prostate cancer, I was hoping that like the vast majority of those struck by the disease he too would live for a long, long time. Sadly, that was not to be.

Two years later, in 1997, while I was in the throes of the Modi Cement takeover, I was required to mourn once again. My close friend Ravi Gupta, who was singularly responsible for creating the Ambuja brand, died of stomach cancer at the relatively young age of fifty-nine.

His passing was a devastating blow to me. He was an enlightened man, my marketing guru, the brand-builder whose counsel I often sought on a variety of things. I hardly knew anything about the concept of marketing or the importance of market research when I first met him.

He led the way and I followed. I thought he was brave to take us on as a client because ad agencies in those days preferred to work with only consumer brands. Ravi took it up as a challenge and achieved the kind of success that turned him and us into pioneers in creating brands out of commodities. In less than three years since we started production, Ravi had successfully transformed Ambuja. We were as much a marketing company as we were a manufacturing company. When I first set up the company, I had never envisaged that marketing would play as big a role in our success, as innovations in manufacturing and finance.

Ravi's imprint was writ large in every new market we conquered. And it still looms large over Ambuja, three decades later with the mnemonic of the giant and the 'I Can' slogan. He and his team had created such a robust template for the advertising of Ambuja that it was relatively easy for those who followed to replicate the success. From the 'Ambuja Parivar Mahotsav' campaign that helped us leap ahead of our rivals in Mumbai, to the Bengali campaign which established our leadership in Kolkata and Bengal and the landmark Boman Irani and Khali campaigns that followed years later, I see Ravi's imprint in each of them. His death was a terrible personal loss.

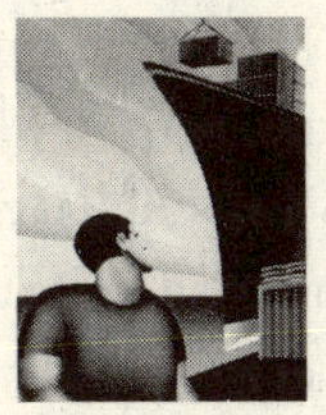

11

A Social Conscience for Ambuja

Learning from Mr Kantisen Shroff • Importance of the Ambuja Cement Foundation • Making development work efficient

There were two people who came to see me unannounced over the years, but went on to play significant roles in the making of Ambuja. I consider it my destiny and fate to have met them in the manner that I did. The first one was Mr Unwalla, the retired concrete specialist from ACC who came to visit me in the late 1980s, about whom I have talked extensively in the earlier chapters. He taught me more about cement than anyone else. His role as an adviser to the company was crucial in the early days as we went on to develop the most durable cement in the market.

The second was Mr Kantisen Shroff, MD, Excel Industries. Excel was one of India's most successful indigenous chemical companies. It was established by him and his brothers in 1941 at Jogeshwari, then a distant suburb of Mumbai. I had long admired the company, but never had any working relationship with them. When my secretary informed me that Mr Kantisen Shroff had come to see me, I wondered why. Both our companies had plants in Gujarat, beyond which we had little in common.

Nearly seventy at that time, Kantibhai or Kaka as he was known, was a simple man with a quiet demeanour. He dressed in ordinary clothes, his appearance belying the fact that he had helped pioneer India's indigenous speciality chemicals and waste management industry. He still ran a company that was admired both by his peers and the stock market. Excel Industries was also one of the rare Indian companies with which the Tatas had a joint venture.

Kantibhai complimented me for what I had achieved with Gujarat Ambuja and added, 'Now that you are doing well you should start doing some community development work in the villages around your plant in Kodinar.' He then proceeded to explain to me why our responsibility as corporate citizens extended beyond shareholders, employees and vendors. Beyond contributing to economic growth, we had an obligation to get directly involved with the upliftment of the rural communities around our industrial plants, he said. This was at least two decades before CSR became mandatory in India and Kantibhai was talking from experience.

Excel Industries had been working in areas like rainwater harvesting, drinking-water distribution, watershed development, encouraging salinity-resistant agriculture, disaster management, health, hygiene and afforestation around their plants spread across Maharashtra and Gujarat for many years. Besides, Kantibhai had been working since the 1960s with the Ramakrishna Mission and later with his own Vivekanand Research and Training Institute, to improve the quality of life of the rural poor in his native Kutch. His wife Chandaben Shroff was well known in her own right as the founder of the Bhuj-based Shrujan Trust, which had been doing pioneering work in preserving and promoting the textile heritage of Kutch and through it empowering women in a deeply conservative society. She was awarded the prestigious Rolex Award for her work in 2006.

In that sense, there was no one better than Kantibhai to lecture me on the need for corporations to contribute towards developing the communities in which they worked. It was what all responsible companies should do, he told me. And I agreed. Of course, he surprised me once again a few months after our first meeting, when I visited him at his Jogeshwari office in suburban Mumbai—I found him seated by an old desk under a large tree. 'During the monsoons, I work from inside the office,' he told me, 'otherwise, I like to work in the open.'

I realized I had a lot to learn from Kantibhai. No doubt I was doing some personal charity work at that time. Since the 1930s, my family had run a free health clinic with a doctor in our hometown of Chirawa. I had taken over its running in the 1970s. In 1977, immediately after my mother was detected with cancer, I started an annual eye camp at Chirawa as well. It proved to be a huge success. At its peak, we conducted more than 15,000 eye examinations and 1,500 surgeries. It was a high point in my annual calendar and gave me the same kind of pleasure as the early success of Gujarat Ambuja. The eye camps continued till 2007 when the Rajasthan government banned eye camps following repeated incidents of botched surgeries.

While the eye camp was my personal charity, I was always acutely conscious of my role as a responsible corporate citizen. That was the reason we made the most substantial investment by any Indian cement company in pollution control at Kodinar. It was also the reason we invested so much to create one of India's greenest factory complexes in Kodinar. We planted more than 1,00,000 trees around the factory in the first few years alone. As a result, the area around the plant is covered by a vast green canopy and overrun by dozens of exquisite birds from around the region. The place is so pretty and quiet that for many years two of India's leading corporate advisers, Mr M.L. Bhakta, who sat on our board and his friend Mr Bansi Mehta of the well-known accounting firm Bansi Mehta & Co, would spend their week-long New Year holiday at the Ambuja guest house next to the plant.

What Kantibhai was suggesting was something different. He wanted Gujarat Ambuja to set up a division that would undertake community development in and around Kodinar. Most philanthropy in those days was in the form of donations to NGOs. His suggestion was that the company should figure out what needs to be done, arrange for funds and get the work done. I told him that while I liked the idea, I did not know how to go about it. He told me not to worry and that he would send someone whom we could recruit to do the work. I asked him who would supervise it, because I had no expertise in the area. He said he would do it, which he did gratis for us in the initial years until we were able to establish our own team.

We started with an investment of ₹15 lakh and a mobile dispensary that went around the villages in Kodinar. Leena Bhatt, the lady who joined us on the recommendation of Kantibhai, looked after the operations. The Ambuja Cement Foundation (ACF) was set up as part of Gujarat Ambuja with the purpose of community development in 1993.

In the early years, the work was concentrated on the dozen or so villages around the Kodinar plant. While the mobile dispensary provided basic health services to the villagers, what they were desperately looking for was a year-round supply of water for home use and agriculture. Despite being blessed with a good monsoon every year and proximity to the sea, these villages suffered from the dual problem of water shortage and soil salinity. The few seasonal rivers in the area would fill up during the monsoon, but the fresh water was lost to the sea through run-offs every year. As a result, the water table had dramatically reduced, the wells were dry and the gradual ingression of seawater into the area was increasing the soil's salinity.

We made it our mission to solve the problem and started by repairing the existing check dams. This helped recharge many of the wells in the area and they retained water through the dry season. The Kodinar watershed programme was taken up with a missionary zeal in the subsequent years with help from the state government and private trusts. We converted our used limestone mine into water reservoirs by shoring up their banks. The reservoirs were then interconnected with channels to enable water to flow from one into the other. ACF has helped repair or build check dams across a region covering over sixty-five villages. We helped create an integrated water-retention system spread over 100 square miles. The reservoirs now store upwards of 12 million litres of water for everyday use by the villagers.

These efforts helped to beat back the saltwater intrusion into the area, which, in turn, has dramatically transformed the soil. From being a government-classified agricultural 'dark' zone because of severe soil salinity, the area is now classified as 'non-saline' and is teeming with thriving farms and orchards, including many in the perimeter of the factory.

The afforestation programme has given the area a massive green canopy. It is probably one of the reasons why the average annual rainfall in the region has gone up from around 750 millimetres to 1,100 millimetres in the last decade. The thick tree cover proved crucial when we approached the Ministry of Environment and Forests (MoEF) for renewing our limestone mining licence. We were apprehensive because Kodinar falls just outside the buffer zone of the Gir forest. The MoEF officials had a tough time locating the active mine on Google Earth because of the thick green cover speckled with the blue hue of the water in the spent quarry-turned-reservoirs.

Starting in the mid-1990s, as Gujarat Ambuja gradually expanded operations to new locations like Himachal Pradesh, Punjab, Rajasthan, Madhya Pradesh, West Bengal and Maharashtra, so did the ACF—it was now a much larger organization focused on a big list of developmental programmes. While Ambuja was responsible for a significant part of the funding, ACF was getting better and better at implementation. Its mandate was clear. All the programmes had to be a joint effort between the community and the ACF. We were going to help the community help themselves. Their participation was vital. Our job was to instil the 'I Can' spirit in the community.

Today, the ACF views the mission of making a community self-sustaining and prosperous through a broad lens. As a result, the foundation's programmes are divided into six categories—Water Resource Management (of which Kodinar is a good example); Agricultural Livelihoods; Women's Empowerment; Skill Development; Health; and Education. These programmes are designed to support people in every area of their lives. And they are tailor-made considering the needs of each place.

At most of our plant locations, agriculture is the mainstay of people's livelihood. In Kodinar, for example, we followed up on the success of our watershed and desalination project by helping farmers improve their farming techniques. We set up a Krishi Vigyan Kendra (KVK) there. KVK is akin to an agricultural research centre and university, staffed by half a dozen scientists and ten other experts. The farmers travel here, spend a few days living in the hostel and are trained in areas ranging from better cropping, use of fertilizers, irrigation methods and use of the latest farm equipment. For those who cannot travel, KVK sends experts to the villages to conduct workshops and seminars.

Besides agriculture, the farmers are trained in animal husbandry, dairy development, poultry, aquaculture, etc. A specially set up community radio station imparts information and knowledge to the farmers in the surrounding villages through expert talks and interviews. ACF also helps the farmers to organize themselves into groups called Farmer Producer Organizations (FPOs) for better bargaining power when collectively purchasing fertilizers, seeds and pesticides and when marketing produce after the harvest. At last count, there were sixteen registered FPOs working under the aegis of ACF, with a membership count of more than 6500 farmers and turnover of more than ₹15 crore.

With my roots in cotton, I was also glad when I was approached ten years ago to get the farmers working with ACF to become part of the Geneva-based Better Cotton Initiative (BCI), a global not-for-profit organization that runs the most extensive cotton sustainability programme in the world. Set up by the World Wide Fund for Nature in 2005, it aims to get farmers to shift to a new farming method that is more environmentally friendly while saving money on reduced use of chemical pesticides, fertilizers and water. It results in better yields and higher income.

Starting with 2,500 cotton farmers in four locations in 2010, the ACF–BCI programme has grown to cover over 1.69 lakh farmers spread across the country. A recent study indicated that as compared to their non-BCI counterparts, the BCI farmers working with ACF use 24 per cent less fertilizer and pesticides, 17 per cent less water, their costs are lower by 14 per cent and their income is higher by 22 per cent. As a result of our work in India, an ACF representative now sits on the BCI global council.

Another critical arm of our rural development strategy has been women's empowerment. It has always been my belief that any development work is only half done until women are involved on an equal footing to men. The key component of ACF's women empowerment programme is the women's self-help group (SHG) and most of its programmes are undertaken through these SHGs.

We started with five SHGs in Kodinar in 1999 and there are now close to 780 SHGs (9637 members) in Kolinar alone and 2601 SHGs across all locations of ACF. Women are counselled on a variety of issues that affect them and their families—including sanitation and the need for proper toilets at home, smokeless *chulhas*, health and the downside of their men drinking alcohol and using tobacco, etc.—through the SHGs. The women are also provided crash courses in income-generating activities such as vegetable cultivation, poultry, animal husbandry and other skills that can fetch them a supplementary income. The women are also taught to use computers. Our 'Internet Sakhis' have so far trained more than 1,00,000 women to use the computer and the internet. The idea is to help the women keep track of family finances, loan repayments and other banking-related activities.

Women also play a crucial role in the various health-related initiatives that ACF runs across all its centres. More than 1,500 women have been trained as government-accredited social health activists. They have been doing excellent work in the areas of maternal and child health. To give one example, in Farraka, a remote area on the West Bengal–Bangladesh border where we began working in 2014, ACF's ASHA workers reduced the prevalence of home births and raised the institutional birth rate from 28 to 85 per cent in just three years. Infant mortality was brought down from 40 to 24 per cent. Similarly, ACF has created a cadre of women called 'Sakhis' for health-related interventions in poor villages around our Chandrapur plant in Maharashtra. These well-trained women go from village to village providing basic healthcare-related advice, especially for women and children.

Another equally important initiative is the Health-Care Centre (HCC) for truckers. It is an essential programme for Gujarat Ambuja, because truck drivers have been vital partners in Ambuja's growth story over the years. The HCC started as an HIV/AIDS awareness and sexually transmitted infection (STI) treatment facility and has now expanded to include vision testing and screening for other diseases. Thousands of truck drivers make use of these free facilities every year.

The single mobile dispensary initiative that launched our community health and sanitation programme in Kodinar in 1993, has now grown to embrace a large swathe of health and sanitation initiatives—community health clinics, diagnostic centres, referrals and linkages to hospitals, immunizations, a focus on maternal and child health, anaemia prevention, screening and early detection of diseases, hygiene-related counselling and building toilets in villages.

The programme that I am most excited about is the Skill and Entrepreneurship Development Institute (SEDI), targeted at young boys and girls from the villages and towns around our factories. It was part of our plan to raise the standard of living of these families by helping children who have just finished school pick up skills that would help them find gainful employment.

They are first provided vocational guidance to help them choose the skill that matches their aptitude. The students are then enrolled for education and training in the area of their interest. Our experts design the courses based on the guidelines provided by the Ministry of Skill Development and Entrepreneurship (MSDE). The courses involve theory and practicals, and cover a wide range of disciplines including automobile repairs, electrical repairs, hospitality industry services, basic software programming, etc. The courses are offered based on our study of industry demand and supply.

As of 2021, our 33 SEDI centres across the country have so far trained nearly 78,000 students. We not only conduct the courses but also try to find them jobs in companies in the surrounding towns and cities. Because we work very closely with several industrial establishments, our placement rate is as high as 74 per cent. And those who do not seek placement are most likely to have gone on to set up their own businesses.

The success of ACF over the last twenty-seven years has been as much a dream come true for me as the achievements of Gujarat Ambuja. I am proud of the fact that it is today among the country's finest CSR operations. What started as a mobile dispensary serving a few villages in Kodinar under the supervision of Kantibhai Shroff now has a footprint that stretches over 2134 villages spread over forty-seven of the country's poorest districts, in eleven states. We started with the primary goal of raising the standard of living of villagers around our plants, but the mandate now stretches far beyond. Many of the places that ACF works in have little or no connection to Ambuja Cement.

Much of the credit for ACF's success goes to Ms Pearl Tiwari, who has been its driving force as its president for two decades. I first met her as a young development professional who had come to seek a donation for an NGO. I liked her persistence and eventually took her on to run ACF when her predecessor left. She currently manages a team of nearly 1,000 professionals based across the country.

I was quite clear from the beginning that the same corporate management principles that made Gujarat Ambuja successful would be employed in the running of ACF. That idea was to be very efficient in everything that we did. Every rupee that we spent had to be stretched to its limit in terms of development returns. Unlike salaries in the NGO sector in India, we pay ACF staff the same kind of corporate salaries that people at Gujarat Ambuja earn. The idea is that they should work with the same sense of empowerment and commitment embodying the spirit of 'I Can'.

It is not surprising then that ACF's Social Return on Investment (SROI), the international measure for evaluating the impact of social projects, has been consistently high for most of our programmes. For example, the Daseran watershed project in Darlaghat scored an SROI of ₹8.44 for every rupee invested. As on date the watershed project in Kodinar has an SROI of ₹13, while SEDI Kodinar is at ₹5.07 and SEDI Chandrapur at ₹4.08.

It is heartening to note that ACF's work has been consistently recognized and feted by governments and industry organizations. We have won CSR excellence awards from many of the states we work in, including Rajasthan, Gujarat and Chhattisgarh. Our work in Bhatapara and Chandrapur won the industry's top honour, the CII-ITC Sustainability Award for Excellence a few years ago. Along with the various state governments and Central government agencies, ACF now partners with some of the biggest private sector companies as part of their CSR effort. As a result, the share of Gujarat Ambuja's contribution to ACF's annual fund corpus has been steadily declining. In 2019, only 30 per cent of the total funding of around ₹150 crore came from Gujarat Ambuja.

This does not, in any way, reflect that Gujarat Ambuja is cutting back. It still contributes roughly 4 per cent of its profits towards ACF annually, as against the legally mandated 2 per cent for CSR. The exciting part is that companies are now approaching us to become partners in many of our projects. That way, they are assured that their CSR money is spent gainfully. They are impressed by the scale and efficiency of what we do and our structured and transparent style of working. Ambuja's share in ACF's overall investment corpus may come down even more in the coming years, which would be a welcome development because it is a clear sign of more development work being done jointly.

Of course, in a country where poverty is still a daunting problem, there will always be much more to do. As I said in my chairman's message celebrating ACF's twenty-fifth year, 'It has been a quarter of a century since we have travelled on this journey and at this juncture we resolve to spread our wings further, taking our work to places where it is needed, beyond our core villages and into new territories that have the potential to prosper.'

12

Powering Ahead

Modi Cement takeover • Strengthening the management bench • New expansions and missed opportunities

In 1996, as I eased back into work after my second surgery, it was quite clear that the cement industry was once again heading for a crisis. After nearly five years of steady and robust growth, demand had begun to slacken. I had by then set up a Corporate Economics Division at Gujarat Ambuja to track the ups and downs of the industry. We were probably the only cement company to do this. Our first chief economist was Ms Kiran Nanda, an experienced economist who was earlier with the Tatas. Her research in areas like housing, infrastructure and economic growth in states around the country came in handy as we looked at expansion over the next decade. Her work was particularly important for me in the two years I was the president of the CMA starting in 1996.

The cement capacity build-up over the previous few years had far outstripped demand growth. Many new plants like ours were coming on stream now. In the three years starting 1995, the total industry capacity increased by 22 million tonnes to top the 100 million mark, while the estimated demand was only around 74 million tonnes. The massive gap between demand and supply portended dramatically low cement prices over the next few years, which was bound to affect everyone's bottom line. And to top it all, power and coal prices had shot up by 40 per cent and freight charges by 20 per cent. Our Darlaghat and Gajambuja II plants had just started commercial production, but thanks to our relentless focus on efficiency and productivity, we were not as severely affected as others. We were still making profits, though not on the scale of previous years.

By 1997, we were transporting close to 2 million tonnes of our production by sea from Muldwarka, which brought down our transportation cost considerably. And we were producing nearly 100 megawatts of electricity at our captive power plants. Consequently, our average power cost was down to around ₹1.30 per kilowatt, as against the ₹4.50 per kilowatt charged by the state electricity boards. Our drive for efficiency brought down power consumption to a new low of around 88 units per tonne, as against the industry average of 121 units.

Neither the crisis in the cement industry nor my two cancer surgeries could curb my ambition to grow. However, I did lower my goals. Before the cancer diagnosis in 1993, I had vaguely thought of setting up an international steel operation. The steel and cement businesses were somewhat similar and there was much talk about large new steel plants coming up in India. Like cement, steel was vital for the country's infrastructure and its demand was expected to grow exponentially worldwide. My thinking was to set up steel plants using the same methods that we had successfully employed for my cement operations. I wanted to do this on the global arena, just as Mr L.N. Mittal was starting to do in those days. Like him, I was in my early forties with lots of productive years ahead of me.

Alas, that was not to be. After my second surgery, I decided to scale back and stick to cement, but with a global footprint. In 1995, we invested in a holding company called Cement International Ambuja Limited in

Mauritius. The idea was to use the Indian Ocean island as a base to set up cement terminals in Africa and in the second stage, move towards setting up manufacturing plants. After some groundwork, however, I thought it over again. I would be competing against giants like Lafarge, Holcim and Cemex. It would involve large investments, which was fine because I was confident about our ability to raise finance. But it would also involve time and energy on my part to kick-start the projects, at least in the early days. It would have required me to travel relentlessly to raise funds and set up operations.

Considering the scale of what I was attempting, I decided that I was not in the best of health to pull it off. As for getting someone else to do it on my behalf, that thought didn't cross my mind. As in the case of Gujarat Ambuja, I wanted to build the foundation myself. With so many opportunities still opening up domestically, I decided to stick to India. The first opportunity came in the summer of 1997 when I was in London on my annual holiday.

I got a phone call from Mr Anil Singhvi, our company treasurer, saying that IDBI and the Washington-based IFC were very keen that we take over the ailing Modi Cement Ltd. I wasn't interested. Our record at takeovers had so far been pathetic, including those initiated by IDBI itself. Singhvi said they were offering us the company for one rupee and that IFC was particularly keen. Both the institutions were having a tough time with the Modis and they felt we were best suited to take over and turn the company around. They offered us all the help we needed. I said I would have to think it over.

The Modis, who till about the late 1970s and early '80s were among the most influential business families in Delhi, had set up the company in 1987. Their 1.15-million-tonne plant set up at the cost of ₹151 crore, was located outside Bhatapara town, about 80 kilometres north of Raipur (now part of Chhattisgarh). In the early days, they had a technical collaboration with Blue Circle, Britain's biggest cement maker. The cement was sold in the largely underserved market of eastern India and IDBI and IFC were among their biggest lenders.

By 1994, Modi Cement was in a bad way, brought about by a combination of poor management and bad marketing. The net worth had turned negative and accumulated losses topped ₹300 crore. The company was declared sick by BIFR and IDBI, the biggest lender, was the court-appointed operating agency. I was privy to news about the company from a young man who ran IFC's India investment office for some years. He used to come and see me to talk about the cement industry. He thought of Ambuja as being the best-run company in the industry.

He told me about the issues he was facing with the promoters and how he had tried to settle the outstanding loan thrice but had failed each time because of the fight between the two promoters. The case had now become an embarrassment for IFC and they were desperate to get out. He had over the years dropped hints about us taking over the company. But knowing the reputation of the promoters, I never responded.

We had worked closely with IFC during our GDR issue and knew them well and I continued to have excellent relations with IDBI. Officials from both organizations came to see me as soon as I was back in Mumbai. They told me they had tried for years to put the company back on the rails, but the Modis had resisted any changes. Their earnest plea made me reconsider my decision and take the offer seriously.

After much thinking, I proposed a takeover plan that would not involve buying out the Modis. I did not want to take the conventional route of taking management control by paying the promoters for ruining the company. I knew any negotiation with them would be futile. Any money that we invested would have to go into the company and not to the Modis. I had been a member of the IDBI Western Committee for many years and a UTI trustee, so I had a good idea about recalcitrant promoters and the desperate desire to hold on to even sick companies regardless of pressure from the banks.

I told IDBI that I would provide them with a plan and they would have to get the Modis to approve it. I would not personally deal with the Modis. The plan was to reduce the company's share capital by 75 per cent, after which new shares would be issued to Ambuja to give us a

95 per cent stake. In return, Ambuja would pump ₹166 crore into the company for its rehabilitation. With this plan, the Modi stake in the company would be reduced to less than 1 per cent.

The institutions forced the Modis to agree to the plan. It was also conditioned on IDBI and IFC taking significant haircuts on their loans—IFC agreed to settle for a payment of ₹65 crore in lieu of their ₹100 crore loan after much haggling and IDBI reduced its interest rates on its ₹100 crore loan to the same level that it was charging Gujarat Ambuja. The plan was finally agreed to by all parties and we took over the company. We got a 1.15-million-tonne cement plant at a bargain-basement price. It was our first success at a company acquisition. For IDBI, it was one of those rare occasions that they were able to sell a sick company that owed them vast amounts of money. Everyone seemed happy.

As soon as the deal was announced, I remember getting a call from the finance head of one of India's most prominent industrial groups. He wanted to talk to me to understand the basics of what I had done. They used the technique for a takeover they were planning at that time.

The Modi Cement plant was in surprisingly good condition despite being shut for a while. The township they built at Bhatapara was impressive, too. Mr D.K. Modi, the youngest son of Mr K.N. Modi and the man responsible for running the company, was genuinely grateful that we had taken over. It helped resolve a long-running feud between him and his brother. He promised to support us in every manner possible. The plant had been shut for several months by the time we completed the legal formalities and took charge in December 1997. We restarted it, renamed the company Ambuja Cement Eastern Ltd (ACEL) and rebranded the cement as Ambuja. The hope was that the new brand name would help sell the cement faster in the company's primary east India market, particularly Bengal.

The acquisition of ACEL presented a great opportunity for me to get the next generation of our family more actively involved in the running of the company's business. A few years earlier, we had inducted my son Pulkit and Vinod Neotia's son Harshvardhan into the Ambuja board as non-executive directors. I thought it would be an excellent idea for Harsh to run ACEL as its MD. He was based in Calcutta, the company's biggest market and the plant itself was more accessible from there than Mumbai. Harsh had never worked in cement, but he ran a construction company and had an interest in architecture. He was well connected with the Bengal government, which I was sure would come in handy for our plan to set up a grinding unit in the state.

When I first suggested Harsh's name to Suresh for the position of ACEL's MD at our annual gathering in Kodinar, he was rather dismissive. He said Harsh did not have any experience in running a cement business. I told him to leave it to me. But when I spoke to Harsh, he wasn't as enthusiastic as I expected. 'I don't know anything about running cement companies,' was his first reaction. I was surprised. Maybe it was nerves. I told him not to worry. 'I will teach you. I am responsible for you and I will guide you on everything.'

He did not want to shift to Bhatapara, so it was decided that he would go there several times a month. He would come down to Mumbai every few weeks to report to and seek advice from other senior colleagues and me. It was not as if we had thrown Harsh in the deep end without any support. The entire top management at Gujarat Ambuja was involved in cleaning up the inefficient operations left behind by the previous management.

Mr Kulkarni and his team took charge of the technical aspects of the plant and got it running to its rated capacity within a few months. Mr Taparia deputed his team to examine the books and found rampant corruption across the company. We knew the names of the people involved, but we did not sack them. At a philosophical level, I believe in the goodness of all men. It is the working environment that makes them corrupt. The atmosphere at Modi Cement, we discovered, was tailor-made for corruption from top to bottom.

When Harsh took charge and with help from Mr Kulkarni and Mr Taparia, put new systems in place, things changed dramatically in a few months. The same people began delivering results. We turned the company around in the first year itself, producing more than a million tonnes of cement. It was a tremendous learning experience for all of us.

In business, the only thing that we can do is create a suitable environment for people to give their best. External factors, such as the economy, government policies, taxation, etc., are beyond our control. What is in one's power is the value system, the culture of hard work and innovation. If we can do that and if we are fair to everyone—employees, vendors and customers—we will be able to build an organization that inspires people to give their best. It is this cultural transformation that we brought about at ACEL in less than a year.

After making a marginal profit in the first year, we made a loss of ₹40 crore the next year. Though production was going up, I was not entirely happy with our performance. Changes were not happening at the pace I had anticipated. We decided that an experienced corporate professional should run the company on a full-time basis. I asked Harsh to look for someone. On his recommendation, we recruited Mr S.N. Toshniwal, a chartered accountant who was at that time running a manufacturing company in Calcutta. He was willing to give that up to join us.

We appointed him as the CEO based out of Bhatapara. Having run a factory, he was comfortable around the plant and proved to be very capable. The day-to-day problems diminished and things picked up steam. To help him with sales and marketing, I sent Mr Atul Desai, one of our brightest managers from Ahmedabad. He did a good job as well. Simultaneously, Mr Kulkarni began working on increasing the capacity of the plant to 1.8 million tonnes, which improved our productivity remarkably. We put up a captive power plant which helped tremendously in dealing with the notoriously bad electricity situation in the state.

Two years later, we invested in a million-tonne grinding unit at Sankrail outside Calcutta. We chose the location because of its proximity to the thermal power plant of Calcutta Electric Supply Company from where fly ash would be available for free, as in Rupnagar and Bathinda. Though Sankrail was nearly 900 kilometres from Bhatapara, it made things logistically easier for the distribution of cement to our primary markets. Besides Bengal, it opened up the entire eastern and north-eastern market for us. That is when we began realizing the full potential of ACEL. Much of the credit for this goes to Harsh and our two professionals, Mr Toshniwal and Mr Atul Desai. Profits began picking up and by 2003, the figure had reached ₹66 crore.

The process of reviving the erstwhile Modi Cement, now ACEL, was arduous. It required a lot of management time and resources. It made me think about augmenting our top management. Gujarat Ambuja was still being run at the top by its founding team. We were now a company producing 10 million tonnes of cement at five plant locations and had three captive ports in two states. My energy level was not the same as it used to be and I had cut down on my travels. I had long felt the need for someone to work with me at the senior level, someone with experience and understanding of the intricacies of managing a multilocational, multifaceted large company.

The name at the top of my mind for many years for this role was Mr A.L. Kapur. He was then the ED and CEO of Birla Corporation Ltd, the erstwhile Birla Jute & Industries Ltd, which owned some of India's best-run cement plants. I had known him since the 1980s, when Gujarat Ambuja was being set up and he was an ED at ACC. He was a chartered accountant who had started his career at Bharat Heavy Electricals Ltd (BHEL) before moving to the government-owned Cement Corporation of India Ltd, where his mentor Col. Satya Pal Wahi had taken over in the late 1970s as MD. After the duo turned the loss-making company around, Col. Wahi joined ONGC (then known as Oil and Natural Gas Commission), which he famously remade into the giant that it is today. Mr Kapur joined ACC, India's largest cement company at that time.

I had long admired ACC for being the ideal professionally managed cement company. I was even more impressed with Kapur *saab*'s wisdom and knowledge the few times I met him. I kept in touch with him and we used to meet intermittently. He left ACC in 1989 after the famous rights issue debacle. He was about to join a Madras-based MNC when I persuaded him to stay back in Bombay and take over as the CEO of the CMA. I was an ordinary member of the CMA at that time, but I realized the vital role the organization could play in influencing government policies at a time when cement had just been decontrolled.

I persuaded the CMA to pay him the same salary as he had drawn at ACC and when he said he did not have a house in Mumbai, we rented one for him at Cuffe Parade. In his two-year stint, he helped reorganize CMA into the strong and influential body that it continues to be today. Once his job was done, he moved to head the cement operations of Birla Jute, which was a Calcutta-based M.P. Birla Group company. I would have loved to recruit him at that time, but I was too wary because we were still only a 7,00,000-tonne, one-plant company.

In 1990, following the death of Ashok Birla on 14 February in an air crash in Bengaluru and the death of his uncle Mr M.P. Birla in July, the affairs of Zenith Industries Ltd fell into disarray. Mr Kapur was persuaded by Mrs Priyamvada Birla (who had taken over as chairperson of Birla Jute after her husband M.P. Birla's death) to take over as MD and put the company back on the rails. A few years, later he returned to Birla Jute to his old assignment, as head of the cement division. Soon after that the MD, Mr J.R. Birla (no relation of the owners), was diagnosed with cancer and died shortly thereafter. Mr Kapur was asked to step into his shoes at the now renamed Birla Corporation.

We remained in contact all through the 1990s and he succeeded me as president of the CMA in 1998. Coincidentally, his son Ajay, a smart young man who was looking for a change from his high-pressure job at

Citibank, joined me as my executive assistant in 1993. He went on to head the marketing operations of the company and was appointed as the CEO in 2014.

When Mr Kapur retired from Birla Industries in 1998, I finally saw it as an opportunity to get him into Ambuja. The company, I felt, had the right size and scale for a man of his stature. And I was desperately looking to augment our senior management to match our pace of growth and expansion. He joined us in May 1999 as a whole-time director and I asked him to look after the Himachal Pradesh operation, Ambuja Eastern and several other new projects. A few months later, he helped recruit his deputy N.P. Ghuwalewala, a chemical engineer who headed the cement operations for Birla Corporation, further strengthening the team.

This was also the time when we received an offer from the Hyderabad-based Visaka Industries to take over an 8,25,000-tonne cement plant in the state. I saw this as another opportunity to get a foothold in the south. But that was not to be, as my old friend Mr Srinivasan swooped in once again from Chennai, sweetened the deal and walked off with the plant. Tired of our failed attempts to take over plants in the region, we decided to set up our own plant in the south. In 1998, we signed a deal with the Andhra Pradesh government for the lease of limestone mines in the coastal Guntur district of the state. The plan was to set up a 2-million-tonne plant at the cost of ₹500 crore.

In our effort to expand the sea-transportation network, we had planned a chain of bulk cement ports around the country. The chain would stretch from Karwar (on the north Karnataka coast) to Mangaluru, Kochi in Kerala and Tuticorin on Tamil Nadu's south-eastern coast. The idea was to expand our Kodinar operations and send cement to these three prosperous states in the south and establish the Ambuja brand name. My big mistake was that I chose Tuticorin as my starting point in south India.

The plan was to invest ₹16 crore to build the port and the onshore facilities, the land for which was acquired in 1998. Mysteriously, problems surfaced soon after. Suddenly everyone in the area became aware of the project and began opposing it. The port workers nearby and the village panchayat were against it. We could never figure out why, considering we would have created jobs and invested in the area. False police complaints were filed against us saying that we had bribed the panchayat president with alcohol for permission to buy the land. It reminded me of what had happened in Mahuva.

Later we found out who was instigating the troubles. I had never thought he could go to such levels. I asked Mr Kapur to sort out the problem. He flew down and met people in Chennai and Tuticorin and came back saying that setting up the port was not a good business decision. I realized my mistake and dropped the project. I also decided never to do anything in Tamil Nadu; I rarely back out of business decisions. My instinct is always to fight back if I feel I am right. It was the only occasion where I did not.

The Tuticorin incident reminded me about a decision I had made a few years earlier of not giving into a senior Union minister's demand for the permission to set up a cement port on the Kerala coast, in Cochin. We had won an open government tender and had planned to invest ₹ 100 crore in the project. It would have helped us send cement to Tamil Nadu and Kerala. But the minister had certain demands. I refused and walked away. It would be another ten years before Ambuja would finally set up bulk cement ports in Kochi and Mangaluru.

Another unsuccessful dream of mine at this time was to set up a cement plant in the then state of Jammu and Kashmir. It had some of the best limestone deposits in north India but only one small cement plant. Insurgency was then still in its early stages. Our people visited Srinagar and spent time with the politicians and bureaucrats to check the business environment. The response they got was similar to what we got in Himachal Pradesh. The state seemed keen, but placed too many preconditions. We also got the feeling that they would not follow through with their promises of concessions and non-interference. We decided to abandon the idea, a decision that I do not regret, considering what has happened in the state since then.

Sri Lanka was another disappointment for me around this time. We were India's biggest cement exporter to that country for many years. We thought it would be worthwhile to set up a bulk cement port and a grinding unit as part of Ceylon Ambuja, a company that we had set up there. We had chosen Galle, on the country's south-west coast, 135 kilometres from Colombo, as our site.

By the time we got permission, we had found that the authorities had allotted the same location to Swiss cement giant Holcim to put up a similar port. As a result, we were forced into a less suitable strip of land where we had problems building the silo and the pipeline. After spending close to $5 million, the port finally began operations in September 2000. But the project never really lived up to its potential. Working with Sri Lankan dealers was difficult and I came away with the impression that the locals were not happy dealing with Indian companies. Holcim, on the other hand, had no such issues with their operations.

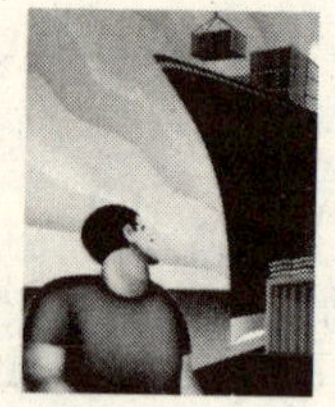

13

The Leap into the Major League

Agony and the ecstasy behind ACC share acquisition • The DLF acquisition • Setting up India's most profitable cement plant

Big changes had been underway in the Indian cement industry since price controls were fully lifted in 1989. The abolition of licensing and the dilution of the MRTP (Monopolistic and Restrictive Trade Practices) Act in the early 1990s accelerated this process. The process picked up pace towards the second half of the 1990s, as a wave of consolidation swept across the industry. Weaker players in the historically fragmented industry were shutting down plants or were being taken over by more efficient companies.

Our Modi Cement takeover was among the many similar deals that happened as part of this process. Others included Visaka Cements which was bought by India Cements; Narmada Cement bought by L&T; the cement division of Tata Steel bought by Lafarge; and Lafarge's buying of the cement division of Raymond Limited. However, nothing in Indian corporate history generated as much controversy, publicity, petty jealousy and heartburn as when we bought the Tata group's 14 per cent stake in ACC in early 2000.

My tryst with the Tatas started when Tata Steel wanted to sell me its cement plants roughly around the time that we were working on the Modi Cement takeover, which concluded in December 1997. Located in Jojobera outside Jamshedpur, the two grinding plants had a combined capacity of 1.7 million tonnes and manufactured hydraulic cement from slag—a by-product of their steel blast furnace located nearby. It is a type of cement that sets and hardens once mixed with water. The company's clinker unit was situated at Sonadih in Raipur district.

Dr Jamshed Irani, Tata Steel's MD, called me saying that they wanted to sell us the plants. It was a far cry from the time I had tried to meet Dr Irani when we were setting up Gujarat Ambuja. Since we were then in the market for a large amount of steel for our civil work, I had thought it a good idea to meet him in person before placing the order. He had given me a two-minute audience at Bombay House before fobbing me off on a deputy. I felt slighted and gave the order to Steel Authority of India Limited (SAIL). Later, as Gujarat Ambuja became a name to reckon with in corporate circles, I was told by industry insiders that Mr Ratan Tata admired what Ambuja had done. So did many others at Bombay House. '*Yeh* Marwari *hai,* ethical *hai,* efficient *hai*. This man has done a fabulous job, created a fabulous brand out of nothing,' was one conversation that was quoted to me.

Dr Irani said he wanted to meet me without any intermediaries. He was friendly and warm. He told me that Tata Steel had decided to get out of cement and wanted to sell its plants. Mr Ratan Tata was keen that Ambuja buy the plants. Besides everything else, they were impressed by our record on pollution control. Their significant concerns were pollution and dust. I was surprised that they asked me instead of ACC, a company in which the Tatas had a stake. It became clear later that this was an indicator of the troubled relationship between ACC and the Tatas.

Jamshedpur in those days was still part of Bihar (Chhattisgarh being formed in November 2000) and my concern was about our ability to handle the local unions, politicians and the government itself. Outside of the Tatas who founded Jamshedpur, no other industrial group had too many good things to say about investing in the state. I was very wary. A few days later, I went back to Dr Irani and told him, 'I am honoured that you and Ratan have decided to invite us to buy these plants and we would like to buy them. But I have heard stories about the problems non-Tata companies have had in Bihar. We will buy them on the condition that the Tatas will continue to be a shareholder in the company. Whether it is 10 per cent or 50 per cent holding, you can decide. But I want the Tatas to be our partner. It will reduce the chances of people creating a nuisance for us.'

My thinking was that since Tata Chemicals had a partnership with Excel Industries in Gujarat, there was no reason they could not partner with Gujarat Ambuja in Jamshedpur. They were strangely reluctant. 'Ratan and I have decided to get out of cement entirely,' Dr Irani told me. I was disappointed at giving up the opportunity, but I felt it was too much of a risk to go in alone. The Tatas eventually sold the division to Lafarge for ₹500 crore, signalling the French giant's arrival in India.

This history with the Tatas was at the back of my mind when Nimesh Kampani of JM Financial, my friend and fellow board member, met me in early 1999. Nimesh was close to the Tata bosses, having been their investment banker for a long time. He told me that the Tatas were looking to sell their 14 per cent stake in ACC and were wondering if I would be interested. To me, the offer represented much more than just an opportunity to buy a stake in India's largest cement company.

―

From my earliest days in cement, I had looked up to ACC. Before the decontrol of cement, it commanded a massive 60 per cent share of the market. The Tatas ran the best and most modern plants, and employed the finest managers and cement technologists in the industry—ACC was to cement what Tata Steel was to steel, Telco was to trucks and Hindustan Lever was to soaps and detergents.

Every cement company professional I admired was from ACC. Though the sheen had worn off in recent years because of misguided diversifications, nimbler and more agile competitors like us and L&T and the simmering friction with Bombay House, the company was still an object of desire in the cement industry and on the stock market. It was India's second-largest cement maker with the best geographical spread across the country, both in terms of its manufacturing facilities and distribution network.

There was no question of rejecting Nimesh Kampani's offer. He introduced me to Mr Noshir Soonawala, the Tata veteran who was the finance director of Tata Sons, the group's holding company and a close confidant of Mr Ratan Tata. The plan was for me to negotiate with him directly. Confidentiality was of the utmost importance since ACC had been such a high-profile and controversial company over the previous decade. I kept the news of the negotiations a secret even from our executive committee members, including close colleagues Mr Kulkarni, Mr Rao, Mr Taparia and Mr Kapur. All of them were recent inductees to the company board. The only senior team member privy to the discussion was Anil Singhvi. He was the company treasurer and would be required to play a vital role in raising funds if the deal went through.

It was not the first time that I was offered an opportunity to buy ACC shares. In 1988, at my father's *baithak* ceremony after he passed away, I remember Nimesh taking me aside to ask whether I would be interested in subscribing to the ACC's failed rights issue. Two of the largest shareholders, the Tatas and Shapoorji Pallonji, had refused to subscribe to their portion because of the company's poor results. Though I was not sure what was happening, the reluctance of these large shareholders to participate in the rights issue indicated a potential problem. I was too new and small to get involved in these big boys' shenanigans. I politely refused Nimesh's offer.

The failed rights issue turned out to be a major scandal. Its roots lay in the fraught relationship between the ACC's headquarters Cement House and Bombay House, though they were just a few 100 metres apart. The origins could be found in the company's history. Associated Cement Companies was formed in 1936 when four of Bombay's most prominent business houses—the Tatas, Khataus, Killick Nixon and FE Dinshaw—merged all eleven of their cement companies into one professionally managed corporation. While the descendants of the other three founders diluted their stakes over the years and moved away, the Tatas had retained their connection through a minority stake and board positions.

The ACC chairman, Mr Nani Palkhivala, had been a forty-one-year-old rising star at Bombay High Court when he joined the Tatas in 1961. He was appointed to the ACC board the same year. Eight years later, in 1969, he became the chairman. 'I believe I was recommended (to be made chairman) because I was a professional manager. It (ACC) has never been a Tata group company,' he would say years later in a newspaper interview in the context of the problems in their relationship.

For the next three decades, he steered the destiny of the company, making sure that the board fiercely guarded its independence. Though a consummate Tata insider with board positions in several group companies, including the holding company Tata Sons, he always gave the impression of ACC being a separate entity. Continuing with the tradition from its founding days, when none of the original promoter logos was used to sell ACC cement, the Tata logo was also never used.

The strained relationship between the Tatas and ACC had become evident for the first time in 1988 when the Tata group had refused to subscribe to its share of the ₹15-crore ACC rights issue (as discussed above). The company was going through a particularly bad time and was desperate to raise money. Still, Bombay House decided to keep away, because of which the issue was in danger of being undersubscribed. Mr Palkhivala then decided to invite non-shareholders to invest and pick up the Tatas' portion of the issue. I was, as I revealed earlier, one of the few outsiders asked to participate and I had declined.

The company's fortunes had brightened once again in the early 1990s when cement prices firmed up. The cash surpluses generated at that time were unfortunately frittered away by the management in unrelated diversifications like tyres, float glass, synthetic ferric oxides and quartz crystals. It was not just about the funds that got diverted, but also the valuable management time and resources that got commandeered elsewhere. Most of these companies were run by managers pulled from ACC. As a result, when the next downturn came in the cement industry in the late 1990s, the company was deep in the red.

In 1995, the Tata group once again refused to participate in the company's ₹313-crore rights issue. Not long after that, the group chairman, Mr Ratan Tata, embarked on a restructuring and consolidation exercise by pushing out established chieftains like Mr Darbari Seth, Mr Ajit Kerkar and Mr Russi Modi and bringing their companies under the direct control of Bombay House. The ACC management under Mr Palkhivala, however, continued to guard its independence fiercely—ACC refused to participate in a plan to allow Tata Sons to raise its stake in the group companies and declined to pay a royalty for the use of the Tata brand name and logo. 'ACC has a strong brand name. It has never sold its cement on any Tata brand. Why should it pay any fees?' was Mr Palkhivala's assertion.

In early 1997, Mr Palkhivala—in an unusually strongly worded response—made his and ACC's position clear on the Tata linkage, in an interview to the *Business Standard* newspaper: 'The board of directors of ACC does not regard ACC as a Tata company or a Tata-controlled company. ACC is run as a professionally managed company. The board of ACC makes every decision after considering whether it is in the best interest of ACC or not.'

To the question of why ACC should not be called a Tata company, he replied, 'Let me ask you, when was ACC a Tata company? For the last thirty years, ACC has not been suggested to be a Tata company. Why should it be called a Tata company now?' And finally, about Tata Chemicals and Tata Tea's stake in ACC, he had this to say: 'These investments were made by Mr Darbari Seth in 1988. He asked me if I had any objections to his companies' investments. I said I had no objections. So, the Tata companies have a stake in ACC.'

The Tatas made one last attempt to bring ACC under their fold. In January 1999, the Tatas made an offer to raise their stake in the company to 20 per cent through a preferential issue. The logic was that the preferential issue, rather than an open public offer, would result in ACC getting some much-needed funds. This time the financial institutions, led by IDBI and UTI who were the biggest shareholders in the company with their 22 per cent stake, refused to back the deal saying that ACC was not a Tata group company and that the offer price of ₹110 a share was too low.

The Tatas then withdrew the board resolution but decided that this was the last straw. Mr Ratan Tata asked Mr Soonawala to find a buyer for their stake in ACC. Mr Soonawala, in turn, authorized Nimesh Kampani to talk to me to assess our interest in acquiring the stake. Separately, it seems they were also in discussion with Lafarge, which had bought their Tata Steel cement plants a year earlier.

I saw the Tata offer as a great opportunity. Beyond my admiration for the company, there were a few other compelling reasons that made this potential investment in ACC worth the effort and the money. First, ACC was not only the largest and the most experienced cement player in the country but also held a unique position in the industry in terms of its presence throughout the country. Second, it had plants in as many as nine states, including the south where we had been desperately looking to set up operations for years. Third, an alliance with ACC would result in a combined cement production capacity of around 20 million tonnes, totalling more than 20 per cent of the Indian cement market. This would make us the largest combine in the country and give us tremendous clout in the industry. Finally, since Lafarge was the rival bidder for this deal, our success would foil their plan of gaining a pan-India footprint in one fell swoop. The French cement conglomerate, with its deep pockets, had the potential to make its Indian competitors' lives miserable in every state where each of us had our plants.

The Tatas wanted to sell their stake in two tranches of 7 per cent each. I later discovered that some of the shares were bought recently and they were looking to cut down on their tax outgo. I was happy with this arrangement because it made it relatively easier to raise funds. Raising money to buy the entire 14 per cent at one go would have been difficult.

The 14 per cent stake came with two board positions, as well as a chairman of our choice. That way, we would be able to influence the company's running without having to make an expensive public offer for an additional stake of 20 per cent, as was required by law at that time. We did not have the money to make a public offer and I would have backed out if that was the deal. I was confident that with our board positions, we would be able to help revamp the company operations in a way that would benefit shareholders. The balance sheet revealed the inefficiency of the company's operations. Its cement production had exceeded the rated capacity only once in the previous twenty years. With this style of working, it was quite clear that the company would never be able to compete with newer players like us.

My negotiations with Mr Soonawala were so confidential that I kept them a secret even from my board members and senior executives. Yet, something curious was happening to the ACC share price through much of 1999. When we first started talking, it was quoting in the region of ₹140. After which, it began climbing steadily despite every indication that the company was doing badly that year. It peaked at around ₹300 towards the end of the year. Either the news of the negotiation had leaked or the Tatas themselves were buying up the shares. I was inclined to believe the latter. After the deal was done and we got possession of their share certificates (this was in the pre-demat days), many of them had recent transaction dates.

In December 1999, when our negotiations with the Tatas were in the final stages, I read a newspaper report that Lafarge was simultaneously talking to the Delhi real estate king K.P. Singh and his son Rajiv Singh to buy DLF Cements Ltd, which had a modern 1.5-million-tonne plant in Rabriyawas in northern Rajasthan's Pali district. The company was known to be poorly managed and the plant had been badly delayed. We never thought of it as a threat to us in the northern market. That would change if Lafarge took over. With its financial muscle and management strength, it could prove to be a tough competitor for us in north India. But there was little I could do about it now, so I ignored the news.

On Thursday that week, I got an early morning call from Mr R.V. Pandit, an old acquaintance of mine, who said he wanted to see me urgently. I went across to meet him at his room at the Taj Mahal Hotel on my way to work. Mr Pandit was a maverick who ran restaurants in Hong Kong and Tokyo and owned a successful B2B publishing house based in Mumbai with magazines like *Imprint* and *Indian Auto Journal* in its stable. He had produced movies like *Maachis* (1996) and *Darmiyaan* (1997). He also owned the famous Mumbai bookstore Nalanda, at the Taj Mahal Hotel. He had over the years developed close personal friendships with top political leaders such as Mr Atal Bihari Vajpayee, Mr L.K. Advani and many RSS functionaries. He had acquired the status of an economic adviser to them and held strong swadeshi nationalistic views.

Mr Pandit, like me, had seen the Lafarge–DLF news report. As soon as I arrived at his Taj suite, he asked me, 'How can you let it happen? How can you let an MNC buy an Indian company?'

I replied, 'What can I do? DLF wants to sell and must have approached Lafarge. I am not in the picture.'

'Are you prepared to buy the company if I arrange for it?' he asked. I said yes without thinking. Mr Pandit immediately picked up the phone and spoke to an officer in the government whom he appeared to know very well. He told him the same thing. 'How can you let a multinational buy an Indian company? You please call Mr K.P. Singh of DLF and ask him how he can do this. I have an Indian buyer sitting here with me.'

The officer called back a little later to say that Mr K.P. Singh was willing to sell the company to an Indian buyer if he got the same price. He added that Mr Singh was not ready to sacrifice on any of the terms and that the deal had to be done the next day because the original plan was to sign with Lafarge the day-after. Mr Pandit turned to me and said, 'You buy now.'

'How can I, at such short notice?' I said.

He seemed unfazed. 'What is there?' he said, implying that he saw no problem.

I promised I would try. I requested him to ask his government contact to set up a meeting and returned to my office, unsure about how to proceed. I knew very little about DLF Cements, other than the fact that it had come up recently and was not doing well. It had accumulated losses of over ₹225 crore and its share price was quoting below ₹10. I asked Anil Singhvi if he would be able to arrange the required funding at short notice if needed. He seemed optimistic and said money should not be a problem since Bank of America (BoA) had been desperately after him to lend us money. 'I will talk to them. They will issue a cheque immediately for even ₹500 crore if we want,' he told me.

The next day was Friday and we flew to Delhi by an afternoon flight as the meeting with the Singhs was fixed for 5 p.m. I requested Mr Ghuwalewala, the former head of the cement division at Birla Industries who had joined us a few months earlier on the recommendation of Mr A.L. Kapur, to come along. If the deal went through, I planned to have him manage the company.

We went straight to the DLF office and the negotiations began immediately with Mr K.P. Singh and his son Mr Rajiv Singh. They did not sound happy at being forced into this situation. It seemed as if they were negotiating under duress. It was not very pleasant to negotiate with an unhappy seller. But we could not back out either, because of Mr

Pandit. At the same time, it was also our big opportunity to stop Lafarge from getting a foothold in north India. We were, after all, eyeing the same market with our large investments in Himachal Pradesh and Punjab.

The negotiations went on late into the night before we were able to arrive at a deal. The reluctant Singhs agreed to sell their entire 21 per cent holding in the company at ₹12.65 a share, for a total value of ₹82 crore. Was it the best price? We don't know because it was not based on any solid research or valuation work. It was based on our gut feeling, not the ideal way to negotiate an acquisition deal. We were flying blind. None of us had seen the plant, so we had no idea about its condition or if there were any other problems. Everything that we knew about DLF Cements was from newspaper clips and a few research reports. I remember Mr Ghuwalewala telling me on the flight that it felt as if we were going to the market to buy a shirt rather than a large company.

I was reminded of a story told to me about how Mr R.P. Goenka bought CEAT Tyres in the early 1980s. Mrs Indira Gandhi, the PM at that time, was on an official tour of Italy when the CEAT owners sought a meeting with her to ask permission to sell the company. They named an Indian industrialist as the buyer. She told them that she would get someone else to pay the same price and buy it. She asked Mr R.P. Goenka, who was close to her, to buy the company and he did.

Later, when someone asked him why he had bought the company without examining the plant or the books, he replied that he knew the person who had negotiated the original deal and was confident he had done a thorough job to arrive at the valuation. I had similar thoughts about this deal. Lafarge obviously would have done their due diligence to arrive at their valuation. The Singhs were not going to sell it to me at a price lower than what Lafarge had offered and it was doubtful that they would overcharge me.

As the evening wore on and we arrived at an understanding with the Singhs, there was still one part of the deal that had to be negotiated. The company had borrowed a considerable amount of money from ICICI at a usurious interest rate of 19.5 per cent. We had informed the ICICI MD, Ms Lalita Gupte, to be on standby for her approval of the deal that evening. Thankfully, she made herself available on the phone from her home in Mumbai, though it was late at night.

She initially refused to budge on the rates when we requested for a cut. I said nobody on earth could pay such a rate and survive. She said they had defaulted repeatedly. They were given the loan at 15 per cent, after which the rates went up. She said she wanted her full payment. After more than four to five hours of negotiation, we finally came to an agreement at two in the morning. We went back to the Singhs after that and told them we had a deal. It was 3 a.m. by then.

We ended up spending nearly ₹350 crore to acquire the company which included a 15-megawatt captive power station. The company was renamed Ambuja Cement Rajasthan Ltd (ACRL). When Mr Kulkarni and his team went to examine the plant, they found that it was a disaster in the way it was run. There were no systems, productivity was low and pollution-control measures were weak. A bigger shock was the fact that the employees, including the CEO, were being paid in cash every month. The factory and mining land deals were not registered, nor had their stamp duties been paid. It was as if the company was running in an alternative universe with its own rules and regulations! We appointed Mr Ghuwalewala as MD and it took years to get the company back on its feet.

Like Modi Cement, I was not entirely happy with this acquisition either. The investment in terms of management time and money to revive it was not worth the purchase cost. It would have been cheaper and more effective if we had put up our own plant. The only benefit was time—a new plant would have taken us at least two years—and by doing what we did, we were able to ward off the immediate threat from Lafarge. We had also now established our own north-west corridor. We were leaders in a long stretch of the market starting from Mumbai and extending across Gujarat, Rajasthan, Haryana, western Uttar Pradesh, Punjab, Himachal Pradesh and Uttarakhand up to (the then state of) Jammu and Kashmir.

We moved fast over the next few years to set up grinding units right across this corridor to augment our position. In addition to Rupnagar, we added Bathinda that serviced southern Punjab, western Uttar Pradesh and Haryana. In 2006, after Holcim took over the management, the company added grinding units in Rauri and Nalagarh to feed remaining areas in Himachal Pradesh and Jammu and Kashmir; Roorkee to service Uttarakhand and neighbouring Uttar Pradesh; and Dadri for south and parts of western Uttar Pradesh. Thus, ACRL was a timely buy to fill a critical geographical gap.

Done with the DLF buy, I had a much-deserved weekend of rest before getting back to close the ACC deal on Monday. Coincidentally, the previous evening all the Neotias—Suresh, Vinod and Harsh—were in Mumbai and I decided to get them on board. We were together when I told them what I was doing and asked for their opinion. Suresh asked Harsh what he thought. He said, 'Let us do it.' Vinod sounded happy and Suresh came on board as well.

On Monday morning, the Tatas told me they were ready to close the deal if we were willing to pay the price they wanted. Lafarge, I heard, had made a final offer of around ₹250 a share. Mr Soonawala asked me if I was willing to improve upon it. Impulsively I said, 'Yes, I am. I would pay substantially more.' To me, at that time, this seemed like a once-in-a-lifetime opportunity and I was not going to let it slip. The Tatas came back with a final figure of ₹370 a share, which was around a 50 per cent premium over the market price on that day. They said it was a take-it-or-leave-it offer. There was no question about me not taking it.

I agreed to their offer, but I had a few conditions. I wanted Dr Subrata Ganguly to step down from the board. In my view, ACC had to make a new beginning. I was not suggesting any change in management, only a change of directors associated with the company's poor performance in the recent past. Dr Ganguly had presided over the decline of the company through much of the 1990s. At the same time, I wanted Mr Soonawala, the Tata nominee, to continue to serve for a few more years. Besides the continuing presence of a director connected with the Tatas, I wanted him for his solidity, experience and reputation.

Mr Soonawala was initially reluctant because the Tatas wanted to break all ties with the company once the deal was done. My intense persuasion over the previous few months had worked. However, he had a warning for me: managing the ACC board was not easy. The whole-time company directors always had their way, he told me. No one was able to stop them from doing what they wanted. I told him that I was sure I would be able to handle them.

Within hours of my agreeing to the price, the Tatas sold us 1.23 crore ACC shares representing 7.2 per cent of their stake in the company, for ₹455 crore on a spot-delivery basis. BoA again provided us with the bridge loan to make the immediate payment. The understanding with the Tatas was that we would buy the remainder 7.2 per cent shares at the same price over the next few months. We agreed to call the deal a 'strategic alliance' between ACC and Gujarat Ambuja, a neutral term if ever there was one.

The deal was just a signed agreement to purchase the Tata shares. There were no accompanying covenants, bank guarantee or piles of legal documents. Nothing prevented me from backing out from the second transaction.

The ACC share price collapsed after the deal was made public. I heard that there was talk among some people at Bombay House on whether I could be trusted to keep my commitment. I was confident though that the Tata top brass trusted me; that was why they had made me the sale offer. Of course I intended to keep my word. That was one of the reasons my reputation went up in Bombay House. Mr Soonawala continued as an ACC director till the time we sold our stake to Holcim in 2006.

Before we made the deal public, I rushed to meet the heads of IDBI and UTI to brief them on the deal and seek their backing. They were among ACC's biggest shareholders. Their support and response were both critical if I had to play any meaningful role in ACC. To my relief, they were more than happy to back us. It wasn't only because of our reputation as the country's best-managed cement company, but also the fact that we had valued the company at a considerably higher price than the price the Tatas had offered them (₹110 a share) for the aborted preferential issue in January.

The chairman of IDBI, Mr D.B. Gupta, told me that he was confident I would be able to help revive the company and expressed his full support. Similarly, Mr P.S. Subramanyam, the UTI chairman, assured me of his full support. He offered me advice on drafting the press release about the deal. His suggestion was to keep it simple and to the point. Their confidence in us was based on the hope that we, with our track record, would be able to put ACC back on the rails after years of poor performance. Getting the financial institutions behind the deal was necessary for the next day's board meeting when the Tatas were to present the deal before the ACC board formally.

That evening I decided to inform our senior executives and the board about the impending announcement the next day. As I have said earlier, except for Anil Singhvi whose help I needed to coordinate with the bankers, I had told no one because of fear that the news might leak. Now when I told them, they were stunned, to put it mildly. They were flabbergasted that I had not discussed it with them. None of them were happy with the deal, wondering if we would be able to do justice to such a large company which had done so poorly in recent years. They felt let down by me in the manner that I had gone about it. I felt awful.

The next day, Mr Soonawala made his formal presentation to the full ACC board, including chairman emeritus Nani Palkhivala, who made it a point to participate despite his deteriorating health condition. Mr Soonawala explained the reasons behind the Tatas' decision to sell, which he attributed to the reluctance of the financial institutions to allow them to raise their stake through the preferential allotment in the previous year.

Mr Palkhivala asked the IDBI and UTI representatives for their opinion. In keeping with what their respective chairmen had told me at my meeting with them, they welcomed the deal. The UTI representative Amitabha Ghosh, as quoted in the board minutes said, 'The strategic alliance between ACC and Gujarat Ambuja was a step in the right direction.' The IDBI representative Mr J.N. Godbole noted, 'Taking into consideration the state of the cement industry, the consolidation taking place and the consequential need for economies of scale and leveraging of synergies, this would be a good alliance.'

The Tatas then recommended that Mr Kapur and I be inducted on the board as additional directors and representatives of Gujarat Ambuja. This was welcomed unanimously. With the board approval in our hands, we issued our respective press releases to make the deal public. Our press release was to the point, presenting the basics of the deal. It talked about the strategic alliance being a significant step towards the consolidation of the Indian cement industry and that I, along with Mr Kapur, had been invited to join the board.

The Tata press release, on the other hand, explained the reason the Tatas had chosen to sell their stake. This included the refusal by financial institutions in late 1998 to allow them to raise their stake to 20 per cent, which they felt was necessary to 'strengthen the financial structure of ACC in order to facilitate its growth'; the fact that the Tatas chose to sell the stake to us because Gujarat Ambuja was 'at present the most profitably managed cement company in the country'; and finally because the 'two major players in the cement industry could pool their strengths as part of the consolidation process which is going on in this industry'. They concluded by stating that, 'Mr Narotam Sekhsaria has been invited on the board of ACC and his experience and guidance will benefit the company and its management.'

The reception in the media the next day was nothing short of historic. The deal made banner headlines across the country. It was hailed as a 'Milestone deal in the history of corporate India', 'Deal of the decade', 'A giant leap forward' and 'A near-perfect strategic fit'. The stock market went euphoric as well. Gujarat Ambuja and ACC stock prices rose to hit the circuit breakers, while the market itself jumped more than 160 points on the back of the deal.

One newspaper analyst summed up the universally positive response saying, 'More than how valuable this deal turns out to be for Gujarat Ambuja and ACC, it could mark a turnaround in how competitors in the Indian industry look at each other. A new era of cooperation among the top players in various other industries could assure them a much better future. In some cases, it could even make companies globally competitive.'

The deal and what happened after that, made me more famous than I would have ever hoped to be. It was as if my life was divided into two parts, before the ACC deal and after. Before the deal, I was known among the cement manufacturers and Mumbai investment bankers as an entrepreneur who ran a very efficient cement company. Now it seemed everyone knew me. The deal was talked about in the newspapers for days and weeks. I spent most of that week fielding congratulatory calls from friends and acquaintances in the corporate and banking world. Many sent flowers.

Among the earliest to call were Mr Vijaypat Singhania of Raymond and Mr Dilip Piramal of VIP Industries Ltd. 'Narotam! It's really amazing. We are proud of you,' Dilip said to me. 'What you have done we would have never imagined. You took over ACC, a Tata company and that too at that price; you had the courage to do it. I salute you.' I had to clarify that it was not a takeover. He still insisted on throwing a party in my honour at the Taj. I told him that it was not the best time. I did not want to be under the spotlight any more than I was at that moment.

None of my friends from the cement world called. I was surprised. Granted, they were rivals, but I knew all of them very well. We would often get together at CMA meetings. I thought they would be happy that I had stopped Lafarge's entry into the country. Instead, there was complete radio silence from their side. It was as if they were upset with me for having upstaged them. I felt that I had made a big blunder by not informing them in advance. I should have explained to them that the Tatas were selling regardless of me buying. And if I didn't step in, Lafarge was waiting to pick it up. Surely, they would have preferred Gujarat Ambuja, an Indian company.

The week after the deal was relatively peaceful. I was inducted into the ACC board along with Mr Kapur. We were welcomed very cordially at our first board meeting and I was unanimously elevated to the position of vice-chairman. Separately, I had excellent interactions with the company MD, Mr T.M.M. Nambiar and the cement division director, Mr M.L. Narula, on the way forward in reviving ACC's sagging fortunes. Contrary to the image projected in the media later, even the financial institution directors could not have been more charming.

My rivals and detractors did not wait for too long. The same newspapers in Mumbai, Delhi and Kolkata which had hailed the deal as a landmark corporate achievement now began poking holes in it. They argued that our plan to buy the 14 per cent stake without making a public offer amounted to cheating the public shareholders and taking over the company via a roundabout route. My induction onto the board and elevation as vice-chairman, in their opinion, was the first sign that we had management control. The tone was tendentious and the analysis seemingly inspired.

Was there any subterfuge or sleight of hand involved in the way we bought into ACC? None whatsoever. Did we plan to do anything beyond what we promised in the press release? Not at all. Though we were now the largest non-financial institution shareholder, Ambuja had only two directors on the fifteen-member board. At no point did we have the numbers to push any agenda that did not have the approval of the majority of the board members. In this situation, there was no way we could have controlled the management, nor did we want to. A follow-up question would be, if not management control, then what was my intention behind buying the Tata stake?

I genuinely believed that ACC had great hidden potential that could be unlocked if we as board members brought in new ideas garnered from our years of running successful cement companies. My thinking was that if I provided constructive advice no one on the board should object, because a healthy bottom line would benefit everyone. We had already spent nearly ₹500 crore on buying the shares and an equal amount would be paid to buy the remainder of the Tata stake.

I very much intended to be an activist director on behalf of the shareholders, with the singular purpose of increasing shareholder value. That is why quite early in my tenure on the board, I instituted a Wednesday meeting with Mr Nambiar and Mr Narula. I planned to spend half a day with them, understand the workings of the company and then advise them on good practices that we had perfected at Ambuja. ACC's vast network of plants was spread over nine states, while ours stretched over seven states. Considering this geography, I felt we could coordinate to avoid price gouging where companies only end up destroying each other. And finally, as a major Indian player, I was worried about the effects of the arrival of deep-pocketed international players in the Indian market. If I had allowed Lafarge to buy the Tata stake, it would have created problems not only for us but also for the entire cement industry. Maybe my friends in the cement industry feared that if we were able to revive ACC, it would create problems for them.

The first one was one of our southern rivals, followed by a young Mumbai industrialist from a prominent family. As ACC had four plants in the south, the Chennai-based industrialist was worried that ACC's plants in Tamil Nadu and Andhra Pradesh would somehow overwhelm him. He considered the south to be his stomping ground and brooked no competition. He was close to the Dravida Munnetra Kazhagam (DMK) which was at that time in power at the Centre, as part of the Vajpayee government. Mr Murasoli Maran, the nephew of Mr M. Karunanidhi, was the powerful minister for industry.

Simultaneously, the Mumbai-based industrialist was working on his contacts in the government. Phone calls went out to the finance ministry whose mandarins feigned ignorance saying they had not blessed the deal. The UTI chairman, Mr Subramanyam, was asked how could he allow this to happen under his watch. Why did he agree to the transaction? Why were other cement companies not allowed to bid for the Tata stake? He was told that he had to get the transaction cancelled, or else his job would be on the line. Mr Subramanyam was not the kind who would stand up to any pressure from government bureaucrats or ministers. He panicked and called me. I was in Singapore on a short holiday with my wife. He told me about the phone call from Delhi and said that I should resign immediately from the board of the company.

'What nonsense,' I replied.

'You don't have the majority and you can't take control of the company,' Mr Subramanyam said. I told him I had not taken control of the company and I reminded him that he had blessed the deal and had advised me on how to draft my press release. 'You come to my office now,' he exclaimed.

I said I could not because I was in Singapore and that he would have to wait. I went to see him after I came back. Explaining what had happened, he said that there was tremendous pressure on him and that I had to do something. I came back to my office and decided to use my contacts in government circles to blunt the criticism. I called Mr R.V. Pandit, who had arranged the DLF deal a few weeks earlier. He was accommodating and immediately called his contacts in Delhi. Following this, the government decided that the matter should be SEBI's headache and that Mr D.R. Mehta, the SEBI chairman, was best placed to handle it.

Despite Mr Subramanyam's histrionics, his representatives on the ACC board and the IDBI representatives on the board continued to be very cordial and supportive in our board meetings. They did not object to my elevation as vice-chairman, nor did they oppose any of the drastic restructurings of ACC's operations that I suggested.

In February 2000, after a great deal of visible pressure from the media and the government, SEBI decided to open an investigation into the deal. I welcomed the announcement hoping that it would calm things down at least for some time until SEBI gave its verdict. But I was wrong. The media attacks continued non-stop. Among the more bizarre ones was a Kolkata-based business newspaper article about Lafarge talking to the finance ministry to make its own 'open offer for 30 per cent of ACC'.

A Mumbai-based business daily ran a story about how 'Gujarat Ambuja has 14 per cent in ACC, but 100 per cent of Management', which I wish was real. Then there was a report in the country's biggest newspaper four weeks after the financial institutions had approved my appointment as vice-chairman saying IDBI had taken 'an in-principle decision that they will not support the resolution to appoint Gujarat Ambuja chairman Narotam Sekhsaria as the vice-chairman of ACC, they have also asked the ACC management to explain the nature of its deal with Gujarat Ambuja'.

At one point, I thought of holding a press conference to clear the misconceptions. But the Neotias felt it would only muddy the waters further. The hope was that it would die a natural death, which it did not. Many of these news reports were fired from the shoulders of the financial institutions and I felt as though I was living in two different worlds—inside the boardroom, the directors of the financial institutions were a paradigm of cooperation and support; outside, in the media, they had their knives out for me.

The business papers were filled with stories about how the financial institutions were desperate to get us out, how they had never approved of the deal. Reports ranged from 'FIs want open offer for Gujarat Ambuja's ACC takeover' to 'FIs divided over the role of minority shareholders' to 'FIs keen to exit ACC'. There was even a report that I was planning to transfer the ACC stake into my private holding company.

Meanwhile, another issue had to be dealt with on an urgent basis. ACC chairman Mr Pallonji Mistry had expressed his desire to retire and I was finding it difficult to find an appropriate replacement. In ideal circumstances, I would have taken over as chairman myself, but these were not ideal conditions. It would have been interpreted as the next stage of our management takeover. There was a string of negative stories when I took over as vice-chairman, talking about how Gujarat Ambuja 'was tightening its hold on ACC'. I thought it would be best to get an outsider as the chairman, a neutral face who would be acceptable to everyone on the board, but should have the public stature to pre-empt any questioning by the press and by our rivals indirectly through their media friends.

I told Suresh about it because he was on good terms with many big-name industrialists across the country. He was at that time on his way to the US as part of a CII delegation led by Finance Minister Yashwant Sinha. He was going at the request of his good friend Mr Rahul Bajaj, who wanted some company. I asked him to find out if Rahul would be interested. On the flight, Rahul asked him, '*Suresh, tumhare ACC ka kya hua*?' Suresh said, '*Kuch hua nahi hai, chairmanship ka matter chal raha hai abhi*. None of us can be chairman,' he added. 'We need an outsider so that it does not look like an Ambuja group company.'

He asked Rahul whether he would be interested. He wasn't. 'If I come as chairman everybody will say I am a friend of yours,' he said. Instead, he suggested the name of Mr Tarun Das, the chief executive of CII, who was also on the same flight. 'He is from CII. Nobody will object. Everyone respects him,' he told Suresh.

Suresh phoned me when he landed in the US. He wanted my opinion. Mr Das had run CII since the late 1960s as the director-general and had been the CEO since the mid-1970s. He was one of the most respected figures in the Indian corporate arena and sat on several boards. I asked Suresh to sound him out. I wanted the chairmanship issue settled immediately, because Mr Mistry had been after the board to relieve him. Suresh and Rahul talked to Mr Das, who agreed immediately. They then went to Mr Yashwant Sinha, who thought it was a good idea. That was the assurance that IDBI and UTI would have no problems in supporting him.

Expectedly, Mr Das's appointment was greeted favourably by the media, though not without some unnecessary twists. Despite our press release explaining how it happened, India's most prominent business daily claimed that 'Mr Mistry is believed to have "selected" Mr Das as his successor—the ACC board unanimously honoured his wishes'. The same press release had details of the pre-planned resignation of Mr Mistry and Dr Subrata Ganguly from the board. The newspaper, though, interpreted it to say, 'Their resignations make way for Gujarat Ambuja to take over the reins at ACC. Ambuja, it is learnt, will buy out the remaining Tata stake and take over the management control, said a source.'

In late April, after all the fire and brimstone in the media, SEBI, having conducted a thorough investigation, stated unambiguously in its ruling that our 7.2 per cent stake acquisition in ACC did not amount to a 'takeover and does not necessitate a public offer to the shareholders'. The takeover code was not triggered because we were neither planning to acquire 15 per cent shares in the company (the threshold for triggering the takeover code), nor were we a majority on the board of directors of the company.

If I thought that was the end of the matter, I was mistaken. Newspaper articles now attacked the SEBI ruling. An appeal was filed by a shareholder before the Special Appellate Tribunal and at the high court. He lost both cases. We were able to prove that the petitioner had no personal interest in the matter and that he was acting on behalf of someone else. The court was upset with him and told him he could not be fighting someone else's cause. The judge asked him if he still wanted to go ahead because if the verdict went against him, he would have to pay us all the legal fees we incurred. He was given two hours to decide, after which his lawyer withdrew the complaint. The judge dismissed the case. Following this, the Special Appellate Tribunal also dismissed the case.

Despite all the legal challenges coming to naught, the media attacks continued for a long time and eventually the continuous volley of barbs got to me. It stressed me out that others were getting affected by it. Gujarat Ambuja's reputation, built assiduously over the years, was now under continuous scrutiny in the minds of employees, friends, family and shareholders who were reading these adverse news reports daily. And it was not just me. Suresh, who had built his reputation among industrialists and businessmen across the country, was distraught. He kept asking me if it was all worth it.

I had no time to rest and reflect. I was determined to get ACC back on the rails in as short a period as possible. We had to wrap up the rest of the ACC deal with the Tatas. Our agreement with the Tatas required that we complete our purchase of the remainder 7.2 per cent shares within one year. The bridge loan that we took for the first tranche of shares had to be paid back. When we bought the first 7.2 per cent tranche of the stake in late December, it was not done through Gujarat Ambuja but through Ambuja Cement Holdings Limited, a new subsidiary company that we had set up.

There was an essential reason for this. Cement is a capital-intensive business and therefore with rapid growth comes the requirement for capital, either debt or equity. Debt would determine the leverage of the business and equity would be at the cost of diluting the shareholders' capital. Every business has to work around a perfect mix of debt and equity. Our strategy always has been to grow without taking on large debts. The only option left was to raise equity capital, which, in turn, would have diluted the equity capital of Gujarat Ambuja. Some of my investment-banker friends advised that I should go for a rights issue. But I felt that we had diluted our equity capital enough in the past for growth.

I took the more innovative approach of getting equity money into the company without taking on debt or diluting the shareholder capital of Gujarat Ambuja. I brought in strategic investors to take a stake in our subsidiary company which held the shares of ACC. We renamed Ambuja Cement Holdings Limited to Ambuja Cement India Limited (ACIL) and sold 40 per cent of its stake to two reputed global investors—American International Group (AIG), through its infrastructure fund; and the Government of Singapore, through its infrastructure investment arm, GIC. They saw a great future for the cement industry in India. They invested a total of ₹372 crore in ACIL. We sold Gujarat Ambuja's 93 per cent stake in ACEL (the erstwhile Modi Cement) to ACIL for ₹415 crore, which resulted in a profit of ₹249 crore for Gujarat Ambuja.

My understanding with the investors was that ACIL would not be a passive holding company. It would set up new cement plants as well as acquire old ones, in which the three partners—Gujarat Ambuja, AIG and GIC—would invest within the proportion of their holdings in the company. We divided the country into two geographical zones to avoid confusion. Gujarat Ambuja Cements Ltd would expand in the north and west, while ACIL would invest in the east and south. Later that year, ACIL invested a further ₹483 crore to buy the Tatas' remaining 7.2 per cent stake in ACC, thus completing our transaction with the Tatas as planned.

Next, ACIL took on the task of setting up a 2-million-tonne cement plant worth ₹600 crore, planned for Nadikudi in Andhra Pradesh as its first project. We had already procured land for it. I made sure I was not on the board of ACIL, since it was holding the ACC share and I was the ACC vice-chairman. The wonderful thing about this new structure was that the strategic investors would provide the additional capital for further expansions, allowing both ACIL and Gujarat Ambuja to grow rapidly. The advantage to Gujarat Ambuja shareholders was that ACIL was a subsidiary company of Gujarat Ambuja. Through the consolidation of accounts, everything came under the umbrella of their mother company.

At ACC, I discovered that years of underinvestment in the core cement business in the 1990s had left the company in a bad way. Its much-vaunted technical capabilities across the various plants were now subpar and there was a terrible shortage of good people to run them. The only good thing was that they had excellent plant locations. Most plants needed modernization and de-bottlenecking. The low cement prices through much of the early 2000s were not helping. For the year ending March 2000, the company made a loss of ₹59 crore.

We needed money for the modernization effort. The first thing that I suggested to the board was to get out of every other business except cement. By June 2000, we had decided to get out of all the non-core businesses set up by the previous MD. Most of these were loss-making or moribund. The money realized through the sale was put back into modernizing the cement plants.

Mr Narula, who headed ACC's cement operations, was among the most respected professionals in the Indian cement industry. An electrical engineer and an ACC veteran, he and I had known each other for a long time. In him, I found a kindred soul to rework the culture at ACC and make it a more cost-conscious and shareholder value-driven organization. For nearly a decade, his efforts at improving the cement operations were stymied because of excessive attention on the unrelated diversification. I assured him that the board would give speedy clearances and the funds for the various modernization projects he had in mind.

He told me about how corruption had become a problem at ACC and I made sure that the board gave him a free hand to get rid of anyone he thought was involved. In our Wednesday meetings, I provided advice and guidance based on our learnings in areas of productivity and efficiency. In keeping with my ethics and principles, I scrupulously kept Ambuja executives from getting involved in this effort. It was only Mr Narula, his boss Mr Nambiar, Mr A.L. Kapur our director at ACC and me.

With the board backing him fully, Mr Narula went all out. In the first year of my stint there, the company conducted as many as 1,700 management development and technical training programmes across all the plants to upgrade employee skills. He finally managed to commission the giant 2.6-million-tonne plant at Wadi in northern Karnataka after a long delay. That had a direct impact on sales and profit. In 2001, for the first time in seven years, the profit figure crossed ₹100 crore. We elevated Mr Narula to the MD's post when Mr Nambiar retired two years later. Once in the saddle, he and I worked even more closely to accelerate the reforms. The progress was painfully slow due to ACC's old plants and large geographical spread across the country.

It would be years before ACC's profits rose to a level of my liking and the stock price rose beyond the ₹370 a share that we had paid the Tatas. By the time Mr Narula retired after five years at the helm, ACC was back to being the blue-chip stock that it was in the 1970s and early '80s. Cement production reached 20 million tonnes. The stock was now trading in the region of ₹1,300.

The ACC drama came at an immense personal cost for me. The pressure that I had to deal with immediately following the ACC acquisition had come from multiple directions. It was not just the barrage of media criticism, SEBI and court hearings and the strain of round-the-clock work involving complex deals, but also the revival plans of Ambuja Eastern and Ambuja Rajasthan and Gujarat Ambuja's expansion plans. There was also the aggravation of managing Suresh's sensitivity towards the ACC media vilification. All this took its toll and my cancer was back by the end of 2000, this time on the other side of my face.

By now though, I had developed enough confidence in Dr Sultan Pradhan to have the surgery done in Mumbai itself at Prince Aly Khan Hospital. This time, part of my other jaw was removed. Dr Pradhan jokingly told me after the surgery, 'I beg you, please don't come back to me for another surgery, there is no place left.' As I had already undergone radiation five years earlier, it was ruled out this time. It was relatively less painful and the healing was quicker. Mentally, it did not bother me as much as it did earlier. But my speech was severely affected this time, which brought a whole new set of problems which I will discuss in the next chapter.

As I was convalescing after my surgery, I reflected on the three significant transactions that we had done in three years—Modi Cement,

DLF and ACC. For various reasons, all of them were done without any planning or strategy. The way I handled them was not how any other large company would have done it. They would have had a complete team in place to handle every aspect of the transactions.

I had only myself to blame for the way I operated. I am impetuous by nature and was in the habit of making decisions on the spot, without thinking. I was lucky to get away with it on most occasions, but there were times when it backfired and I was left to rue my actions. My essential learning from the ACC experience was that like every other company, I should have had a professional team of specialists handling the media. That was my biggest failing.

My other stress was about handling Suresh Neotia. The ACC problems bothered him no end. He regretted giving the go-ahead for the deal after reading what was being said in the media. 'We were doing well on our own, then why did we have to do this?' he asked me.

Ironically, the period when we were battling the negative fallout of ACC was among the best years at Gujarat Ambuja, even by our high standards. Our total cement production now topped 10 million tonnes, a remarkable jump from just 7,00,000 tonnes a decade earlier. We were exporting more than a million tonnes of cement a year, roughly around 40 per cent of the country's exports. The efficiency and capacity improvement steps initiated by Mr Kulkarni and his team added more than a million tonnes of additional cement from our existing plants in Kodinar to our total production every year. We were among the earliest manufacturing companies in the country to initiate a comprehensive company-wide ESOP scheme for our directors and employees, soon after SEBI introduced the scheme in 1999.

And the expansion continued apace. The first phase of the long-planned Bathinda grinding unit in Punjab was now operational, receiving clinkers both from Ambuja Rajasthan and the Himachal Pradesh plant. The grinding unit at Sankrail, outside Kolkata, was now onstream, supplying cement to Bengal and other parts of east India. To cap it all, in June 2000 we began work on our single-biggest cement plant yet, the

2-million-tonne facility at Chandrapur, 150 kilometres south of Nagpur in Maharashtra.

We named it Maratha Cements. It was as if we had saved the best for last. After our experience in Himachal Pradesh, I had told myself that our next new plant would be in a place where everything was easy—land acquisition and topography, permissions, procuring power and limestone and the market for the cement itself. Maratha Cements turned out to be that venture. We had the choice of putting up the plant either in Nadikudi in central Andhra Pradesh, or Chandrapur on the eastern tip of Maharashtra. We opted for the latter because we were based in Mumbai, so access was more straightforward and the state government was eager to help us. Chandrapur was investment-starved in those days.

The region's central India location gave us access to underserved areas in northern Andhra Pradesh and southern Madhya Pradesh. There were four large cement plants in the area owned by the most prominent players in the industry—ACC, L&T, Birla Cement (M.P. Birla Group) and Manikgarh Cement (Century, B.K. Birla Group). They did not worry us because all these were old plants set up in the 1970s and '80s.

Chandrapur was a dream location for a cement plant for other reasons. All the primary raw materials were available within short driving distances. The area had high-quality limestone deposits, as many as twenty-seven working coal mines, four thermal power plants, including the 3,340-megawatts Chandrapur Super Thermal Power Station, which ensured plenty of fly ash and excellent rail and road connectivity because of the many industries around. Apart from all this, the state government considered the area to be underdeveloped and was willing to provide plenty of incentives and land.

After all that we went through in Darlaghat and Mahuva, this seemed like a walk in the park. The best part was when I went to meet the then Maharashtra chief secretary, Mr Arun Bongirwar, to find out the modalities for the mandatory meeting with the CM. Mr Bongirwar, who was from Nagpur himself, told me, 'Why do you need to meet the CM? It is better to keep away from politicians. If you have any problem, you come to me.' Some years later, after he retired, I asked Mr Bongirwar to serve on the board of Ambuja Cement Foundation and he was gracious enough to accept.

The Maharashtra government was very keen on this project because most of the industrial investment in those days had gone to the Mumbai–Pune–Nasik belt. No one was interested in the underdeveloped eastern part of the state, maybe because of the long distance from Mumbai. Even the existing cement companies had hardly invested any money in upgradation since their plants were set up. 'You don't need to meet anybody and I want to see who stops your file,' Mr Bongirwar told me. And true to his word, we never had to go back to the government for anything. It was the same sage advice that Mr Khan had given me in Gujarat many years earlier.

The Maharashtra State Electricity Board (MSEB) also helped us make history, albeit inadvertently. When we approached their office for power, they turned us away in the usual arrogant manner of a monopoly electricity provider. They said there was no excess power at that time, which we knew could not be true. I told my people that we would not go back to them. We would set up our own thermal power plant. Coal was not a problem since plenty was available from the nearby mine. We decided to set up a 40-megawatt power plant simultaneously with the plant.

As far as I know, ours was the first large industrial plant to come up in the country without being linked to the state electricity grid. We discovered that it was cost-effective as well. Besides saving crores in MSEB installation and wheeling charges, our cost of generating power was in the region of ₹1.70 or 1.80 per unit against the grid power cost, which was ₹9. Even taking plant depreciation into account, our price was under ₹3 a unit.

The Maharashtra government's industrial development agency SICOM's processes were so efficient that our land acquisition took under six months, which was remarkable by Indian standards. Civil work started in June 2000. Mr Kulkarni and his team set another record by starting trial production in just eighteen months and well within the ₹600-crore budgeted cost. Commercial production started a few months later and within six months we were running the plant to full capacity.

The only issue we faced at the construction stage was from a local MP who periodically threatened to create problems for us under one pretext or the other. Mr Vilas Deshmukh, one of our senior engineers (he recently retired as the company's chief manufacturing officer), who was in charge of the land procurement process, did a great job pacifying him. He made sure that the problem never got out of hand. Villagers in the surrounding areas had some initial apprehensions about how the emissions from the plant would affect their farms and livelihood. To calm their fears, we took many of them to Kodinar and showed them what we had done there and how agriculture thrived all around our plants. They were more than convinced.

The Chandrapur plant was a landmark for the Indian cement industry on many fronts. Its raw mill was the biggest in the world at that time. At 150 metres, the preheater was the tallest in the country. And we built what many believe is the longest train platform in India for our railway siding. Further, despite commercial internet being in its early days in India, we connected our raw mill directly to the software development centre of the German suppliers Gebr. Pfeiffer & Flender. It enabled them to run real-time maintenance checks that reduced our downtime considerably.

Simultaneously, our sales and marketing team did a remarkable job of getting the distribution network in place before the start of commercial production. Besides Maharashtra, the market stretched across a vast swathe of the surrounding states, including Madhya Pradesh and Andhra Pradesh. As a result, we were able to sell everything we produced despite the presence of all the legacy brands in the area, including those of L&T and ACC.

Maratha Cements, our plant at Chandrapur, was a remarkable testimony to how efficient the team led by Mr Kulkarni had become in putting up a giant cement plant. Similarly, the sales and marketing team under the leadership of Mr Ajay Kapur, my erstwhile executive assistant, proved that when needed, they could establish the Ambuja name anywhere in the country in double quick time. Chandrapur was also an incredibly proud achievement for me. It became our most profitable plant almost overnight and the highest profit-making cement plant in the country. Our profit margins in the early days were as high as 35 to 40 per cent, which was and still is unheard of in the industry. Two decades later, Chandrapur is still Ambuja's most profitable plant.

Maratha Cement, in many ways, represented our mastery over the art of cement making. It was the culmination of fifteen years of hard work, the coming together and distillation of all our learnings, experience and knowledge. In less than two decades since we started, the group's cement capacity had grown eighteenfold to 13 million tonnes. We were now the best-known cement brand across Maharashtra, Gujarat and Rajasthan in western India; Haryana, Delhi, Punjab and Himachal Pradesh in the north; and in West Bengal in the east.

14

The Long Goodbye

Selling the ACC stake • The search for a successor • Handing over the reins to Holcim • End of the Sekhsaria–Neotia era

By 2003, we had achieved yet another important landmark, that of exporting nearly 2 million tonnes of cement, the only Indian company to do so. We were now responsible for as much as 53 per cent of the country's cement exports. Muldwarka that year handled a record 4 million tonnes of cargo, including our imports (coal, gypsum and furnace oil).

Chandrapur was my last big project. Its success gave me the perfect opportunity to re-evaluate my career and my life itself. I had been at it for more than twenty years now. How long did I want to continue like this? I felt I had reached the peak of what I could achieve. I knew cement so well that I could set up a plant anywhere and make it viable. I could take any loss-making plant, turn it around and make it successful. I could write more than one book about cement.

I had understood every aspect of the cement business: project finance and execution, manufacturing, marketing, sales and finance. I knew more than most people about cement, because for much of my life I was a hands-on manager in touch with every aspect of the company's working. I did not believe in only issuing instructions from the comforts of a wood-panelled office. I felt as much at home at my manufacturing facilities as in my office in Mumbai.

The rethink about my priorities did not happen overnight. It had been on my mind since my third cancer surgery. I felt it was God's way of telling me that I had been given enough leeway and I shouldn't try to push my luck further. Surgery had severely affected my speech. I now felt constrained, especially when talking to outsiders. My interactions with people became much less. It was this handicap that put the thought of retiring from the business into my head the first time. The cancer had made me weak and physically vulnerable. I did not have the kind of energy that I had in the 1990s.

The Neotias empathized with me. They were also at an age where they wanted to take it easy. Vinod had told me several times that he wanted to retire. By then, he had cut down on the time he spent at the Ambuja office in Mumbai to a bare minimum. And Suresh not only wanted to retire himself but had always advised me to do the same for the sake of my health.

I had achieved everything that I had set out to do in life. I was a small trader who became a successful industrialist. My father was a modest businessman whose most generous gifts to me were ethics, spirituality and the belief that if you work hard, you will achieve your goals. I was lucky to get into chemical engineering and blessed to have had the option of joining my family's cotton-trading business despite my engineering degree.

Fortunately, I did well in everything I tried my hand at, including manufacturing a commodity about which I knew very little. I was able to assemble a great team of professionals from the earliest days and together we built the country's most successful cement company. I had structured and executed the biggest Indian corporate deal of the era. Now I had a seat at the high table of the captains of the Indian industry. I had made enough money for several generations of my family. Doubling that was not going to change things any further.

Did I want more money, a few more zeros added to my personal wealth? No. Did I want to own a yacht or a plane? No. Did I want to build a mansion? No. I still lived in the same house where I grew up as a child. These things never attracted me. I never wanted to become a Birla or an Ambani. I had no ambition to establish a family business dynasty. All I wanted in life was to go on holidays with my family, be with friends, eat good food, read a good book and have a nice drink.

It was the simple pleasures of life that I longed for, rather than leaving behind a family legacy. I was fifty-four, too young to retire, many would say. But in my mind, I was ready to give it all up. Considering the state of my health, I did not see myself doing this high-stress job in my sixties and seventies. There was also another practical issue at the back of my mind. Most of the small group of senior executives, who had helped build the company over two decades, were themselves close to retirement or getting there. Considering my health and state of mind, I was not sure I had the energy to build a new team.

Sure, I would have loved to have one of my children run the company. But my son Pulkit, who had been on the board of Gujarat Ambuja since the mid-1990s, was not interested. Similarly, my nephew Harsh, who was also on the board, was averse to shifting to Mumbai. My daughter Padmini was already married into another family. The two Neotia brothers, my partners and co-promoters, were already in retirement mode. It was now increasingly clear to me that the Sekhsaria–Neotia control of Gujarat Ambuja was in its last stages. Unlike the vast majority of other Marwari business houses, ours was a one-generation gift that would end once I called it a day.

Would I feel a sense of loss when I gave it all up? Not really. The Bhagavad Gita, which has been my companion through thick and thin, had prepared me. Like many others, my big takeaway has been the chapter about duty and devotion called 'Karma Yoga'. It speaks about unselfish action and doing one's duty without being attached to the fruits of one's labour. I had done my job to the best of my ability.

It was not just holidays and reading that I had in mind after retiring. I planned to become a full-time investor and manage my own money by setting up a family office. Managing money was a passion for me. Gujarat Ambuja had one of the best treasury operations in corporate India and several of Mumbai's most successful investment bankers used to come to me for advice. In my utopian future, I would be living out of a home on an island in Tahiti in the South Pacific and managing my investments remotely like Howard Hughes.

I had, at one point, harboured dreams of getting into finance and insurance in a big way. The government had opened up the insurance sector to private players in 2000 and we had experience in successfully running two housing finance companies since the 1990s. Home Trust Housing Finance, a wholly-owned subsidiary of Gujarat Ambuja, operated out of Kolkata and we were equal partners with HDFC in GRUH Finance, a rural housing finance company based out of Ahmedabad.

The growing success of HDFC in the 1990s had prompted me to seriously look at scaling up our housing finance operations to become a serious player in the business. It is a business that is based on brand credibility and tight controls in the lending operation and Gujarat Ambuja excelled in both these areas. When I suggested this to Suresh a few years ago he was dismissive, '*Kaise sambhaloge*? (How will you manage it?) Your health is not good. Harsh does not take much interest. Pulkit does not take any interest. *Phir kiske liye kar rahe ho yeh sab*? (So whom are you doing all this for?),' he asked me. But that did not deter me.

A year later, a lender to one of our numerous acquisitions wanted to be repaid urgently. Though we had never defaulted on the payments, he was insisting on being paid back and had been harassing Anil Singhvi. Singhvi came to me saying that they were putting tremendous pressure on him. I told him, 'Let the market improve and we will pay him back.'

He said, '*Nahi saab,* we've to do something symbolic.'

I asked him what he meant by symbolic.

He said, 'Let's sell the two housing finance companies.'

I told him I did not want to sell them. 'These are companies that I have built,' I said, 'and I have big plans for them.' I asked him to stall the lender.

He stalled the lender for three months, after which he came back to me saying that the lender was again insisting on being paid. That is when I told him in disgust to go ahead and sell the two companies. I asked him to meet Mr Deepak Parekh, the MD of HDFC, who I knew would be more than happy to buy them. He paid us ₹60 crore for the two companies. We made a handsome profit, but I regretted selling them. They were good companies, growing fast with virtually no non-performing assets. We could have built them into something bigger. The sale dashed my plans of getting into finance.

The sale also brought home the fact that I had to do something more significant about the debt we had taken on for the purchase of ACC shares. The market dynamics had changed dramatically since our deal and it had left me a bit worried. In 2001, Grasim had acquired the 10.45 per cent stake that Reliance Industries owned in L&T and had further increased its holding to 14.9 per cent through market purchases. To ward off a hostile bid on the whole company, L&T had agreed to sell its entire 16-million-tonne capacity cement division to Grasim.

Several other large companies were also talking to the media about their intention to get into cement. All this had me concerned that someone would make a hostile bid for ACC. After all, we owned only a 14.4 per cent stake, the value of which was less than half of the ₹370 a share that we had paid. The stock price of ACC had been stuck in a rut through much of the early 2000s. If someone were to be attracted by this low stock price and make a bid for the company, I would be left nowhere. Though the company itself was doing well after the restructuring initiated by Mr Narula, cement prices were way too low in that period for the changes to have any significant impact on the bottom line.

~

Cement prices started picking up in late 2003 and so did the ACC share price. The company had finally started doing well under Mr Narula's stewardship. It was the best time to put my plan into action, to look for a buyer for both the ACC shares and eventually Gujarat Ambuja itself. And I knew exactly to whom I wanted to sell. For more than ten years, since the Narasimha Rao government initiated economic liberalization, I had had frequent visits from executives of two European cement conglomerates—the French company Lafarge and the Swiss firm Holcim—the two international giants who were actively looking at India at that time.

At various points, they had both indicated their desire to buy us. I was never interested. I did offer them minority stakes in Gujarat Ambuja, but they were not keen. They wanted to buy us outright. Now that I was ready, I wanted to initiate a conversation with Holcim. From my experience in talking with these companies over the years, I found the Swiss to be less aggressive and more reasonable. I decided it was going to be Holcim. I was not interested in Lafarge.

Was I hypocritical in wanting to sell to an MNC when I had spent the better part of the previous three years talking about saving the Indian cement industry from Lafarge? Absolutely not. From my ACC experience, I had concluded that my competitors viewed Gujarat Ambuja as a bigger enemy and threat than Lafarge! It seemed fair to sell to Holcim.

After a brief chat with the Neotias, who were more than happy about my decision, I asked Singhvi to initiate a discussion with Holcim to sell the ACC stake, which we held through ACIL. Holcim sounded interested and agreed to negotiate. But before we could start a substantive discussion, they backed out saying that the timing was not right. I read later that they were in the middle of another big deal in Europe, the $4 billion-takeover of Aggregate Industries, the giant British building-materials company. I asked Anil Singhvi to lay low. I was not interested in selling to anyone else. The discussions went into cold storage for a year.

Holcim came back in late 2004 saying they were ready to talk once again. Within a few weeks, we were able to arrive at a stage where a deal looked possible. My condition was that I would not sell the ACC shares at a price lower than our purchase price. I must get the price and something more. Holcim was interested in buying Gujarat Ambuja as well, but I was not ready. I told them to restrict the conversation to ACC. After many rounds of discussions, we were able to get a fair valuation. They agreed to pay an enterprise value (EV) of ₹4,500 per tonne for the ACC shares. This was 20 per cent more than what Grasim had paid a year earlier to take over L&T's cement division, which was much more profitable than ACC.

The plan was for Holcim to buy AIG and GIC's 40 per cent stake in ACIL at ₹370 a share, paying a total of ₹897 crore. Simultaneously, it would invest another ₹2,576 crore to buy an additional 27 per cent holding in ACIL from Gujarat Ambuja, taking its stake to a controlling 67 per cent. At this point, ACIL would cease to be a Gujarat Ambuja subsidiary and become a Holcim company. The money from Holcim would be used by ACIL to make an open offer for 20 per cent ACC shares at ₹370 a share. That would raise ACIL's stake in ACC to a controlling 34 per cent and Holcim would take over management control. Gujarat Ambuja would retain a minority position with 33 per cent share in ACIL.

Once the finer details of the deal were finalized, I briefed our executive committee of directors about my decision. Besides the Neotias and Singhvi, who were involved in the negotiations, no one from Gujarat Ambuja was privy to our discussions with Holcim over the previous few months. I had been worried about the consequences of the news leaking out. None of the executive committee members were involved in the running of ACC and none of them had any reservation or objection to the deal I had worked out.

We signed the deal with Holcim in the third week of January 2005. A press release announced that Holcim would immediately invest $800 million in ACIL, the single-largest foreign direct investment in an Indian cement company ever. The press release projected the deal as a 'strategic partnership to realize value-creating projects in India and participate in the growing cement industry in the country' and stated that 'Gujarat Ambuja and Holcim aim to strengthen their cement trading activities in South Asia, the Middle East and other countries on the Indian Ocean rim. The two companies would be exchanging their experiences and Holcim intended to use India as a platform for its IT and R&D procurement and to source talented Indian manpower.'

Most of the press reports that followed focused on the ticket size of the deal. There was intense speculation as to why we had decided to sell the ACC stake so early after buying it. I had fun reading the reports after all the negative press I was subjected to in the earlier years. Some said that it was a smart move on my part to own more of ACC without spending any of our money (we still had 33 per cent in ACIL, while ACIL would eventually own more than 50 per cent of ACC). According to one of the press reports, 'In effect, GACL (Gujarat Ambuja Cements Ltd) will own more of a company that it could not have owned completely in the first place.'

Others talked about us not being able to afford to increase our stake in ACC and being fearful of a hostile bid, something that was closer to my thinking. Another analyst hypothesized that we sold because we had no use of ACC anymore. He claimed that we had achieved our mission of establishing 'price stability' in the various cement markets of the country. Some saw a connection between Holcim paying ₹370 a share for the ACIL stake and Gujarat Ambuja paying ₹370 a share for ACC three years earlier. They interpreted it to mean that the deal was a 'fire sale' where we had just about managed to get our cost price for the shares. This was an erroneous analysis. Gujarat Ambuja had already made a profit of ₹250 crore by selling the Ambuja Eastern plant to ACIL.

We had managed to pay off the debt we took on to buy the ACC shares and still retained a 33 per cent minority stake in ACIL. Besides, we had successfully kept international competition out of our vital northern markets at a crucial moment in our growth. Thus ACC had proved to be a beneficial buy for Gujarat Ambuja, even if its performance did not measure up to my expectations in the short run.

The stock market provided an unalloyed welcome to our deal. Both Gujarat Ambuja and ACC share prices firmed up through much of 2005, doubling by the end of the year. Holcim was lucky that the share price was quoting around ₹350 when they made their mandatory public offer for 20 per cent shares in May at ₹370 a share. It received a good response and they were able to raise their stake to 34 per cent. The year-end saw the departure of Mr Soonawala from the ACC board and with that the end of the company's connection with the Tatas after nearly seventy years. I was grateful to him for having continued on the board for so long, after the Tatas had exited five years earlier.

The mental and physical strain of intense negotiations took its toll once again. Cancer returned with a vengeance. I was back at the Prince Aly Khan Hospital in Mumbai for my fourth surgery, once again in the hands of my good friend Dr Sultan Pradhan. He was not happy that he had to remove a bit more of the remaining section of my jaw. The only silver lining was that my hospital stays and the period of convalescence at home gave me time to think about my future. Having gone under the knife for the fourth time in a little over a decade, I was now convinced, more than ever, that it was time for me to sell my stake in Gujarat Ambuja. I was ready to walk away from the company that I had founded and run for nearly twenty-five years. My body was not able to take it anymore.

Holcim had been in continuous touch with me and I decided it was time to start talking to them about GACL. I called the Neotias to tell them of my plan. Suresh, though in agreement with my decision to give it all up, wondered if instead of selling our stake I would reconsider convincing Pulkit or Harsh to take over. I explained to him why that was not workable. As a final alternative, he suggested Padmini taking over the company. That also, I told him, was not a feasible option at that point, though she was well qualified with degrees from the London School of Economics. Eventually, he agreed to give me a free hand if and when I wanted to sell.

I asked Anil Singhvi to call Holcim once again to inform them about my decision this time to sell our GACL stake. He was utterly taken aback. 'You are still young. What will you do if you sell?' he asked me. I told him this was going to be an exploratory meeting. I was not sure if I wanted to sell. I instructed him to keep the process confidential, as was the ACC share sale the previous year.

Once Holcim and I agreed on the broad parameters of the deal, I spoke to Suresh and asked him to accompany me to Zurich for a meeting with Holcim chairman Rolf Soiron and CEO Markus Ackermann. The two Swiss gentlemen, one a highly respected corporate statesman and the other a cement professional with work experience around the world, were charming and gracious. This deal for them was bigger than anything else they had done till then outside Europe. India was the world's second-largest cement market. It would catapult Holcim into a leadership position in a country where their big European rival Lafarge had stolen a march on them in recent years, by acquiring two plants of a total capacity of 5 million tonnes (the cement divisions of Raymond and Tata Steel). Holcim's only condition for us was that we should sell our entire stake to them.

We were able to negotiate an even better deal than the one for ACC. As against the ₹4,500 per tonne that they paid for ACC, we got them to agree to ₹9,000 per tonne for GACL. The premium was the price for acquiring India's most efficient and profitable cement maker. The deal would involve Holcim acquiring the 24 per cent stake held by the promoters in GACL, in stages starting from January 2006 when it would buy 14.8 per cent of the shares. This would be followed by an open offer for a further 20 per cent of the company's shares a few months later. The deal ensured us a minimum price for the share, or the prevailing market price, whichever was higher.

Simultaneously with the open offer, management control of GACL would be transferred to Holcim. I would step down as MD of GACL and give up my day-to-day responsibilities in favour of a Holcim appointee. As with ACC, I negotiated the right to be consulted on the appointment of the new MD as long as I retained my connections with GACL and the Ambuja Foundation. I was to be chairman of all three till the age of seventy-five. Again as with ACC, where I was designated vice-chairman till Mr Tarun Das retired, I would be the vice-chairman of GACL till Suresh Neotia stepped down. The idea behind this arrangement was to ensure a smooth transition to the next phase of the company and to maintain continuity with the previous management and culture.

Rather than wait till Holcim formally took control of the GACL management after their public offer, I planned to resign as soon as Holcim bought the first tranche of the promoters' stake in January 2006. It would allow the new MD to ease into his position by the time Holcim took over after the public offer a few months later.

Whom should I choose to be my successor? This was the most challenging question I had dealt with in a long time. I was quite clear that I did not want to bring in someone from outside. It had to be someone from the inside. The choice was between the five executive committee members and directors of the company—Mr Kulkarni, Mr Taparia, Mr Rao, Mr Singhvi and Mr Kapur. Except for Mr Kapur, all of them had the distinction of being with the company from the earliest days. Two of them had joined even before the company had acquired land for the first plant. It was a very tight-knit group of men who had worked closely with me to build the company from the ground up. Their attachment to GACL was at a personal and emotional level.

Mr Kapur had run Birla Industries before he joined us, so in that sense, he was the most experienced but was already seventy-one. Similarly, Mr Rao was seventy-four. Mr Kulkarni had been my de facto deputy for the twenty years we had worked together. He was sixty-three and approaching retirement. Mr Taparia was fifty-five, but I wanted to appoint someone younger, who could steer the company over the next two decades. Singhvi fit the criterion. He was only forty-six, with many more years ahead of him. Though his experience was primarily restricted to the company's treasury operation, my feeling was that he would grow into the job.

Singhvi was ambitious by nature, which I viewed as a positive thing. He was a chartered accountant from Jodhpur who had joined us in 1986 while still in his twenties. He had a sharp mind and the ability to grasp complex financial issues. We had worked closely on many big deals, including ACC and Holcim. He knew my mind and my business philosophy. He was the only person outside of the promoters' family who knew about the Holcim deal as he was by my side during both the negotiations. Taking everything into consideration, I decided that Singhvi would succeed me as MD of Gujarat Ambuja.

The details of the deal with Holcim were wrapped up in a few weeks in late 2005. And as in the case of ACC, besides the Neotias and Singhvi, no one in the company was aware of the momentous changes that lay ahead. A few weeks before signing the deal, I had the unenviable task of informing the executive committee members about the heartbreaking decision to sell my stake and step down from the company which we had jointly built over the previous two decades. I anticipated even more problems in breaking the news of my decision to appoint Singhvi as the MD after me.

When the day came, it was tougher than I had expected. They were shocked and numbed by my decision. They felt completely let down. 'How could you do this?' was the overwhelming sentiment I saw on their faces. I had a detailed chat with each of them separately. I explained the reasons for my decision—my fragile health, my speech impediment after repeated surgeries and the doctor's advice to slow down. I told them why Holcim was my choice as the partner to carry forward our joint legacy. They had promised continued investment in growth and to maintain the culture of efficiency and productivity that we had fostered over the years.

I kept the most sensitive subject, concerning Singhvi, for the end. That came as an absolute shock to all of them. I told them that his relative youth was the only reason I picked him. None of them agreed with my reasoning. It was the first time I realized how unpopular Singhvi was among his colleagues. Despite the reservations of his fellow directors, I did not feel the situation warranted a rethink. My feeling was that once Singhvi took over, he would carry the team with him. After all, they were his seniors in terms of work and experience and it would be in his interest to have them on his side. I sought and got a promise from each of the directors that despite their objections, they would fully support and cooperate with Singhvi to continue the Ambuja growth story.

By early December 2005, the news of the impending deal was leaked by someone to the business papers. The stock market viewed it favourably and the Gujarat Ambuja share price inched up gradually. It helped us realize a much better price for our stake than we had anticipated. The deal was executed on Monday, 30 January 2006. In the first stage of the transaction, Holcim bought 14.78 per cent of our 24 per cent stake in the company at ₹90 a share. They paid an additional ₹15 per share to prevent us from setting up a competing cement company in the years ahead.

After founding the company and running it for nearly twenty-five years, I resigned as MD the next day. Despite all the preparations, it was an emotional moment for me as I passed the baton to my chosen successor Anil Singhvi. It was the end of a hugely eventful era for me. I hoped that he would take Ambuja to newer heights.

With the information about our decision to sell the stake having already appeared in the media, the only newsworthy bit was the scale of the deal. It was even bigger in monetary terms than the ACC deal the previous year. Holcim paid us a total of ₹2,142 crore for our stake and had set aside a further ₹2,520 crore to buy an additional 20 per cent share of the company through an open offer in April. Newspapers talked about the Holcim–Gujarat Ambuja deal being part of a new trend, where giant MNCs were finally paying good money to take over well-run Indian companies. There was no backlash against us for selling out to an international conglomerate.

After a few days of euphoria, I was hit by a pang of guilt at having let my people down. It was not only about my senior team, but also the employees at the plants and offices across the country whose hard work and loyalty had made it possible for us to be so successful. I decided to make a farewell visit to all our plants and offices and hold open-house meetings to thank everyone and explain the reasons behind my decision personally. I assured them that things would be as good or even better under Holcim and that their future was safe with them. Their love and warmth touched me as they bid me goodbye.

Our shareholders were always our backbone and most of them had stayed with us through thick and thin. They had, of course, been rewarded sumptuously by Ambuja's performance over the years. The Ambuja share price had jumped more than 420 times over the previous two decades—₹10,000 invested in the company IPO in 1985 was now worth more than ₹42 lakh. I was not surprised then that the shareholders continued to have faith in the Ambuja stock even without the Sekhsaria–Neotia team at the helm, which to me was the hallmark of a great institution. The founders might move on, but the company should continue to do well.

The share price climbed steadily all through 2006. The unanticipated downside of this was that the Holcim public offer at the pre-decided price of ₹90 a share in April 2006 got an inadequate response. The share price had already crossed ₹100 by then. Besides the small shareholders, we, the promoters, also benefited considerably from the rising stock price as our contract had mandated us to sell the second tranche of our stock (close to 4 per cent) in November 2006. The stock kept its upward momentum in 2007 and we were the beneficiaries again when we sold the third tranche of our holdings (close to another 4 per cent). The price had now climbed to ₹154 a share.

Holcim tried once again in late 2007 to increase their holding with another public offer for 20 per cent of the outstanding stock, at a much higher price this time. The response was slightly better, but still netted only 5 per cent of the shares. It helped push their holding to a relatively comfortable 45 per cent. By then, they had taken over the management control of the company by inducting three of their directors into the board of GACL—Holcim CEO Markus Ackermann, executive committee member Paul Hugentobler and Nirmalaya Kumar, a professor of marketing at London Business School. I transitioned into my new role as the non-executive vice-chairman with relative ease. I was finally able to take my mind off Ambuja and start planning for a new future as a philanthropist and investor. I had my freedom and peace of mind.

Today, nearly fifteen years later, besides being the chairman, I still feel a close bond with Ambuja and everything that is happening there, including the work that is being done by the Ambuja Cement Foundation. I visit the company plants occasionally and keep in touch with many of my former colleagues.

I must be honest in admitting that if someone had told me in 2005 that this is how I would feel about the company in 2021, I would not have believed them. Having committed to remaining the chairman of the company till the age of seventy-five, I am still very much involved in the big decisions. The arrangement allows me to make sure that the company continues with the values and culture that shaped its first two decades and made Ambuja one of the most admired names in India's corporate world.

That was the reason I chose to talk only to Holcim to sell our stake and not ask for three or four competing bids. Maybe I could have got a better valuation in that process, but it would have probably made me sever my links with Ambuja. That was the motivation behind my decision not to approach any Indian business house to sell our stake. Ambuja is my legacy and I intend to guide its destiny, even if it is from an arm's length, for as long as I can.

15

Some Last Thoughts

Lessons from five decades on the frontline of business and investment

The year 2021 marks fifty-one years since I first started working. I spent my first ten years as a cotton trader, the subsequent twenty-five steering Ambuja and since then I have been running our family office with help from my son Pulkit and daughter Padmini, both of whom now work full-time with me. Padmini also runs our two philanthropies, the Narotam Sekhsaria Foundation, which enables non-profit organizations and social entrepreneurs to make a sustainable and lasting impact on society; and the Salaam Bombay Foundation, which helps needy children stay in school and then get them involved in after-school activities in the areas of sports, arts and culture. Over the years, both these organizations have helped thousands of young people find new meaning in their lives. These pursuits have made my post-retirement life immensely fulfilling and rewarding.

Life for me these days, as a result, is as hectic and exciting as it was when I was running Ambuja. What I see when I look back is a long and satisfying journey. It has had everything in it—thrills, challenges, obstacles, successes, failures, happiness, disappointments, luck, misfortunes, mistakes, missteps, moments of agony and periods of euphoria. Every experience has been an occasion for me to learn something. Each of them provided me with lifelong lessons that made me better as a person and as a manager.

I have distilled some of those learnings into a list here, in the hope that it will be useful to everyone:

- The ups and downs of life are inevitable. The best way to tide over them is by being positive and dedicated to one's values, regardless of how testing the circumstances.
- Business is essentially about creating the right kind of culture and work environment where everyone can thrive and realize their potential. If people are unable to perform, it is imperative to bring about necessary changes. I have seen underperformers achieve tremendous results with the smallest of changes.
- The right work culture is one that combines ethics, values, integrity, transparency, fairness and accountability with a performance mindset. It should provide an ideal setting for everyone to give their best, which is the springboard for success.
- It is a given that environmental consciousness is good for the planet. But what is not widely known is that it is good for business as well. It was a vital ingredient of our success over the years. Like ethics, fairness, integrity and transparency, caring for the environment has a direct beneficial impact on the bottom line as well. Even consumers feel happy about buying from companies that are eco-friendly and run their business ethically. That is one of the reasons we were always able to command a premium price for our cement.

- Business success is incomplete without a social conscience. In a country like ours where poverty is still endemic, it is incumbent on every business, big or small, to do their bit to ameliorate the suffering of its poorest, in whatever way they can. The satisfaction in bringing the tiniest bit of joy to their lives is good for your heart. It helps you sleep better at night knowing that you are a 'giver' and not just a 'taker'. It makes you a better person and a better manager.
- The 'I Can' philosophy that I have talked about extensively in the book encapsulates my work philosophy. Here are some pointers:
  - If you energize the soul of your people, the body and mind will follow and they will do extraordinary things.
  - In any business relationship, everyone must be a winner, including your outside partners. Win-win relationships lead to more robust organizations.
  - Every investment in business should build wealth.
  - Be agile in action. Be agile in spotting risks and opportunities.
  - Integrity is walking the talk and doing what you think is right.
  - Doing the obvious is easy. Look beyond and do the difficult things.
  - Making little improvements every day is good for one's spirit and the company's bottom line.
  - Trust begets trust.
  - Frugality should be a way of life.
  - Everything I have learnt is based on the belief that life is simple, not complicated. So is business. Keep it simple and whatever you do, make sure you never compromise on your values. Success will come; so will happiness.

Afterword

My father has the curiosity of a child.

He starts the day with a walk, accompanied by his favourite music or a podcast. He carefully observes everything around him—fellow walkers, joggers, milkmen, newspaper delivery boys, birds, flowers on trees, clouds, the sky—he doesn't miss a thing. He is always joining the dots. He doesn't just follow the daily weather pattern. He is continually analysing what it means for agriculture and the economy, how it will impact the livelihoods of people and the last mile of rural distribution networks. He observes the fitness bands and smartwatches on the wrists of runners and wants to know if this is a new trend in connected wearables and whether the trend is here to stay. Is it too urban? Is it very niche? Is there a possibility to make it affordable for a larger number of people? Can it be made to serve a bigger purpose? Can it be part of a universal healthcare system?

Once home, he reads the newspapers and makes notes in the margins that are addressed to different people at the office. All through my childhood, the newspapers I read at home had his markings. It is said that reading is a means of thinking with another person's mind. In the case of Papa's annotated newspapers, you are thinking with the minds of two people.

His interests are wide-ranging. They go beyond the usual business, economy, markets and politics into areas like music, literature, cinema (he loves Hindi films), sports (he watches every cricket and tennis game he can) and, very often, food. He has a take on which tea shop at Veraval has the best *khari* biscuit and tea, which dhaba to stop at for kachori on the way to Chirawa and where to get the best pistachio teacake in London. He is always seeking, continually discovering and constantly sharing food titbits.

The newspapers travel with him to work and his staff scans the articles with his notes and sends them to the relevant people. He is very prompt in reading and responding to every document shared with him and expects the same of you. Prepare yourself thoroughly before meeting him, for he engages with you methodically and rigorously on every topic.

Whenever we discuss a new investment opportunity at our Family Office meetings, he will always have a question about, 'What is this going to teach you?' His curiosity is infectious. And over the years, his thirst for learning has become part of the DNA of everyone around him. He is of the opinion that even if nothing comes out of a discussion, one should have learnt something from it. He always encourages us to study and learn from failure. Business schools, he feels, should focus equally on case studies of business failures as they do on successes.

His energy and impatience are a potent combination that keeps everyone on their toes, both in the office and at home. He thinks so fast that the rest of us can barely keep up. He's just as focused on the execution as he is on the conception of an idea. He often leaves detailed instructions on how everything should be done.

He is always open to hearing you out if you have a suggestion or a better approach to solving a problem. More often than not, you will find that he has carefully thought through every aspect of the issue, including the solution that was just suggested. I remember his cancer surgeon, Dr Shaha, once laugh and say, 'The only time I can have my way with your father is when he is under general anaesthesia.'

Clarity of purpose and courage of conviction are two qualities deeply ingrained in Papa. He will understand a situation clearly, come up with a plan in granular detail and then proceed to implement it with surgical precision. I recall an instance where we had spent weeks preparing a bid for a company. In the days leading up to the bid, there was much chatter about how parameters other than those we had used could determine the winner.

I wondered if we should have a relook at our bid document, but Papa would have none of it. He said we were clear on the fundamentals and our bid was based on it. Everything else was just noise and it should not muddle our thinking. Our bid went through and I learnt the value of filtering out the noise. In a world where media is an endless scroll at our fingertips and there is so much fake news, the ability to shut out the noise is a gift indeed.

Papa has always shunned mediocrity and pursued excellence. He leads by example and never gives up. In recent decades, with his speech impaired by multiple surgeries and radiation, he practises speech therapy diligently, even at seventy. He continues to conduct all his meetings and AGMs himself, making every effort to ensure that everyone understands him. He often says life is like a river. It has many twists and turns. You cannot influence its course, but you can learn to navigate it.

Ours was among the first formal Family Office set up in India. I clearly remember how charged and energized he was at the prospect of creating something new in uncharted territory. His blueprint for the Family Office made no mention of capital, save to say that we are the trustees of the wealth for future generations and that capital preservation was the starting point. He chose instead to focus on people and work culture.

He emphasized that a robust value system is what will hold the organization in good stead. Fairness, honesty, integrity and transparency are not negotiable in his book. He holds nothing dearer than reputation and trustworthiness. He always says that building a reputation takes a lifetime, but all it takes to destroy it is a single act. The same is the case with trust. For him, our office must be a harmonious place where people come not just to work but also for personal advancement—intellectually, economically and socially. The most significant investment we make is in our relationships. Our work must serve a higher social cause and that must be our biggest motivation.

He believes that you should be as much a giver as you are a taker. People who give evolve into better people. He's always giving, not just as a philanthropist, but also as a parent, friend, mentor and patriarch. And he does it invisibly and anonymously, away from the gaze of people. He guards his privacy zealously and does not enjoy the spotlight. He never fails to remind us that we should talk more about failures than successes and learn from what other people have to say.

Papa is my rock. He has an immense reservoir of courage to face any adversity. No matter what the stress, he always shields our family from it. He has an incredible capacity to compartmentalize issues. He never makes us feel that we are getting in the way or interrupting him. He invariably finds time for the family. Whether it is to take our calls on the busiest of days, take me out for coffee to catch up, or go on family holidays, he is never too occupied. He believes that he should be readily available as a parent and that both the quality and the quantity of the time he spends with us matters.

Just before my eighteenth birthday, he had to leave for his first cancer surgery in New York. Despite being in tremendous pain, he told me calmly and matter-of-factly that it was just a minor medical procedure and that he would be back soon. On my birthday, eighteen spectacular bouquets of red roses arrived at home. The flowers and fragrance filled my room and I could feel his presence despite the distance.

Papa is very spiritual and deeply philosophical. And he is a big believer in destiny. I have seen this during the good times and the not so good. 'Everything happens for the best. There will be some good even in the worst of things that happens to us. You will get to understand it with time,' is his favourite mantra. Talking of his illness, he once said to me, 'Cancer is the best thing ever happened to me. It has kept me humble. All the good work we did around cancer would never have happened otherwise. It was destiny.' Cancer strengthened his eternal faith in the Almighty. Papa's beliefs are rooted in Vedic philosophy. To this day, he reads the Gita whenever he seeks peace or inspiration.

According to him, life will have many ups and downs and we go through adversity to savour the good times. 'It's like enduring a dark night to enjoy what the beautiful dawn has in store. Remember that everything in life is transient, so do not attach too much importance to the highs or lows. Both will pass.'

The best education I have had and continue to have, is by being my father's daughter. For that, I will always be grateful. The story you just read of his journey, his struggles, his philosophy and insights from his life in his own words, will, I hope, provide the future generation of businessmen and entrepreneurs some valuable learnings and influence them to follow a path of strong values even as they seek to fulfil their dreams.

Every girl will tell you her father is her hero and I'm no different. My father is my world and I'm proud of how he has shaped my world view. With his thoughts, with his words and his deeds, he continues to be my guiding light.

October 2021

Padmini Sekhsaria

Appendix I

Dramatis Personae
Family

Basantlal Sekhsaria: Great-grandfather

Banarsilal Sekhsaria: Grandfather

Satyanarayan Sekhsaria: Father (adoptive), Banarsilalji's brother.

Nagarmal Sekhsaria: Father

Bimla Poddar (Bai): Sister (adoptive)

Bimal Kumar Poddar: Brother-in-law (husband of Bimla Poddar)

Surendra Sekhsaria: Brother

Janardan Sekhsaria: Brother

Nalini Sekhsaria (Nilu): Wife

Pulkit Sekhsaria: Son

Padmini Sekhsaria: Daughter

Suresh Neotia: Co-founder, younger brother of Bimal Kumar Poddar

Vinod Neotia: Co-founder, younger brother of Bimal Kumar Poddar

Harshvardhan Neotia: Son of Vinod Neotia

Appendix II

The Team that Built Gujarat Ambuja Cements Ltd (GACL)

Suresh Neotia (1936–2015): founding director, chairman, May 1988; stepped down from the board as chairman in September 2009

Vinod Neotia (1939–2009): founding director; stepped down from the board in January 2006

Bhaskar Shovakar: Joined November 1982 as senior vice president; left August 1984

S.S. Bhandari: Joined April 1983 as financial controller; left April 1995

M.M. Hirpara: Joined June 1983 as project engineer; retired in December 2011

P.B. Kulkarni: Joined August 1983 as project manager; retired in January 2009

B.L. Taparia: Joined November 1983 as assistant company secretary; retired in March 2019

G.C. Kotwal: Joined August 1984 as joint president; died March 1986

J.P. Desai: Joined July 1986 as manager (technical services; retired in January 2019

P.C. Jain: Joined May 1985 as general manager (commercial); retired in Oct 1998

Anil Singhvi: Joined February 1986 as deputy manager (finance); left in April 2007

Rashmi Kampani: Joined February 1986 as sales adviser; retired in June 2011

A.V. Rao: Joined November 1990 as construction adviser; remained as chief-projects till March 2010

Sudhansh Gupta: Joined August 1993, as senior vice president (port & shipping); will retire in February 2022

Associates

T.V. Chidambaram: registrar, Bombay University

Dr M.P. Jain: director, GACL (1983–89); managing director, Andhra Cements Ltd

H.K. Khan: chairman, GACL (1983–86); chairman and managing director, GIIC

N.N. Pai: chairman and managing director, IDBI; died October 2008

Dilip Swadi: Swadi Automobiles

S.A. Dave: chairman, UTI

M.L. Bhakta: director, GACL; Partner, Kanga & Co

Nimesh Kampani: director, GACL; non-executive chairman, JM Financial Limited

A.L. Kapur: director, Gujarat Ambuja

R.C. Sinha: managing director, CIDCO; retired in May 1994

Index

Acknowledgements

At the outset, I would like to give thanks to the Almighty and to my parents, Ma and Babuji, for their blessings and the values they imparted to me, making me the person I am today. Over the years my sister Bimla, whom I fondly call Bai, has been my guide and support. My wife, Nilu, has been my pillar. My children, Pulkit and Padmini and grandchildren, Mrinalini, Tanvi, Vaidehi and Nirvaan, have been my joy and biggest inspiration.

The Ambuja Story would not have been possible without the people who built it alongside me. Mr P.B. Kulkarni, Mr S.S. Bhandari, Mr B.L. Taparia, Mr Rashmi Kampani and Mr A.V. Rao have all been founding fathers of Ambuja. As also many of the distinguished directors like Mr ML Bhakta and Mr Nimesh Kampani, who sat on our board from the earliest days and enriched the company with their wisdom and guidance.

I also want to thank Neeraj Akhoury, the current managing director of Ambuja Cement and Ajay Kapur, the managing director when I started work on this book, for their support in helping me document many aspects of the company's history. I am also grateful to our partners at LafargeHolcim, especially Mr Martin Kriegner and Mr Jan Jenisch, for their encouragement in this endeavour.

I have always been a private person. The success of Ambuja notwithstanding, I have never been keen to seek the public eye. So much so that not long ago I had the pleasure of talking to a gentleman on a flight who, when told that I was from Ambuja, asked me if I knew Narotam Sekhsaria. In the years after I exited Ambuja, many people, including family members, asked me to write about my journey. My daughter Padmini persisted the most, telling me that it was not just for my colleagues who helped build Ambuja, or for me, but also for future generations—for grandchildren and great-grandchildren, for students of business, for entrepreneurs and young professionals embarking on their career and looking to build India's new industrial enterprises. The techniques, the ethos and the values that went into making Ambuja will hopefully inspire them to do even better.

I resisted the idea of writing a book for a long time, until I began to see the merits of Padmini's suggestion. I realized that my reluctance was probably a cover for my lack of courage to take on the project. Then serendipitously, I met Radha who offered to work with me. Radhakrishnan Nair is a gifted business writer and a master of his craft. He has been instrumental in my developing the courage to pen my thoughts and put together my varied experiences into what has now become this book.

I am also grateful to Ritu and Alok Nanda for bringing this book to life with their thoughts, guidance and support.

Finally, I am indebted to all the employees of the company over the years and our various partners and shareholders. Their trust in everything we did has made *The Ambuja Story* possible.

About the Author

Narotam Sekhsaria is the chairman of ACC Limited, Ambuja Cements Ltd, and Ambuja Cement Foundation, which runs one of India's most extensive CSR programmes. He also manages the Narotam Sekhsaria Foundation, a leading philanthropic funding agency.